Going Deeper With God

PETER C. HORRELL

Ark House Press
arkhousepress.com

© 2025 Peter C. Horrell

All rights reserved. Apart from any fair dealing for the purpose of study, research, criticism, or review, as permitted under the Copyright Act, no part may be reproduced by any process without written permission.

Unless otherwise stated, all Scriptures are taken from the New International Translation (Holy Bible. Copyright© 1996, 2004, 2007, 2013 by Tyndale House Foundation. Used by permission of Tyndale House Publishers Inc., Carol Stream, Illinois 60188. All rights reserved.)

Cataloguing in Publication Data:
Title: Going Deeper With God
ISBN: 978-1-7642813-4-8 (pbk)
Subjects: REL006110   RELIGION / Biblical Meditations / General; REL012020 RELIGION / Christian Living / Devotional; REL012120   RELIGION / Christian Living / Spiritual Growth.

Design by initiateagency.com

Thanks

To Brian & Rosy Allbutt, Graeme & Carol Cooksley, Dave & Liz Cave, Larissa & Lucy Khan for their assistance in printing these Meditations. And to my wife, Caroline, for your support and encouragement that has enabled us to work together abroad and at home in the service of Jesus our Saviour.

PREFACE

"GOING DEEPER WITH GOD" is written for those who have a yearning for a closer walk with God. *"As the deer pants for streams of living water, so my soul pants for You, O God"*, refers to a longing for a deeper intimacy with God. It means a whole-hearted desire to experience a deeper dimension of His presence in our lives. (Psalm 42:1)

In his writings, Peter challenges us regarding our own relationship with God. He covers many aspects of life, both temporal and spiritual; aspects that no doubt, many of us have personally reflected on, or struggled with, or even just wondered about, and hoped for insight or wisdom for the matter at hand.

Peter writing here, draws on his full life experiences, experiences that are extensive in scope, and that have taken him across the world to different cultures as a missionary and church planter, or kept him in Australia and New Zealand as a pastor and teacher. As with many such writings, one can see the "footprints" where the writer has walked through life, and they reflect the solace, the support, and the strength that have been drawn by Peter from God, both through a personal and real relationship with Him, and from the words of counsel and truth from the Scriptures.

It was a privilege to be invited to preview the compilation, (and suggest some light editing amendments), and in the reading and checking,

I appreciated the wisdom and insights I gained, as will, I am sure, those who open the following pages, and read and reflect on the words and Scriptures, that make up this devotional writing.

Peter's Autobiography also makes for interesting reading. With a touch of humour, he openly and candidly shares his early life as an orphan, his time in the British army in Kenya and his love for adventurous living. Ending up as a penniless drunk and a homeless derelict he was literally 'fished off' a street in Auckland, New Zealand. What followed reveals to all of us what God can do with a life fully committed to Him. Read it. You will be blessed.

Graeme Cooksley

TABLE OF CONTENTS

Intimacy With God 1
A Loaf of Bread 3
The Image Of Christ 5
Silent Before God 7
Fear The Lord And Gain Wisdom 9
The Value Of Affliction 11
Numbering Your Days 13
Insidious Pride 15
Precious Deaths 17
Wholehearted 19
Walk In The Spirit 21
Don't Lose Heart 23
Time Is Precious 25
Praise In Infirmities 27
Jesus Our Example 29
The Dark Night Of The Soul 31
Saved By His Life 33
Throwing Pearls Before Swine 35
God Sees The Heart 37
He's Still Working On Me 39
Humility 41
Taming The Tongue 43
Reflections On Death 45

The Kingdom Of God	47
"Love Not The World"	49
Battle For The Mind	51
A Blank Cheque?	53
Down But Not Out	55
Source Of Contentment	57
Resisting Temptation	59
A Fruitful Tree	61
Limiting The Limitless God	63
The Ways Of God	65
Loving And Hating Life	67
The Love Of Solitude	69
A Good Conscience	71
The Inner Life	73
The Cross	75
The Discipline Of The Lord	77
Perfect Peace	79
Crucified With Christ	81
Keeping The Peace	83
Feeling Faint?	85
Pay-Back Time	87
A Lowly Esteem Of Ourselves	89
Uneducated And Untrained	91
True Worship	93
Anger	95
Forgetting The Past	97
Clay Pots	99
My God! Why?	101
The Power Of Forgiveness	103

Stand Still ... Be Still	105
Spiritual Sluggards	107
Complete In Christ	109
To Die Or Not To Die	111
Prayer Without Words	113
The Source Of Defilement	115
Secure In God's Right Hand	117
Don't Lose Your Reward	119
"If"	121
"I Have Chosen You"	123
Old Age	125
What's In A Name?	127
Francis Ridley Havergal	129
Two Aspects Of God's Will	131
Trust—Delight—Commit—Rest	133
The Christian's Hope	135
Our Unseen Guardians	137
Lord Of Our Circumstances	139
Why Does God Allow It?	141
Chasing The Wind	143
Self-Denial	145
The Greatest Commandment	147
"Amazing Grace"	149
The Battle For The Mind	151
The Judgment Seat Of Christ	153
The Sins Of Presumption	155
Hide And Seek	157
Thinking As God Thinks	159
Lost In Adam – Restored In Christ	161

Death Better Than Birth	163
A Light On My Path	165
Struggling With Sin	167
The Christian's Thought Life	169
The Anointed Christian	171
The Folly Of Wealth	173
The Whole Amour Of God	175
God's Co-Workers	177
Prisoner Of The Lord	179
The Return Of A Backslider	181
Lasting Impressions	183
The Great Liberator	185
A Grand Epitaph	187
"He Abides In Us"	189
Sleep Will Be Sweet	191
A Voice In The Night	193
Faith Over Fear	195
Gain Through Loss	197
The Lord Is Leading	199
Faith And Doubt	201
"Be Holy, Because I Am Holy"	203
Grieve Not The Spirit	205
Heart Burn	207
A Change Of Mind	209
A Bottomless Abyss	211
Fanning The Flame	213
Confidence Toward God	215
The Divine Whisper	217
Christian Suffering	219

"Give Me Neither Poverty Nor Riches"	221
"Never Nurse A Grudge"	223
This Side Of The Valley	225
The Wings Of A Dove	227
Grow In Grace	229
The Growing Christian	231
Three Different Levels Of Living	233
Two Aspects Of God's Peace	236
Four Ways To Know Christ	238
Four Ways God Speaks To Us	240
What Jesus Took To Himself	244
A Portrait Of An Ideal Christian	246
Sacrifices To God	248
Five Christian Priorities	250
A Fourfold Description Of The Christian	254
Milk Or Meat?	256
Inviting God's Scrutiny	258
Quick To Listen - Slow To Speak	260
Question Time!	262
Assurance	264
The Humanity And Divinity Of Christ	266
More Of Jesus Less Of Me	268
Jesus Is The Foundation	270
Blessed With A Bad Memory	272
A Call To Holiness	274
What Is Your Gift?	276
Faith – Hope – Love	278
"I Consider Them Rubbish"	280
The Search For Satisfaction	282

Where Is Your Treasure?	284
The Lamb Of God	286
Head Knowledge Or Heart Knowledge?	288
The Lord's Prayer – Father	290
The Lord's Prayer – Heaven	292
The Lord's Prayer – Kingdom	294
The Lord's Prayer – Your Will	296
The Lord's Prayer – Daily Bread	298
The Lord's Prayer – Our Debts	300
The Lord's Prayer – Temptation	302
Never Look Back	304
The Point Of No Return	306
"Never Take Revenge"	308
Dead To Sin But Alive In Christ	310
What Are We Living For?	312
A Great Cloud Of Witnesses	314
Return The Question	316
Scorched But Escaping The Flames	318
"Christ Is All I Need"	320
"Abide In Christ"	322
"The Eye Of Faith"	324
Set Apart For Himself	326
The Day Of Vindication	328
Heavenly Minded	330
Humility	332
Holiness To The Lord	334
"I Am" The Bread of Life	336
"I Am" The Light of the world	338
"I Am" The Door to the sheep	340

"I Am" The Good Shepherd	342
"I Am" The Good Shepherd	344
"I Am" The Resurrection & the Life	346
"I Am" The Way – Truth – Life	348
John 3:16 God	350
John 3:16 Loved	352
John 3:16 World	354
John 3:16 Son	356
John 3:16 Whoever	358
John 3:16 Eternal Life	360
The Seven Deadly Sins - Pride	362
The Seven Deadly Sins - Lies	364
The Seven Deadly Sins - Murder	366
The Seven Deadly Sins - Wickedness	368
The Seven Deadly Sins - Impulsiveness	370
The Seven Deadly Sins - Falsehood	372
The Seven Deadly Sins - Trouble Maker	374
The Mount Of Temptation	376
The Mount Of Teaching	378
The Mount Of Prayer	381
The Mount Of Transfiguration	383
The Mount Of Prophecy	385
The Mount Of Triumph	387
The Mount Of Commission	389
Let Us Fear	391
Let Us Be Faithful	393
Let Us Be Bold	395
Let Us Be Mature	397
Let Us Be Sincere	399

My Lord - My Strength - My Redeemer 401
Poetry 403
   Beyond The Furthest Star 403
   Resplendent In Your Holiness 404
   Lord Of All Creation 405
   Sovereign Lord, King Of Kings 406
   My Tower Of Strength 407
   Jesus The Light Of The World 408
   Thank You, Lord 409
   Spirit Of God 410
   Prince Of Life 411
   From Every Nation 412
   Alpha & Omega 413
   Endless Is The Universe 414
   How Great You Are Lord 415
   Your Love 416
   Forever In Your Debt O Lord 417
   From Eternity Into Time 418
   I Am His New Creation 419
   The Lord Of Hosts 420
   You Gave Me Life 421
   Your Love Reached Out To Me 422
   Precious Is Your Love 423
   God's Purpose 424
   Eternal Spirit 425
   Saviour And Lord 426
   Christ's Return 427
   Christ - The Image Of God 428
   How Excellent Your Name 429

Holy Communion 430
How Wonderous Your Love 431
Thanksgiving & Petition 432
Poem For A Christian Funeral 433
A Christian's Lamentation In Old Age 434
Perfect Peace 435

INTIMACY WITH GOD

To enjoy intimacy with God is to be on the same page as God. It means being in one accord with His eternal plan for your life. It implies being in harmony with all He wants to do for you. What He has written on His page is for your good, both in time and eternity. The following are some indicators that reveal whether you are living on God's page or on your own page.

If you are living on God's page, you will hate what He hates and love what He loves. You will not love the world. You will hate the sin and the pride that lurks within your own heart. Your longing is to be free from its power and to be made perfect in God's holiness. Living with God on His page, He will not be just _part_ of your life; He will be your _whole_ life. Your heart will be fixed on Him.

To live on His page is to be able to hear God's still small voice in your heart. A sense of His peace and presence evades your whole being that mere words cannot explain. You just know He is with you as you become aware of His protective presence and care. Your love for Him and His love for you will make you perfect in His love. To be made perfect in God's love is to have no difficulty in forgiving others who may offend you. No grudge, envy or bitterness can ever take root in your heart when you are made perfect in God's love.

If you are living on His page, you will love solitude to spend "alone time" with Him. During such precious times no selfish request will ever come from your lips, and no idle word spoken. You want to hear Him speak to you, so your own words will be few. Spontaneous thoughts of praise and thanks will fill your heart as you wait silently before Him.

When living on His page the most fervent desire of your heart is to become more Christlike. You will know that this is His ultimate intention for you. Regardless of any personal loss, nothing will be more important than your desire to see God's will come to fruition within you. NOTHING. Nothing on earth will tempt or persuade you to take one step back from the open grave that awaits you. On the contrary, you will cry out, *'O to be absent from the body and present with the Lord'*. (2 Corinthians 5:8). You will long look forward to hearing His call, ready to exchange your mortality for immortality, and to be forever with your heavenly Father and His Son, Jesus, in heaven.

A LOAF OF BREAD

Mark 6:41

"Taking the five loaves and the two fish, and looking up to heaven, He blessed and gave thanks then broke the loaves and gave them to His disciples to distribute to the crowd."

Such a small loaf that can teach us something to aid us in our walk with the Lord. It might seem so insignificant as hardly worth mentioning yet ….. well, let's just let the loaf tell us what happened.

"I remember being carried in a lunch box by a small boy where a large crowd of 5000 people were gathered. I think we were on the side of a mountain where they all came to listen to a miracle man who was able to heal the sick. I heard some talk about there not being enough bread to feed them all. There were five of us tucked together in that lunch box, or where there seven? I can't remember. I heard someone say what use are they to feed so many people. I think *they* were referring to us.

Then I felt someone picked me up and things began to change. I was in the hands of Someone who held a firm hold on me. I felt myself being raised up and heard a voice blessing and giving thanks to God and then his hands slowly began to break me in pieces. I could not understand what was happening. I felt weak …confused.

So, what does that small insignificant loaf teach us? Before Jesus can use us, we must be in His hands. That speaks of our 100% commitment to Him. Never think you are too insignificant to be used by God. He chooses the weak and the foolish, the ordinary and the untrained to serve Him. (Acts 4:17; 1 Cor. 1:27; 2 Cor. 12:9). It isn't what you can do for Him but what He can do with you and through you. Just as Jesus used that small loaf to serve Him, so he can use us to serve Him. But we must be in His hands.

"And Jesus broke the bread". Before He could use it, He had to break it. Before we can be truly useful to Jesus, we must first be broken. Broken of our self-confidence, broken of our self-importance, broken of our pride until we become aware that it is only in Christ's strength alone, we can serve God. This can be a humiliating experience but done under the hand of God will result in a useful and blessed service for Jesus.

Jesus looked up to heaven. He took the loaf, blessed it, gave thanks and used it to meet the needs of many people. Such can be your life if you are in Christ's hands. "Take my will and make it Thine,

> It shall be no longer mine.
> Take my heart it is Thine own,
> It shall be Thy royal throne"

Frances Ridley Havergal (1836-1879)

THE IMAGE OF CHRIST
Romans 8:29

"Called to be conformed into the image of His Son"

As a silversmith continued to look down into a pot of liquefying silver, his apprentice asked, "When will you know when the silver is pure? "When I see a mirror-like refection of my own face in it", he replied. "Any remaining impurities will distort my features." When God created Adam in His own image it does not mean that God is in human form. The image of God refers to His moral, spiritual and intellectual nature. (Gen.1:26-27). Through disobedience Adam lost the image of his Creator and became morally, spiritually and intellectually deficient. Like a rogue gene Adam's flawed nature has been passed down through the generations.

Jesus Christ is the image of the invisible God who came to restore that image in fallen humanity. (Col. 1:15-17). Like the silversmith, God must remove the impurities in our lives so He can begin to see a mirror-like reflection of Himself in our hearts. Removing those impurities in our lives will test just how strong our faith, our love and our obedience is to Him. He will use everything, even the nasty things we face in life, to achieve His grand purpose of transforming us into the image of His Son, Jesus. (Rom. 8:28-29).

There is nothing more important in your life or in mine than that God's ultimate intention be fulfilled in us. *NOTHING*. We must learn to see things from God's perspective. The impurities that God must deal with include self-will, self-righteousness, self-serving, and pride. Thomas Â Kempis writes, *'rare it is to find one who is wholly free from the blemish of self-seeking'*. The Holy Spirit's work in our lives is to bring about our transformation to the likeness of Christ.

Jesus is our role model. In Him we see what God wants to see in us. That is His ultimate intention for everyone who has turned to Him in faith and made Him Lord of their lives.

> *"Oh, make me clean!*
> *Purge me from every stain,*
> *Let me Your image gain,*
> *In love and mercy reign*
> *Overall, within."*

H. B. Beagle (b – d unknown)

SILENT BEFORE GOD

Ecclesiastes 5:2-3

"Do not rush into speech, let there be no hasty utterance in God's presence. God is in heaven; you are on earth; so, let your words be few."

Before barging into God's presence with a list of your own petitions spend time in silence before Him. Allow Him to calm your spirit. This silence will allow you to hear His *'still small voice' in* your hearts. Elijah was seeking to hear the voice of God during noise and turmoil, but God told him to look within his own heart and listen. (1 Kings 19:11-13). It is only in silent meditation that you can hear His whisper within you.

A listening ear is of far more value than an overactive tongue. You cannot listen to what God is saying and talk to Him at the same time. Compose yourself. Learn to keep your thoughts from roving. Let God's peace sweeps over your soul. Think upon His mercy and love and the blessings you have received from Him.

The command *'Do not rush into speech'* is advising you not to go charging into His presence with hasty and thoughtless words. Hasty words come from the lips not from the heart. It is more important for you to listen to what God wants to say to you rather than what you want to say to Him. He already knows your needs, and His promise is already fixed;

He will supply your needs. He already knows the yearnings of your heart so thank Him in anticipation and in faith for what He is going to do for you.

> *"Blessed is the soul which hears the Lord speaking within ... blessed are the ears that gladly receive the pulses of the Divine whisper ... blessed are those ears which hear the Truth which teach inwardly ... blessed are the eyes which are attentive to the things within ... blessed are they who are eager to give themselves to God ... blessed are they who wait silently before God".*

Thomas Â Kempis (1380-1471)
The Imitation of Christ

FEAR THE LORD AND GAIN WISDOM

Proverbs 9:10

"The fear of the Lord is the beginning of wisdom, and the knowledge of the Holy One is understanding"

The fear of God was widespread in the Middle Ages. The people were taught that God was a harsh and unforgiving Judge who demanded time be spent in Purgatory to atone for their sins. They would have to suffer the torments of Purgatory for some indefinite time before being allowed into heaven. Medieval art displayed pictures depicting struggling souls in agony in the fires of Purgatory. In the Middle Ages the fear of God was a cringing fear. They believed God was unforgiving and merciless in His judgment.

True *"fear of the Lord"* is to recognize God as the Creator of heaven and earth. It is to acknowledge His power, His absolute holiness, His majesty, sovereignty, and supremacy that will inspire a fear in never wanting to disobey His laws. It inspires awe, reverence, and holy fear. *"The fear of the Lord is the beginning of wisdom"*. No man is truly wise till they fear the Lord. His wisdom is more precious than silver and gold. (Prov. 3:13-15).

Man craves knowledge, but without wisdom he is only a walking encyclopaedia. Many people high in academics have shipwrecked their lives through lack of wisdom. God's wisdom is not learnt in the academic world. Wisdom is a gift from God. *"If you lack wisdom, pray to God, who will give it to you. God gives generously and graciously to all'* (James 1:5).

Paul's prayer for the Christians in Colossae was that *'God would fill them with the knowledge of His will, with all wisdom and understanding that His Spirit gives'* (Col. 1:9). The only fear of God you should harbour in your heart is the fear of losing what God has predestined you to be on the last Day.

> *"Thus, Wisdom's words discover*
> *Thy glory and Thy grace,*
> *Thou everlasting lover*
> *Of our unworthy race!*
>
> *Thy gracious eye surveyed us*
> *Ere stars were seen above.*
> *In wisdom, thou hast made us,*
> *And died for us in love"*
>
> William Cowper (1731-1800)

THE VALUE OF AFFLICTION
Psalm 119:71

*"It is good that I have been afflicted, that
I might learn Your decrees"*

King David, the writer of this Psalm, writes from experience. Throughout his life he was afflicted in many ways. His psalms reveal his cries for help when his life was often threatened. He was exhausted through having to continually be on the lookout for the soldiers of King Saul who were intent on taking his life. He often had to hide in caves to keep ahead of them. *"Arise, O Lord! Deliver me, O my God! Listen to my cry for help. I am worn out with groaning"*. David was sorely tested with afflictions. Yet he could still write, *"It is good that I have been afflicted"*. He was able to see that his afflictions were a blessing in disguise.

Your love for the Lord is not a guarantee of being protected from the afflictions associated living in this world. You live in a fallen world of sin, corruption, war and disease that makes it impossible for you not to experience suffering in some way or another. God is not the author of your afflictions and neither does He like to see you suffer. But God will use those afflictions in whatever form they may come to you for your eternal benefit.

Your afflictions will cause you to flee to God. Your thoughts inevitably will turn to God. You will seek His comfort and assurance in opening your heart to Him. Your afflictions will also teach you something about yourself. Christians have testified how their faith was sorely tested during a time of illness not knowing whether they were going to survive. Their faith in God was tested. Their love for God was tested. Their courage to face death was tested. In the end they say with David, "*It is good that I have been afflicted, that I might learn Your decrees.*" Martin Luther stated, "*I never knew the meaning of God's word until I came into affliction. I have always found it one of my best schoolmasters*".

Paul wrote "*that in all things God works for the good of those that love Him, who have been called according to His purpose.*" (Rom. 8:28). He works all things for your good and for His glory.

> *"His purposes will ripen fast,*
> *unfolding every hour:*
> *The bud may have a bitter taste,*
> *but sweet will be the flower".*

William Cowper (1731-1800)

NUMBERING YOUR DAYS
Psalm 90:12

"Teach me to number my days, that I might apply my heart to wisdom"

"We are more anxious to count the stars than our days, and yet the latter is by far more practical". J. Calvin. (1509-1564). You cannot number the days you have yet to live. That is known only to God. The way to number your days, however, is to live as if the present one is your last. The only certainty you have in life is that you shall die. Therefore, "*It is prudent to think of death - to think upon our own mortality*". C. H Spurgeon. (1834-1892).

"Lord, teach us to make each day count, to reflect on the fact that we must die, and so become wise", wrote David. (Ps.39:4). "We can never apply our hearts to wisdom except we number every day as our last." Augustine. (354-430). God's wisdom is to act as if you could see the whole of your life in one glimpse, or as if you could see its end. You could then make reparations before that happened. Hindsight would be irrelevant.

The wisdom of God consists in making full use of the uncertain time allotted to you. How long you live is unimportant. It is how you live that is important. Be your days be many or few, you are encouraged to use them in applying your heart in seeking God's wisdom. You only are given one life. What you do with it will determine your eternal destination. Your life is like a shadow that quickly passes away.

The psalmist wrote *"the fear of the Lord is the beginning of wisdom"*. Fear of offending a holy and righteous God results in obedience to Him. To be wise is to be prepared for when your days come to an end. No one knows when their days will end, therefore it is wise to always be ready to hear God's summons when He calls your name.

> *"Be Thou my wisdom and Thou my true word,*
> *I ever with Thee and Thou with me, Lord:*
> *Thou my soul's shelter and Thou my high tower,*
> *Raise Thou me heaven-ward, O power of my power"*

Mary Byrne (1880-1935)

INSIDIOUS PRIDE

Proverbs 16:18

"Pride goes before destruction, and a haughty spirit before a fall"

In his epic poem, "Paradise Lost", John Milton writes about the pride of Satan who declared, *"I will exalt my throne above the stars of GOD: I will be like the HIGHEST"*. (Is. 14:12-17). Milton goes on to quote the devil as saying, *"Better to reign in hell than to serve in heaven"*. J. Milton (1608-1674). Satan would rather *'reign'* than *'serve,"* and his pride cost him his place in heaven and brought sin and ruin on earth.

Pride, that high sense of one's personal status, is the most hateful thing in the sight of God. Pride poisons the heart, soul, and mind. 'It hardens the heart from loving and forgiving others. It hardens the soul against correction and warnings, refuses to admit wrong and is a forerunner and cause of men's ruin' (Pro.16:18) *"A proud man is always looking down on things and people; and, of course, if you are looking down, you cannot see something that is above you."* C. S. Lewis. (1898-1963).

No matter how committed you are to Christ, none of us are free from the insidiousness of pride in our hearts. *"I have within me that great pope, SELF"*. Luther (1483-1546). Pride is essentially self-worship. Thoughts of self-grandeur have their roots in pride. Pride is taking to us the credit for something that God has accomplished. Pride seeks the praise and glory that belongs to God alone.

You shall struggle with pride till your dying day, but it need not control you. *"Humble yourselves under the mighty hand of God, that he may exalt you in due time,"* Peter (1Peter 5:6). Far better for you to humble yourself before God than to be humbled by another. The only pride you should ever cherish in your heart is what God has done for you in Christ. (2 Cor. 10:17-18).

> *"Show me, as my soul can bear,*
> *The depth of inbred sin.*
> *All the unbelief declares,*
> *The pride that lurks within:*
> *Take me, whom Thyself has bought,*
> *And bring into captivity*
> *Every high aspiring thought*
> *That would not stoop to Thee"*
>
> Charles Wesley (1707-1788)

PRECIOUS DEATHS
Psalm 116:15

"Precious in the sight of the LORD is the death of his faithful servants".

A Christian friend was close to death. As I took my final leave she quietly said with a serene smile, Peter, *"I will see you in heaven"*. There was not a flicker of anxiety in her demeanour. She was looking forward to meeting Jesus and Jesus would be looking forward to welcoming her home.

"Precious in the sight of the Lord is the death of His faithful servants. Death ends His eternal purpose for them. The host of heaven bust out with songs of joy when the soul of another believer is added to the number of their ever-increasing heavenly family. They see the soul's removal from its physical body as a time for rejoicing. Death has set them free from all its afflictions and sufferings associated with living on earth. That soul has been far removed from all physical pain, grief, and adversity that they had experienced on earth.

'Precious in the sight of the Lord' are His *"faithful servants'* who have served Him faithfully and whom He can now reward for their faithfulness. The work of sanctification started by God's Spirit whilst they were in the world has come to its end. The Lord takes delight in seeing the finished work of His Spirit in the souls of His redeemed. He has walked

with them through their pilgrimage on earth, empathized with them in their trials, grief and pain, and has understood the conflict, and the temptations they had to face. Death is their great liberator.

Jesus now welcomes them home. They are His treasure, His inheritance. He bestows upon them their rewards for their labours on His behalf (Eph.1:14,18; 2 Cor.4:7). 'We are precious in His eyes, both living and dying; For whether we live, we live unto the Lord; or whether we die, we die unto the Lord" (Rom. 14:8)

> "For ever with the Lord! Amen, so let it be.
> Life from the dead is in that word, its immortality,
> Here in the body spent, absent from Him I roam,
> Yet nightly pitch my moving tent,
> A day's march nearer home."
>
> James Montgomery (1771-1854)

WHOLEHEARTED

Psalm 119:2

"Blessed are they that keep His testimonies, and that seek Him with their whole heart"

To keep His testimonies in the heart you must heartily embrace them with your whole heart. His testimonies are enshrined in His Word. Jesus said, *"Search the Scriptures for they testify of Me"* (Jn.5:39). They testify to the truth that Jesus is the Messiah, the Saviour of the world. They testify His sacrificial death on the Cross for the sins of mankind. They testify to His rising from the dead and His promise to return as the Judge of all mankind. They testify and bear witness to God's love, holiness, justice and mercy.

His testimonies are forever preserved in the Word of God. Knowing them, you should believe them, believing them, you should love them, and loving them you should keep and obey them.

> *"O send Thy Spirit, Lord, now unto me,*
> *That He might touch mine eyes, and make me see:*
> *Show me the truth concealed, within Thy Word,*
> *And in Thy Book revealed I see the Lord."*

Mary A. Lathbury (1841-1913)

To seek and obey His testimonies with your *'whole heart'* implies a sincere and undivided heart. A divided heart fluctuates and is never fixed on one objective. To seek Him with the *"whole heart"* is to show your sincere desire to be conformed to His will, and to learn His ways. *"My heart is fixed, O Lord, my heart is fixed"*, cried David. Like David, you ought to be able to say, my heart, O Lord is fixed solely upon You. (Psalm 57:7)

> *"A heart resigned, submissive, meek,*
> *My great Redeemer's throne:*
> *Where only Christ is heard to speak,*
> *Where Jesus reigns alone".*
>
> Charles Wesley (1707-1788)

WALK IN THE SPIRIT

Galatians 5:16

"Walk in the Spirit and you will not fulfil the lusts of the flesh"

The command to walk in the Spirit indicates choosing between two different lifestyles. One is choosing to fulfill the desires of the flesh resulting in a lifestyle of wickedness, and the other in choosing to walk in the Spirit resulting in a life-style acceptable to God. (Galatians 5:22-23). To walk or live in the Spirit is not an option but a command. It is the only way that enables you to have victory over sin.

"Flesh" is not to be taken as equivalent to the body. Medieval teaching that the body was the cause of sin resulted in bodily abuse. Flesh refers to the lower and sinful nature inherent in all humanity. Those who live on this lower level have their lives formed by it, and the result is spiritual death.

Those who walk in the Spirit have their lives transformed by the Spirit. They constantly receive His impulses to mind and do the things of the God. The Spirit gives them the strength and the motivation for holy living. Those who walk in the Spirit please God and hate the sin in their own lives. Christian's ought to hate the weakness of their flesh that drags them down to defeat. Victory is found only by walking in the Spirit. *"Walk in the Spirit, and you will not fulfil the lusts of the flesh"*

*"The Holy Spirit, Lord alone
Can turn our hearts from sin.
His power alone can sanctify
And keep us pure within."*

Fanny Crosby (1820-1915)

DON'T LOSE HEART

Galatians 6:8-9

Let us not become weary in doing good, for at the proper time we will reap a harvest if we do not give up"

"The issue of the life to be
We weave with colours all our own
And in the field of destiny
We reap as we have sown".

John G. Whittier (1807-1892)

Matthew Henry (1662-1714) wrote, *"Our present time is seed time; in the other world we shall reap as we sow now"*. Paul writes, *"at the proper time we will reap a harvest if we do not give up"*. This ought to encourage Christians all over the world who are involved in sowing the seeds of the Gospel wherever they live. Weary though their task may be the time is coming when they shall see fruit for their labour.

The rule of sowing and reaping has never changed. There is a time lapse between sowing the seed and reaping the harvest. Farmers do not plant their crops one day and reap the next. There must be time for the seeds to germinate and come to maturity before the harvest.

Likewise, the seed of God's word sown in the heart needs time to mature before the reaping. It may take a short time, or it could take years depending upon the state of the persons heart when they first received the Word. But you can be certain God will bring in the harvest.

Paul is telling his fellow Christians not to become *"weary in doing good"*. A missionary who is faithfully toiling on some foreign field, a Sunday School teacher instructing her young pupils every Sunday, a pastor in faithfully preaching God's Word can become weary in "doing good" if they see no fruit for their labour.

But the promise is sure. The day is coming when the Lord will harvest the seed they have sown in the hearts of those who received it.

> *"Go labour on spend, and be spent,*
> *Your earthly loss is heaven's gain,*
> *The joy to do the Master's will.*
> *No toil for Him is done in vain"*
>
> Horatius Bonar (1808-1889)

TIME IS PRECIOUS

Ephesians 5:16

"Redeeming the time for the days are evil"

Countless would be the number of people on their deathbeds who would gladly give all they ever possessed to add more time to their lives. With little time left to them they would reflect upon their past with regret in how they had wasted in their lives in pursuit of the possessions they were now about to leave behind. If given a second chance they would give all they possessed to have more time added to their lives. But it is too late.

"Tempus Fugit" — "Time Flies" — inscribed in Latin on old clocks. It acts as a reminder how quickly time passes every time we glance at the clock. *"What is your life?* James answers his own question. *"Your life is no more than a mist, seen for a little while and then dispersing"* (James 4:14). Ask any elderly person, and they will tell you how quickly their life has flown by.

Someone has said, *"Yesterday is history. Tomorrow is a mystery. Today is a gift. That's why it is called the present"*. Each day you live is a gift for you cannot be certain of a tomorrow. Don't just take it for granted that it will occur.

You live in evil times. You live in dangerous times. Nuclear clouds are threatening total annihilation over the whole world. Climate change has passed the point of no return. The writing is on the wall for those who have the eyes to see.

Paul urges us *to "redeem the time for the days are evil"* The best way to redeem the time is to use it by serving Jesus Christ. Time is short. We do not know when He will return or when our own lives will end. No Christian should harbour regrets over how they had lived their lives on earth when on their death bed. Meanwhile let us "Redeem the time for the days we live in are evil".

> *"There will come a time when all your labour and troubles cease. Do what you can. Labour faithfully in My vineyard, said Jesus, I will be your reward"*

Thomas Á Kempis (1380-1471)
Imitation of Christ

PRAISE IN INFIRMITIES

2 Corinthians 12:9

"And he said unto me, my grace is sufficient for thee: for my strength is made perfect in weakness. Most gladly therefore will I rather glory in my infirmities, that the power of Christ may rest upon me".

What Paul's infirmities were, remained a mystery. It might have been an ongoing sickness or some physical hindrance that left him weak on his missionary travels throughout Asia Minor. Some have suggested it was bad eyesight. Whatever it was it was a nuisance, a hinderance because it sapped his physical strength and left him physically weak in his service for Christ. Three times he asked the Lord to remove his infirmity and three times his request was denied. Jesus said, *"My grace is sufficient for you: for my strength is made perfect in your weakness"*.

Paul learned that the negative in his life was a positive in the hands of Christ. Despite his weakness, he came to understand that Christ's power within was sufficient to enable him to do what Christ had called him to do, so much so, that he began to *"glory in his infirmities, that the power of Christ may rest upon him"* (2 Cor.12:7-10). Not only did he accept his ailment, whatever it was, but he was able to rejoice knowing that it was because of his weakness that the power of Christ rested upon him.

Who can tell what is best for them. Though God always listen to your petitions He does not always give you what you ask. He sometimes denies your request because of His foreknowledge into your future. He knows what is best for you. Whatever physical infirmities you may bear you will find Christ's power sufficient to sustain you and use you for His glory.

> *"No strength of our own or goodness we claim.*
> *Yet since we have known the Saviour's great Name,*
> *In this our strong tower for safety we hide,*
> *The Lord is our power; the Lord will provide."*

John Newton (1725-1807)

JESUS OUR EXAMPLE

1 Peter 2:21

"That we should follow in His steps"

A non-Christian said to a pastor, *"Jesus is the finest example of how we all ought to live'*. 'True', he replied, '*but first you need Him as a Saviour*. It is only a love for Jesus that will motivate anyone to want to follow in His steps. Peter wrote, *"Christ suffered for you, leaving you an example, that you should follow in His steps"*. The apostle tells us Jesus is our example and following in His steps is to live the way He lived.

This implies being ready to forgive: From the Cross He cried, *"Father, forgive them, for they know not what they do"* (Luke 23:34). When Peter asked, *"Lord, how often am I to forgive my brother if he goes on wronging me? As many as seven times?* Jesus replied, *"I do not say seven times; I say seventy times seven."* Peter was to show to his brother an infinite amount of mercy and forgiveness. Jesus is telling Peter not to keep count (Matt. 18:21-22). Those that follow in Christ's steps ought to be prepared to do the same by not keeping count of how many times you forgive others.

To follow in His steps is to do the will of God by living your life in utter obedience to all that He requires of you. *"Father, if its not be possible for this cup to be taken away unless I drink it may your will be done"* (Matthew

26:42). To follow in His steps is to reach out to the poor, the helpless, the sick the lonely, the homeless and the prisoner. (Matt.25:34-40).

To follow in the steps of Jesus implies a life wholly dedicated to God. It means a willingness to do the will of God, regardless of personal cost. When you finally end your earthly pilgrimage, you shall discover that following in His steps has led you straight into His kingdom where He awaits to welcome you.

> *"All the way I'll Walk with Jesus, through*
> *the sunshine, through the gloom,*
> *Though His blood-marked steps may lead*
> *me, to the garden, to the tomb.*
> *Jesus, keep me closer—closer, step by step, and day by day.*
> *Stepping in Thy very footprints, walking with Thee all the way".*

Albert B. Simpson (1843-1919)

THE DARK NIGHT OF THE SOUL
Psalms 13:1; 88:6

"You have put me in the lowest pit, in darkness, in the deep"
"Why, O Lord, do you hide your face from me?"

The epic poem, "The Dark Night of the Soul", by the Spanish poet, St. John of the Cross, (1542-1591) is synonymous with travelling the *"narrow way."* (Matt 7:13-14). The poet describes his soul's anguish in his pursuit of a closer union with God. He calls it *"The Dark Night of the Soul"* because of the spiritual dryness, confusion, and uncertainty that invaded his own soul. John questioned his salvation. He felt totally abandoned by God, harboured doubts about God's existence, and the afterlife.

The psalmist went through this same experience of the 'Dark Night of the Soul'. *"Why Lord, do you hide your face from me?"* He appears to reproach God by implying he did not deserve to be cut off from Him. *"Have I not cried unto you? stretched out my hands to you? called upon you daily? have earnestly sought your face?"* (Psalm 88; Ps. 6:3; 42:5-6; 43:5).

Many of the most notable Christians in history have spoken of their own dark night of their soul. According to her letters released in 2007, the saintly Mother Teresa of Calcutta, confessed to times of spiritual darkness she experienced during her ministry in India. To feel abandoned by God is indeed a torment felt more intensely in devout Christians who have a fervent passion in following Christ.

Jesus Himself experienced this darkness, and the sense of abandonment when He cried from the cross, *'My God, my God, why have you forsaken me?* The three-hour darkness that covered the whole land prior to His death could well symbolize the darkness He felt in His own soul. (Mt. 27:45)

There are times when you will feel as if God is a long way away from you. You may even think you have been abandoned by God. Passing through your 'Dark Night of the Soul' can be a testing time. But even if you think He has *hidden His face* from you, your face is never hidden from Him. He could no longer abandon you than He could His Own Son.

> "While You wait in gracious wisdom and my doubts begin to rise,
> I recall Your loving kindness, and I lift my hopeful eyes.
> While Your hand withholds the answer,
> I will not withhold my heart.
> I will love you in Your silence, I will trust You in the dark."

Barbara H.

I have endeavoured to discover the surname of Barbara H. but without success. Whoever you are thank you for your poem)

SAVED BY HIS LIFE

Romans 5:10

"For if, when we were God's enemies, we were reconciled to him through the death of his Son, how much more, having been reconciled, shall we be saved by Christ's life"

> "O happy day that fixed my choice,
> On Thee my Saviour and my God.
> O Happy day, happy day,
> When Jesus washed my sins away."
>
> Philip Doddridge (1702-1751)

Indeed, *'happy'* is the day when someone responds to God's call and embraces Jesus as their Saviour. Happy is the soul that finds peace with God through Christ. Happy is the repentant sinner who knows their sins are forgiven, and now know they belong to God's family. That *'happy day'*, however, is only the beginning of what God has in store for those that have *"fixed their choice"* on Him.

There is far more to God's purpose than just saving you from Hell and providing a home for you in Heaven. You ought to try to see things from God's perspective. Christ's death reconciled you to God, but that was only the beginning of God's eternal plan for you. Paul wrote, *"being reconciled to God through the death of his Son, how much more... shall we be saved by His life!".*

Though you have been saved from the penalty of sin, you now need to be saved from the power of sin within you. Jesus did not die to save you <u>in</u> your sin, but to save you <u>from</u> your sin. The death of Jesus saved you from sin's penalty. The resurrected life of Jesus within saves you from sin's power. His resurrected life enables you to live in victory over its power. God's eternal plan from all eternity is that you be transformed into the image of His Son. That transformation begins here on earth.

In his hymn, "Love Divine, all Loves Excelling", Charles Wesley's petition was, *"Take away our love of sinning."* That petition is what God desires from you. As you allow Christ to live and control your life, you will discover what it means to *'being saved'* from sin's power.

> *"Finish then Thy new creation,*
> *Pure and spotless let us be,*
> *Let us see Thy great salvation,*
> *Perfectly restored in Thee:*
> *Changed from glory into glory,*
> *Till in heaven we take our place,*
> *Till we cast our crowns before Thee,*
> *Lost in wonder, love and praise."*

THROWING PEARLS BEFORE SWINE

Matthew 7:6

"Do not give dogs what is holy, and do not throw your pearls before pigs, lest they trample them underfoot and turn to attack you".

In Jesus' day pearls were the costliest of all jewels. They had become symbols of the preciousness of truth. When Jesus said, *"do not give to dogs what is holy"*, He was referring to the truths written in God's Word.

The words of Jesus are allegorical, but their meaning is clear. Dogs and swine have no appreciation for beauty or value. To throw anything of value to them is to see it trampled underfoot. The dogs and swine symbolize some people who have no appreciation of the value of the Gospel.

Jesus is saying do not persist in offering what is precious and holy to those who continually reject it, otherwise they could defame God's holy name. Some well-meaning, but unwise Christians, make the mistake of barging in and trying to force-feed unbelievers into listening to them even though they have not the slightest interest in wanting to listen to what they have to say. A discerning Christian will be able to sense whether the one they are speaking to is receptive or otherwise to what they wish to share.

Jesus made it clear to His disciples that they were to *'kick the dust off their heels'* and move on when a city indicated it had no interest in listening to the Gospel (Matt. 10:11-14). There is a *"time to keep silent and a time to speak"*, and we need God's wisdom when we do so (Eccl. 3:7). We need sensitivity to the promptings of the Spirit in witnessing to others. We need His guidance to guide us to those He has already prepared, and who already have a sense of their spiritual need. They are out there, but we need the Spirit's guidance to lead us to them, and them to us. (Acts 8:26-40).

> "Come gracious Spirit, heavenly dove,
> With light and comfort from above:
> Be Thou our guardian, Thou our guide,
> O'er every word and step preside."
>
> Simon Browne (1680-1732)

GOD SEES THE HEART
1 Samuel 16:7

"The LORD does not look at the things man looks at. Man looks on the outward appearance, but the LORD looks at the heart."

The world estimates a person's worth by their outward appearance. Samuel made the same mistake about Saul. Samuel was impressed with the appearance of Saul. He must have been a tall, fine-looking young man, talented and likeable. *"Surely"*, thought Samuel, *"this is the Lord's anointed."* (1 Sam.16:6). But God investigated the heart of Saul, and what He saw did not please Him. It seemed as if God was using Saul as an example in how <u>not</u> to form an opinion of someone else.

The heart (the core of a human's moral, ethical and spiritual being) is where God looks and judges a person's worth. He sees its motives, intent, and character. It's what is on the inside and not the outward appearance that is of worth to God.

The Pharisees wanted to appear pious before the crowds. They walked among the people in their long robes craving their greetings. Jesus, however, saw right through their hypocrisy. He saw their hearts. *"You are like whitewashed tombs, which look beautiful on the outside but on the inside, are full of the bones of the dead and everything unclean..."* (Matt, 23:27-28, Luke. 20:46).

We live in two worlds, the outward and the inward; the former is open to the eyes of the world. They see us and appraise us by our outward appearance. The inward is open to the eyes of God. He reads our hearts like an open book. Nothing is concealed from Him.

> *"Search me, O God! My actions try*
> *And let my life appear.*
> *As seen by Your all-searching eye,*
> *To mine my ways, make clear.*
>
> *Search all my sense, and know my heart,*
> *Who only canst make known,*
> *And let the deep, the hidden part*
> *To me be fully shown."*
>
> F. Bottome (1823-1894)

HE'S STILL WORKING ON ME
Philippians 1:6

"Being confident of this very thing, that He who began a good work in you will perfect it until the day of Jesus Christ"

God will always finish the good work of transforming His people into the image of His Son Jesus. That is His ultimate intention for you. It will take time, but He will complete it in His own good time. Though it is the work of His Spirit within you, He needs your cooperation in accomplishing it. Paul wrote, *"Work out your own salvation in fear and trembling; for it is God who works <u>in you</u> to make you willing and able to obey His purpose"* (Phil. 2:12). You are not a robot that God manipulates to obey His will. He has put within you a willingness to obey His will in fulfilling what He has planned for you.

His *"good work"* begins now at your new birth (John 3:1-11). You are a babe in Christ but need to grow to spiritual maturity. You can only grow, however, by your obedience to God. God can only carry out the good work and bring it to perfection in the lives of those who obey Him.

If any believer is lukewarm in their relationship with Christ, they will fall far short of the reward that was intended for them. Your obedience to God will result in His perfect will finding its fulfilment in your life. In every believer there ought to be a whole-hearted desire to become more Christ-like in character.

This is God's ultimate intention for you. He will work all things for your good in achieving His goal. The time will come when you shall be presented before His glorious presence perfect and without fault with great joy. (Jude 24). Until that time comes, God is still working on you.

> *"Fill Thou my life, O Lord My God'*
> *In every part with praise,*
> *That my whole being may proclaim*
> *Thy life and Thy ways"*

Horatius Bonar (1808-1889)

HUMILITY
1 Peter 5:6

"Humble yourselves therefore under the mighty hand of God, that He may exalt you in due time"

"Who among us will be the greatest in the kingdom of heaven? It was a question the disciples asked Jesus. Perhaps they each were hoping they would be named above the others as the greatest. In answering, Jesus took a child, and replied, *"Whoever humbles himself like this child is the greatest in the kingdom of heaven."* (Matt.18:1-4). A child is the best example of humility. They know nothing of pride; they are not puffed up with their own importance.

One of the godliest and most prized aspects of a person's character is humility. It is so important that even God took note when Moses walked in humility. (Num. 12:3). It was the reason God was able to use Moses in such a mighty way. He was the meekest of men. God was able to use him in saving His people out of slavery in Egypt.

Pride comes before the fall. Many a preacher has risen to the top of the charts only to come crashing down to earth because they have embraced in their hearts the adulation of the crowds. Those who exalt themselves before man will in due time be humbled. Those who humble themselves before God will in due time be exalted. When a Christian has a genuine understanding of God's awesome power, His splendour and His holiness, they will voluntarily bow the knee in humble servitude before Him. They that really know God, will humble themselves under His mighty hand.

"And Jesus, being found in appearance as a man, he humbled himself and became obedient to death, even death on a cross". (Phil.2:8). Humility is greatly prized by God.

"Do nothing out of selfishness or conceit,
but in humility consider
others as more important than yourselves"
(Phil. 2:3).

"The saint that wears heaven's brightest crown,
In deepest adoration bends;
The weight of glory bows him down,
Then most when most his soul ascends;
Nearest the throne itself must be
The footstool of humility"

James Montgomery (1771-1854)

TAMING THE TONGUE
James 3:8

"But the tongue can no man tame; it is an unruly evil, full of deadly poison"

Our tongue can often get us into strife. It is such a small member that can do enormous damage. James likens it as to fire that can set aflame a whole forest. He likens it to deadly poison. Like poison that slowly spreads through the body the tongue can spread slanderous words that poisons minds against others. What may seem to be harmless words can devastate families, marriages, friendships, and even churches. The tongue is capable of hurting and inflaming the emotions of many, many people. *'Death and life are in the power of the tongue'* (Pro.18:21).

James uses images of the horse's bit and the ship's rudder, both to do with the power of control to hammer home this truth. The rudder controls the ship. The bit controls the horse. But who can control the tongue? James does not represent it as impossible, but as extremely difficult.

We cannot swallow back our words once spoken. But we can swallow our pride in asking forgiveness from someone we have offended with our words.

"Angry words, O let them never
From the tongue, unbridled slip,
With the soul's best impulse
Ever check them,
Ere they soil the lips.
Angry words are quickly spoken,
Bitter thoughts are rashly stirred,
Fondest links of life are broken,
By a single angry word".

Horatius R. Palmer (1834-1907)

REFLECTIONS ON DEATH

Psalm 102:11

*"My days are like the evening shadow;
I wither away like grass."*

Our bodies, however strong and healthy cannot stand forever in good health. As we age nature will slowly take its toll and consume our strength. Death is inevitable. George Barnard Shaw put it this way: *"The statistics on death has never changed. One out of one person dies"*.

The psalmist compared our days to an *"evening shadow"* about to disappear altogether. He saw life's sunset rapidly approaching as he declined in years and *"wither away like grass"*. Most people don't like to think of death. C. H. Spurgeon said, *"It is wise to think of death but in their short-sightedness, most people think only of living"*. Attending a funeral service reminds them of death for a short while, but memory begins to fade, as they are once again get caught up with the delights of living their lives.

"Show me, O Lord, my life's end and the number of my days; let me know how fleeting is my life." (Ps. 39:4). This petition of King David ought also to be your own. Whether your days be long or short on earth is not important. It is how you live them that counts. For the followers of

Christ death is not the end but the beginning. It is a transition from the earthly realm into the heavenly realm.

The Brevity of Human Life

"My end, Lord, make me know,
My days, how soon they fail;
And to my thoughtful spirit show
How weak I am and frail.

To Thy eternal thought,
My days are but a span;
To Thee my years appear as naught,
A breath at best is man.

Man, lives in empty show,
His anxious care is vain,
He hoards his wealth, and does not know
Who shall possess his gain?"

Psalm 39 (The Cyber Hymnal)

THE KINGDOM OF GOD

Luke 17:21

"Behold, the kingdom of God is within you"

When Jesus was asked, "When is the Kingdom of God coming?" He replied, *The Kingdom of God does not come with your careful observation, nor will people say, "It is here or there because the Kingdom of God is within you".*

God's Kingdom does not come with pomp and ceremony. No one will see it come because it is of a spiritual nature and escapes the scrutiny of men. God's Kingdom is established within the hearts of His people. Every kingdom has a throne upon which sits a king from which he rules. The throne in God's kingdom are the hearts of His subjects. He alone has the rightful place upon that throne, and He will not tolerate rivals. Anything else in the life of a Christian that takes the place of Christ is an idol that needs to be removed.

> "The dearest idol I have known,
> Whate'er that idol be,
> Help me tear it from thy throne,
> And worship only Thee".

William Cowper (1731-1800)

Wherever God rules in the hearts of His people there is His Kingdom. Jesus said, *"This gospel of the kingdom will be preached in the whole world as a testimony to all nations, and then the end will come"*. (Matt. 24:14). Until the end comes, we have His Great Commission to continue to preach the gospel to all nations. (Matt. 28:16-20). When we pray the Lord's Prayer, we pray, *'your kingdom come, your will be done, on earth as in heaven'*. In doing so we are asking for the extension of His kingdom to reach the most distant and isolated parts of the world.

Jesus said, *"this gospel of the kingdom will be preached in the whole world as a testimony to all nations, and then the <u>end will come</u>,"* that is, He will come when the task of witnessing to all nations is complete. (Matt. 24:14). We all have our part to play in the extension of His kingdom by sharing the Gospel of Christ and in doing so we hasten His return.

> *"Master, speak! Your servant hears,*
> *Waiting for Your gracious word;*
> *Longing for Your voice that cheers;*
> *Master let it now be heard.*
> *I am listening, Lord for Thee!*
> *What have You to say to me?*
>
> Frances R. Havergal (1836-1879)

"LOVE NOT THE WORLD"
1 John 2:15

"Do not love the world or the things of the world. If anyone loves the world, love for the Father is not in him".

Just as light and darkness cannot coexist, neither can love of the world and love for God coexist. Love of the things of the world, and love for God is impossible. You cannot serve two masters. Either one or the other will have priority. This is the test of where a Christian's true love lies. *"Do not love the world or the things of the world."* Three times Christ designated Satan as the prince of this world who holds the world's inhabitant under his evil influence. (John 12:31; 14:30; 16:11). The world is in open rebellion against God having rejected and crucified His Son, Jesus.

The love for the 'things' of the world have proved too much a temptation for many who have been enticed back into its corrupt ways. The love they once had for God has been replaced in their pursuit for what the world can offer. We do not know whether it was to seek fame or fortune, or to satisfy the desires of his carnal nature that caused Demas to turn his back on Paul. *"Demas has forsaken me having loved this world"* (2 Tim.4:10).

Don't flirt with the world for that is the first step towards loving the world. If your love for God is fervent the things of this world will have no attraction for you. Your hearts desires will be heavenward, and you shall seek with all your heart the things of heaven not the things of the world.

> *"Turn your eyes upon Jesus,*
> *Look full in His wonderful face;*
> *And the things of earth will grow strangely dim,*
> *In the light of His glory and grace"*

Helen Hewarth Lemmel (1864-1961)

BATTLE FOR THE MIND

Eph. 6:16

"Above all, taking the shield of faith, that you shall be able to quench all the fiery darts of the wicked"

The devil's *'fiery darts'* are silent, invisible, and fly as swift as soundless arrows. Paul calls them *'fiery darts'* because they ignite everything they touch. The devil infuses into the mind fear, doubt, guilt, disobedience, anger, lust, rebellion, anxiety, revenge, hate – the list is endless! It is not uncommon for us to experience these attacks on a regular basis. The devil's attack on our minds is relentless. Unclean thoughts can be injected into the mind on the most solemn occasions. In church, during the Communion Service, a Prayer Meeting …Then can follow a sense of guilt and torment for having had such wicked thoughts when it is the devil himself who has infused them into our minds.

The devil wants to control the mind. He already controls the minds of hundreds of millions of people in the world. They are unaware they are his slaves in carrying out his will in this fallen world. The Christian's mind is a battle ground over which the devil is fighting for control. He will continue to bombard our minds with his fiery darts up to our dying day. Victory is ours. Paul writes, *"Above all, taking the shield of faith, that you shall be able to quench all the fiery darts of the wicked"*.

Our faith in Christ acts like a shield that extinguishes these fiery darts of the devil. *"Faith means the ability to apply quickly what we believe, thus enabling us to repel everything the devil does or attempts to do to us"*. Martyn Lloyd-Jones (1899-1981).

> *"Increase our faith! On this broad shield,*
> *All fiery darts be caught;*
> *We must be victors in the field,*
> *Where You for us has fought".*

Francis R. Havergal (1836-1879)

A BLANK CHEQUE?

John 14:13-14

"And I will do whatever you ask in my name, so that the Father may be glorified in the Son. You may ask me for anything in my name, and I will do it."

Wow! What a promise! Has Jesus handed us a blank cheque? Can I have that new car? A new motorbike? A new house? That big new Television? These two verses from John's gospel are the favourites of the 'name it and claim it' by the so-called Prosperity Churches. 'Pray for what you want, the preacher says, and just tac the name of Jesus on the end of your petition, and it's yours. If you don't get it, says the preacher, it's because you lack faith.'

This interpretation of using this promise as a blank cheque is a complete distortion because it is taken way out of its context. This promise is for the disciples of Jesus. Not for us. Jesus was preparing to face the cross thus ending His mission on earth. He was commissioning His disciple *"to go preach the gospel to all nations baptizing them in the name of the Father, the Son and the Holy Spirit"*. (Matt 28:19-20).

After about three years of ministry in Palestine Jesus' time in the world were coming to an end. He would die on a Cross. But His disciple was commissioned to take the Gospel to the ends of the earth with its message of salvation. Jesus is promising them His help. He will give them everything they needed to further His great Commission in making disciples of all nations. It is in that context that His promise is given. It has everything to do with helping them fulfill that Commission.

To "ask in the name" of Jesus implies asking for something consistent with His will. I am not asking something selfish for myself; but asking for the something according to His will. Selfish prayers will never be answered.

James wrote, *"When you ask something in prayer, you do not receive it because you ask with wrong motives, that you may spend what you get on your pleasures"*. (James 4:3).

> *"Teach me to pray, Lord, teach me to pray,*
> *This is my heart-cry, day unto day;*
> *I long to know Thy will, and Thy way,*
> *Teach me to pray, Lord, teach me to pray."*

Albert S. Reitz (1879-1966)

DOWN BUT NOT OUT

Psalm 145:14

"The Lord upholds all those who fall and lifts up all who are bowed down".

"If you think you are *standing firm, be careful that you don't fall*" is a reminder to be careful you don't fall. (1 Cor. 10:12). Paul is warning against becoming complacent in our Christian Walk. We are all in danger of falling into sin but more so if we do not understand the nature and the power of sin in our lives. We need to recognize that we are weak and feeble, and continuously in need of God's divine aid and strength.

The Lord, however, shows His compassion when one of His followers do fall into sin. He knows the weakness and the frailty of our bodies and sympathizes knowing how imperfect we truly are. (Psalm 103:14). In a moment of weakness some have let their guard down and given into the weakness of the flesh that has caused them sorrow and regret. They carry a heavy load of guilt and shame that some find difficult in forgiving themselves for what they have done.

King David was guilty of adultery with Bathsheba. He was also guilty to being responsible for the killing of her husband Uriah on the battlefield. Can you think of anything worse? An adulterer and an accomplice to murder? David was deeply sorry for what he had done and humbled himself before the Lord in repentance. And the Lord lifted him up and made him a great King. David could later write, *"The Lord upholds all those who fall and lifts up all who are bowed down"*.

To be bowed down is to be truly repentant and humble before the Lord God, and those the Lord will lift again. The Lord does not despise or reject them. He draws near and holds them if their fall humbles them before Him. They who fall may call themselves a fool for their weakness. But if they are truly humble before Him the Lord does not call them a fool. He lifts them up and encourages them to continue their walk with Him.

> *"Fear not, I am with you; O be not dismayed,*
> *For I am your God, and will still give you aid;*
> *I'll strengthen, help you, and cause you to stand,*
> *Upheld by my righteous omnipotent hand."*

Richard Keen (c. 1787)

SOURCE OF CONTENTMENT

1 Tim. 6:6

"But godliness with contentment is great gain"

Paul is writing to Timothy about the perils the love of money causes to those who have set their hearts upon money. The phrase "money is the root of all evil" is often misinterpreted when in fact the quote specifically refers to the love of money as a potential source of evil. (1 Tim 6:10). People who love money are controlled by money. They don't own money. Money owns them. It becomes their master. They have an insatiable craving to want more, and the more they have the more they want. They can never have enough. And, like Ebenezer Scrooge, those that love money are loath to part with it.

There can never be true contentment in the life of anyone who is addicted to the love of money. No matter how much they have it can never bring them lasting satisfaction. Some of the most unhappy and less contented people on earth are to be found among the wealthy. Hollywood is full of them!

Contentment in life can never be gotten by how much wealth you have. It comes through having peace with God, forgiveness of sin, freedom from a guilty conscience, and a steadfast hope of heaven. It refers to a state of heart and mind completely independent of all outward things. It is a calm and satisfied feeling; a freedom from murmuring and complaining.

True contentment comes from what God provides for us in Christ. He alone can satisfy the deepest longings of the soul. It requires little of this world's goods to satisfy a Christian who considers themself a pilgrim on their way to heaven. Even though they may have little of this world's goods they will find full contentment in living a life in a close relationship with Jesus Christ.

> *"There is a peace within me,*
> *That has sprung from deep contentment.*
> *With my Lord, who's All in All.*
> *For my delight is in this Living One,*
> *Who is Himself, my everything".*

Author unknown

RESISTING TEMPTATION

1 Cor. 10:13

"No temptation has overtaken you, but such as is common to man; and God is faithful, who will not allow you to be tempted beyond what you are able, but with the temptation will provide the way of escape also, so that you will be able to endure it"

You are not alone in your temptations. Christians all over the world face the same temptations as you do. None are exempt. Temptations will come to you in varies ways, via the world, the flesh and the devil. The beginnings of temptation always start in your mind. Your mind is the most vulnerable part of who you are, and the devil will use it to tempt you into sin. Herein is the need to use the shield of faith to quench his fiery darts. (Eph. 6:6).

To be tempted is not sin, but to surrender to temptation is sin. Not to reject unclean thoughts will result in a strong imagination, a sense of delight and then consent. All temptations that come to you are limited in their power by God according to your ability to bear it. God does not tempt you. (James 1:3) He does not infuse evil thoughts into your mind. When you are tempted, the devil will often condemn you for being tempted, but that condemnation is from the devil that you must reject.

God knows how much pressure you can take. He makes a way of escape from temptation so that you do not fall into sin. You will not be tempted beyond your ability to bear it. Temptation is an opportunity for you to grow in your faith. In Christ, we have the victory.

"Yield not to temptation, for yielding is sin;
Each victory will help you, some other to win,
Fight manfully onward, dark passions subdue,
Look ever to Jesus, He will carry you through.

Ask the Saviour to help you,
comfort, strengthen, and keep you;
He is willing to help you;
He will carry you through".

Horatio R. Palmer (1834-1907)

A FRUITFUL TREE

Psalm 1:3

"He will be like a tree planted by the rivers of water, which gives its fruit at the right time, whose leaves will ever be green"

Bishop J. Hall, (1574-1656), wrote, '*Look wherever you like in the Bible, and you shall never find any true Christian compared to anything but a fruitful tree*'. "The righteous will be like a tree planted by the rivers of water which gives fruit at the right time whose leaves will ever be green". The likeness between a righteous person and a fruitful tree is they both yield fruit. As water maintains the life of a tree so it can bear fruit, likewise the indwelling life of the Spirit of Christ enables the believer to bear spiritual fruit. That fruit is *love, joy, peace, patience, kindness, goodness, faithfulness, gentleness and self-control*". (Gal. 5:22).

There is only one way we can evaluate the life of a professing Christian, and a Christian preacher. There can be no pretence. Jesus said, *"By their fruit you shall know them"* (Matt. 7:8-20). Do they show righteousness, humility and faithfulness in the way they live? The world judges us, not by our words but by our deeds. It is not what we say that is all important, but the way in which we live our lives before others. This is how the world evaluates us.

Like a tree planted by the rivers of water from which it receives its nourishment and gives its fruit at the right time, so our lives are spiritually in union with Christ thus able to bear the fruit of the Spirit. (John 15:5-8).

"I'd rather see a sermon than hear one any day;
I'd rather one should walk with me than merely tell the way.
The eye's a better pupil and more willing than the ear,
Fine counsel is confusing, but example's always clear;
And the best of all the preachers are
the men who live their creeds,
For to see good put in action is what everybody needs.

I soon can learn to do it if you'll let me see it done;
I can watch your hands in action, but
your tongue too fast may run.
And the lecture you deliver may be very wise and true,
But I'd rather get my lesson by observing what you do;
For I might misunderstand you and the high advice you give, But there's no misunderstanding how you act and how you live."

Edgar Guest (1881-1959)

LIMITING THE LIMITLESS GOD
Psalm 78:41

"Yes, they turned back and tempted God, and limited the Holy One of Israel".

The Israelites had been slaves of the Egyptians for about 400 years. God had promised to give their ancestors, Abraham, Isaac and Jacob, the Land of Canaan for their inheritance. The time had now come for them to leave Egypt and occupy this Land. Under the leadership of Moses, Pharoah was finally persuaded to let God's people go.

During their trek from Egypt to Canaan, about 840 Km (5,270 miles) they began to rebel against Moses. They questioned his leadership, blamed him for their lack of food and water, and accused him of deliberately leading them into the desert to kill them. They even threatened to stone him to death.

When they reached Mount Sinai, God gave to Moses the Ten Commandments, the fourth of which commanded, *"Don't make or bow down to idols. I am the Lord your God"*. This commandment they disobeyed by making an idol in the shape of a bull and then worshipped it as their God. This provoked God to anger. On the edge of the Promised Land, He turned the Israelites back into the desert and for forty-years they wandered in the wilderness.

There is a lesson to be learned from this event. God bought them *OUT* of their slavery in Egypt so that He could bring them *INTO* all the blessings He had prepared for them in Canaan. He never intended them to wander around in a desert but, because of their disobedience, they bought it upon themselves. Likewise, for the followers of Christ. He saved us out of our slavery to Satan to bring us into all the blessings He has planned for us. Don't be a saved Christian wandering about in a spiritual desert. God has a plan for each of us, but it depends upon our obedience to Him whether He can fulfil that plan in each of our lives. Yes, we can limit the limitless God in what He wants to do for us.

> *"Lord my will I here present Thee,*
> *Gladly now no longer mine:*
> *Let no evil thing prevent me*
> *Blending it with Thine"*

>   Charles W. L. Christien (1839-1926)

THE WAYS OF GOD

Psalm 103:7

"He made known His ways to Moses, His deeds to the people of Israel"

It was to Moses, the humblest man on earth that God made known His ways. For forty days Moses was alone with God on Mount Sinai where God made known to him His commandments, His statues and ordinances. The Ten Commandments he gave to Moses are rules for all humanity and are as important today as they were thousands of years ago. He made known to Moses the importance of respecting Him, the God of all creation, being honest, honouring our parents, and being good neighbours.

His ways He made known to Moses, His deeds to the people of Israel". The Israelites saw God's deeds. They saw His power when He turned the River Nile into blood. He sent plagues of frogs, gnats, flies and locusts over Egypt. God's mighty hand of judgment fell heavily upon the land of Egypt in defence of His people from the Egyptians. He led them through the Red Sea as on dry land. He fed them with manna, bread from heaven, in the wilderness. He protected them from their enemies.

The ways of God. The deeds of God. There are some Christian groups that place an emphasis upon seeing the "deeds" of God, His *"signs and wonders*" in their church meetings. They want to see God's deeds, His miracles taking place in their midst. Jesus said to such people, *"Unless you people see signs and wonders, you will by no means believe"*. (John 4:48). Faith based solely on miracles is very shaky ground upon which to base one's faith. Our faith is based solely upon the finished work of Jesus on the Cross of Calvery.

It is far more profitable for our spiritual growth and understanding to seek to know God's *"ways"*. Spending time with Him alone we gain insight into what He desires of us and what He wants to do for us. *"Show me your ways, O Lord, teach me your paths"* (Psalm 25:4)

> *"Teach me Thy way, O Lord, Teach me Thy way!*
> *Thy gracious aid affords, Teach me Thy way!*
> *Help me to walk aright, More by faith, less by sight.*
> *Lead me with heavenly light, Teach me Thy way!"*

Benjamin M. Ramsey (1849-1923)

LOVING AND HATING LIFE

John 12:25

"He that loves his life shall lose it; and he that hates his life in this world shall keep it to life eternal"

"Love" and "hate" in this verse point to the thought of *preferences* toward life rather than actual love or hate. Those who *'love life'* spend their time in pursuit of the wealth and the pleasures the world has to offer with little thought of God. They are earth-bound in their thinking and prefer to have the things of the world rather than the riches that God offers them in Christ. Their love of life, with its temporal pleasures will result in them losing the life that God offers to them in Christ, i.e. eternal life.

Jesus said, *"He that loves his life shall lose it; and he that hates his life in this world shall keep it to life eternal"*. This suggests we should not make this life on earth our 'be all and end all'. On the contrary, we should avoid doing so. Caring more about our physical life we lose the true purpose for our living. If we truly love God and know God, we will not pander to temporal things. We will think ahead on our eternal future. Our preferences will always be wanting to live and serve Jesus regardless of any sacrifice to ourselves.

To hate life is to hate the sin in one's own life. They hate the world with its corrupt system, its wars, and its widespread cruelty. Those who hate life have already been touched by God's love and will put Christ first in seeking to do His will rather than putting their own interests first. Their focus will be on the things of heaven rather than the things of earth. In sacrificing their own life to live only for Christ will result in having life eternal.

> "Earth holds no treasure but perish with using,
> however precious they be;
> Yet there's a country to which I am going:
> Heaven holds all for me.
> Why should I long for the world with its sorrows,
> When in that home o'er the sea,
> Millions are singing the wonderful story,
> Heaven hold all to me".
>
> Heaven holds all to me,
> Brighter its glory will be;
> Joy without measure will be my treasure:
> Heaven holds all to me"

Tillit S. Teddie (1885-1987)

THE LOVE OF SOLITUDE
Matthew 14:23

"After he had dismissed the crowd, he went up on a mountain apart to pray. Later that night, he was there alone"

Though Jesus liked to spend His time with people there were times He wanted to be alone. He often sought solitude and dismissed the crowds and even His own disciples that he might spend time alone with His Father. He chose a place where He could have His mind free from having to think about the needs of the crowds that always followed Him. Unlike us, He did not have the same reasons for prayer as we do. He did not have to confess sin for He was without sin. (John 8:45-47)

Jesus was subject to all the temptations of man. Having taken on the form of a human being He endured temptation like all men, yet without sin (Heb. 4:15). He would have prayed for strength in facing and overcoming the many temptations that crossed His path. And He would have prayed for the courage He would need to finish His Father's mission as He faced an agonizing death on the cross. The fact that Jesus was aware of His need to seek solitude and prayer should also motivate you to do likewise.

There are times when you need to disengage yourself from the outside world. As you shut the door on all its distractions you are inwardly refreshed as you wait before God meditating on who He is and what He has done for you. It also allows God to speak to your own heart, and what He wants to say to you. And what He wants to say to you is more important than what you want to say to Him.

> "Alone with God, the world forbidden.
> Alone with God, O blest retreat!
> Alone with God, and in Him hidden.
> To hold with Him communion sweet"
>
> Johnson Outman (1856-1922)

A GOOD CONSCIENCE

1 John. 3:21

"If our conscience does not condemn us, then we can approach God with confidence"

Kant, the 18th cent. German philosopher said there are two things that fill me with awe: "The starry heavens *above me and the moral law within me*". Where there is a moral law there must also be a Lawmaker. That Lawmaker is God and His moral law within accuses or excuses us of wrongdoing. Humans are the crowning glory of all God's creation having been endowed with the faculty of conscience.

Paul has much to say about the different kinds of a conscience. There is a good conscience, a bad conscience, a condemning conscience, an evil conscience, a seared conscience, and an abandoned conscience. (1 Tim.1:5; 3:9; 4:2. 1 Cor. 8:12, Titus 1:15; Heb. 10:22). The conscience acts like a bridge between man and God. It is God's only link to man and if seared as with a red-hot iron, God's link to that person is lost forever. They have crossed over God's the red line. (Rom.1:24). It is the Holy Spirit's only avenue of approach in bringing the conviction of sin to a sinner.

Christian's ought to strive to maintain a good conscience. It means holding short accounts of wrongs committed, being quick to forgive others and a longing to please God in every way. Doing so we can boldly approach the throne of grace with confidence and obtain mercy and find help in time of our need. (Heb. 4:14).

> *"Lord, how secure and blest are they,*
> *Who feel the joys of pardoned sin?*
> *Should storms of wrath shake earth and sea,*
> *Their minds have heaven and peace within"*
>
> Isaac Watts (1674-1748)

THE INNER LIFE

Ephesians 3:16

"I pray that out of his glorious riches he may strengthen you with power through his Spirit in your inner being"

In his petitions for others, it is interesting to note what Pual did *not* ask God for on their behalf. There is no mention in his prayers for their health, their financial needs, for protection against persecution or from dangers they faced from their idolatrous neighbours. There is no doubt Paul was concerned for their physical welfare but first and foremost he was mostly concerned for their spiritual welfare.

In comparisons to Pauls, our own prayers for others can appear to be rather shallow and selfish, and short-sighted. We tend to focus upon their physical well-being with little thought for their spiritual. I'm not suggesting we do not pray for the health and the physical needs of others, but I have yet to hear a prayer like Pauls uttered in a prayer meeting!

There are times when we can lose our inner man's strength with God. The soul can reach a point of weakness where there is no more energy in Christian living. Perhaps this can be due to taking care of the needs of the outer man and paying less attention to the needs of the inner man. The Holy Spirit can give us a fresh infusion of His power that will strengthen us in our inner being to becoming strong in spirit. He longs to do so.

In our own private petitions for others another let us focus upon their spiritual needs just as Paul did. Each of us need the power of the Spirit in our inner most being, and so, when we make that request for ourselves let us also make it for someone else too.

> *"Holy Spirit, Power divine,*
> *Fill and nerve this soul of mine,*
> *Kindle every high desire,*
> *Perish self in Thy pure fire"*

Samuel Longfellow (1819-1892)

THE CROSS
Matthew 16:24

"Whoever wants to be my disciple must deny themselves and take up their cross and follow me"

"Take up your cross, nor heed the shame,
nor let your foolish pride rebel:
for you the Saviour bore the cross,
to save your soul from death and hell."

Charles W. Everest (1814-1877) wrote about the cross for he saw God's love revealed to him in sending Jesus to die on a cross for his sins. His sins had been forgiven, he was at peace with God, and knew he had eternal life with Jesus in heaven. He was so moved by what Jesus had done for him that he wrote this hymn to express his love for Him. But Charles did not simply write about the cross. He took to heart what Jesus said, *"Whoever wants to be my disciple must deny themselves and take up their cross and follow me"*

To deny oneself has nothing to with giving up things we like, but the giving up of ourselves to Jesus Christ. It is to live for Christ and to fully identify with His rejection, shame, suffering, and death. The thought of taking up a cross must have sent a shudder of horror through the disciples when Jesus spoke these words to them. The cross was an instrument of death. Crucifixion was an ancient form of execution in which a person was either tied or nailed to a cross and left to hang until dead. Death would be slow and excruciatingly painful.

To bear the cross and follow Christ is to be willing to face criticism, ridicule, opposition, misunderstanding, hardships, ostracism and even death. His call for us to take up our cross is a call to engage in radical self-denial. When we sing the hymn "*Jesus, keep me near the Cross*" let us also add, And Lord, help me '*bear the cross*' and faithfully follow You.

> "Take up your cross, the Saviour said,
> if you wouldst my disciple be;
> deny yourself, the world forsake,
> and humbly follow after me.
>
> Take up your cross and follow Christ,
> nor think till death to lay it down,
> for only those who bear the cross,
> may hope to wear the glorious crown.
>
> Charles William Everest (1814-1877)

THE DISCIPLINE OF THE LORD

Hebrews 12:6

"The Lord disciplines the one he loves, and he chastens everyone he accepts as his own"

God will not turn a blind eye to the shortcomings of those whom He loves. Like any responsible Father He will protect, correct and lovely discipline His children so they grow up to be mature and godly in life. Without His discipline we'll never know what would have happened to us if He had left us to our own devices. There is no doubt that our lives would never reach the state that God intends them to be.

How does God discipline those whom He loves? In the first place to be disciplined by God shows you are loved by God. God works everything together for good those whom He loves and who in turn love Him. Paul wrote: *"all things work together for good for those who love God, to those who are called according to His purpose."* (Rom. 8:28).

God does not cause trouble or pain, but He can use trouble and pain in our lives as discipline to build us up in our faith. His methods of discipline may vary. Loss of income, physical sickness., hardship at home and the troubles associated with just living in the world are often God's ways of building us up to be what He wants us to be.

Looking back on his own difficulties the Psalmist would write: *"It was good for me to be afflicted so that I might learn your decrees"*. *"Before I was afflicted, I went astray, but now I obey Your word"*. (Ps. 118:12; 119:67-71). Far better to be under the discipline of God than to be left to our own devices.

> *"Have Your own way, Lord! Have Your own way!*
> *You are the potter; I am the clay.*
> *Mould me and make me After Your will,*
> *While I am waiting, Yielded and still"*

Adelaide A. Pollard (1862-1934)

PERFECT PEACE

John 14:27

"Peace, I leave with you; my peace I give you. I do not give to you as the world gives. Do not let your hearts be troubled and do not be afraid."

Peace for most people is a state of freedom of the mind from anxieties, troubles, and worries that confront us any time in life. This kind of peace is temporary and can last until another trouble sets in. The peace the world offers is to avoid open conflict between nations. They call absent of war peace, but as history teaches, that kind of peace is short lived.

The peace that Jesus gives is an inward and lasting peace that surpasses all human understanding. (Phil.4:7). This peace doesn't eliminate conflict or trouble but gives you the ability to endure it. Those that have the peace Jesus imparts rest in the sure knowledge of knowing that He is in control of all the painful events that can take place in life. Neither grief, nor pain, sickness nor sorrow nor even the threat of death itself can take that peace from those to whom Jesus has given it.

The peace that Christ wants to impart to you is gained by accepting Him as your Saviour and making Him Lord of your life. There is no other way you can have true peace in your heart.

"Peace, I leave with you; my peace I give you. I do not give to you as the world gives. Do not let your hearts be troubled and do not be afraid." My prayer for you, my reader is:

> "Now may the Lord of peace Himself give you peace
> always in every way. The Lord be with you."
>
> 2 Thess. 3:16

> "Peace, perfect peace,
> In this dark world of sin;
> The blood of Jesus whispers,
> Peace within".
>
> Edward H. Bickersteth (1825-1906)

CRUCIFIED WITH CHRIST

Galatians 2:20

"I am crucified with Christ: nevertheless, I live; yet not I, but Christ lives in me..."

If Paul had been literally crucified with Christ, obviously he would not have been around to write his letters to the churches. Only the two thieves who were with Jesus on Calvary's Hill were crucified with Him. Paul is saying he was crucified with Christ mystically. When Jesus was crucified, Paul considered himself as being crucified with him. He died with Jesus. In the past Paul lived the way of the world but that way was over. His old way of living had been nailed to the cross. 'I have been crucified with Christ', he said, 'I no longer live but Christ lives in me, and He gives me victory over sin.' (2 Cor. 5:17; Rom 6:4).

What Paul wrote about himself is true of all who have put their trust in Christ. When a new believer is baptized by emersion they are symbolically baptized into Christ's death. When they emerge up from the waters they are symbolically raised to newness of life. They have testified to all that their former sinful way of living has been left behind and from hereon they will live and walk in the newness of life that is in Christ.

'I live', said Paul, *yet not I, but Christ lives in me*". The sinful nature within us is still very much alive and cannot be overcome without God's power.

But the Spirit of Christ within gives us that power to say "no" to sin and "yes" to God.

> *"I've reckoned myself to be dead unto sin,*
> *And risen with Christ, and now He lives within.*
> *The life more abundant He gives unto me,*
> *This overflow of life gives me full victory."*

James M. Kirk (1854-1945)

KEEPING THE PEACE
Romans 12:18

"If it is possible, as far as it depends on you, live at peace with everyone"

"*If it is possible*" implies that it is not always possible to live at peace with everyone. It seems as if Paul himself was often in conflict with both Christians and Jews. He argued with Barnabas about the suitability of Marcus accompanying them on their second missionary journey. Their dispute was so heated they split up and went their separate ways. (Acts 15:37-39). It is unrealistic to think we can live peacefully and in harmony with everyone including some fellow Christians. We are to seek peace but then it does not always depend upon us. There are some hard heads who simply will not reconcile with others.

We cannot control someone else's outburst of anger or criticism aimed at us. But we can try to control our own reaction to such outbursts. For their assaults against us we are not answerable, but we are answerable for how we react toward them. Just as it takes two to tango, so it takes two to argue.

Each of us have our own opinions about things, and when these opinions clash with others it can result in bad feelings, angry words, divisions, and rivalries. We ought never be accused of originating a quarrel with another person that will break the peace. One of the fruits of the Spirit is *"long-suffering"*, and there can be a short supply of that on some occasions.

Keeping the peace, however, is never to be at the cost of comprising with known sin. Two of the seven churches mentioned in Revelation were guilty of doing exactly that. They turned a blind eye to sin in the lives of some of its members just to keep the peace. They did not want to "rock the boat" and so they received a stern rebuke from the Lord. (Rev. 2:12-17; 18-28).

> *"Pour down Thy Spirit from above,*
> *And bid all strife and discord cease.*
> *Join heart to heart in mutual love,*
> *O reign among us Prince of Peace."*
>
> James Montgomery (1771-1854)

FEELING FAINT?

Psalm 142: 3

"When my spirit is faint within me, you are there to watch over my steps."

This Psalm is referred to by Bible commentators as the "Cave Psalm". David was hiding in a cave from King Saul who was trying to kill him. Along with thirty-seven of his "mighty men" he used the Cave Adullam as his fortress. He was trapped by Saul's men and felt there was no way of escape but only by a miracle. David was overwhelmed feeling weak in spirit under his present affliction yet his trust in God was such that he could say, *"When my spirit is faint within me, you are there to watch over my steps."*

There are times when we can feel just as David felt when overwhelmed with the pressures of life. Nowhere has God promised us health, wealth, and prosperity but He has promised to care for us and to sustain us to the end, (Heb. 13:5-6). We do not how God watches over our steps, but we can rest assured He does, particularly when we are faint in spirit. Nothing about us is hidden from His sight. He knows our weaknesses and *"remembers we are but flesh, a passing breeze that does not return."* (Psalm 78:39).

"All the way my Saviour leads me.
What have I to ask beside?
Can I doubt His tender mercy?
Who through life has been my Guide?
Heavenly peace, and Oh such comfort,
Here by faith in Him to dwell,
For I know whatever befalls me,
Jesus does all things well,
For I know whatever befalls me,
Jesus does all things well."

Fanny Crosby (1820-1915)

PAY-BACK TIME

Matthew 7:1-2

"Pass no judgement, and you will not be judged. For as you judge others, so you will yourselves be judged, and whatever measure you deal to others will be dealt back to you."

Every judgment a person makes against another becomes the basis for their own judgment. Such is the fixed and unchanging law of God. The advice Jesus gives to us is not to pass judgment because the way we judge others, is the same way in which we shall be judged. Judgment time is pay-back time.

Unlike the sanctimonious Pharisees and Sadducees who were quick to pass judgement upon the common people without any thought for the people's feelings we should not be hasty to judge anyone. We cannot know the pains, regrets or the yearnings in the hearts of others. How can any judgment be just and true if we do not know the heart of the one, we judge? If we knew what some people have had to go through, we would not judge them at all.

To judge a person without knowing the whole story is why Jesus said *"Pass no judgement, and you will not be judged. For as you judge others, so you will yourselves be judged, and whatever measure you deal to others will be dealt back to you."*

John Stott (1921-2011) said, *"Jesus does not tell us to cease to be men* (by suspending our critical powers which help to distinguish us from animals) *but to renounce the presumptuous ambition to be God* (by setting ourselves up as judges)."

> *"Thou Judge of quick and dead, before whose bar severe,*
> *With holy joy or guilty dread, we all shall soon appear.*
> *Our erring souls prepare, for that tremendous day,*
> *And fill us with a watchful care and stir us up to pray."*

Charles Wesley (1707-1788)

A LOWLY ESTEEM OF OURSELVES

Genesis 18:27

"And Abraham answered and said, behold now, I have taken upon me to speak unto the Lord although I am but dust and ashes."

In pleading to God to spare the city of Sodom, Abraham admitted he was bold in asking Him not to do so. He was aware of being in the presence of Almighty God, the Creator of heaven and earth whom he held in awe and before whom he acknowledged he was nothing more than dust and ashes. He felt unworthy to be in God's presence and confessed his unfitness in being so.

"*I am but dust and ashes*", a frail, feeble, mortal creature unworthy to speak to God. This was not feigned humility. Abraham knew God, and those that know God most will fear Him most. They will stand in awe and reverence and acknowledge the vast distance there is between them and God.

> "Alas! And did my Saviour bleed,
> And did my Saviour die?
> Would he devote that sacred Head,
> For such a **worm** as I?
>
> Isaac Watts. (1674-1748)

This thinking was prevalent in the days when this hymn was written, perhaps because there was a higher view of God and a deeper sense of sin. Look up into the night sky and contemplate upon the vastness of the stars above and you will begin to understand how small you are in God's creation. Like Abraham, Watts and many others it will have a humbling effect upon your soul that gives you an awareness of your own smallness and unworthiness before an almighty and powerful God.

"Whenever we find that our religious life is making us feel that we are good-above all, that we are better than someone else, we can be sure that we are being acted upon, not by God, but by the devil. The real test of being in the presence of God is that you either forget about yourself altogether or see yourself as a small dirty object."

C. S. Lewis (1898-1963)

UNEDUCATED AND UNTRAINED

Acts 4:13

"The Council were amazed to see how bold Peter and John were ... to learn they were uneducated and untrained ... but realized they had been with Jesus"

'*Unschooled and ordinary*' would hardly be the kind of reference a church would like to receive about a candidate applying to be their pastor! This comment was made by the Jewish Council before whom Peter and John stood accused of non-Jewish activities. They had just healed a crippled beggar. The Council were amazed at their boldness and noted they had been the companions of Jesus.

This summed up Peter and John's success in making such an impact on the crowds to whom they were preaching. *"They had been with Jesus."*

They had been with Jesus for about three years, and along with James, they appear to have been Jesus' closest associates. Peter, James and John went up with Jesus on the Mount of Transfiguration. (Matt.17:1-8). On the morning of the resurrection, Mary Magdalene ran directly to Peter to inform him, and John what had happened. (John 20:2). For about three years they had been with Jesus. They walked alongside of Him; they listened to Him and had been eyewitnesses to His miracles. They saw and they learned by spending time with Him.

Isn't it amazing what God did with those *'ordinary, uneducated and untrained'* men! No follower of Jesus is ever too *ordinary* or *unschooled* to be useful to Him. Never underestimate your value to God. It will surprise you what He has accomplished through the lives of those who were *'unschooled'*. God chooses *the foolish things, the weak things, the lowly things to shame the strong and the wise so that no one can boast before Him.* (1 Cor. 1:27-29). If God can speak through an ass; He can speak through me. (Numbers 22:21-33).

> *God did not choose philosophers, nor orators,*
> *nor statesmen, nor men of wealth and*
> *power and interest in the world to publish*
> *the gospel of grace and peace. Not the wise man after*
> *the flesh ... God sees not as man sees.*
> *He has chosen the foolish things of the world,*
> *the weak things of the world ... men of mean birth,*
> *of low rank, of no liberal education, to be the preachers*
> *of the gospel and planters of the church.*
> *He is a better judge to serve the purposes of His glory."*
>
> Matthew Henry's Commentary (1662-1714)

TRUE WORSHIP

Psalm 29:2

"Give to the Lord the glory due to His name. worship the Lord in the beauty of holiness"

There is an inspiring lifting of the soul as we join in heartfelt praise to the Lord. Be it in a cathedral, a church, a small chapel or at home, our hearts are stirred as we sing the great hymns of the Christian faith or the contemporary songs of our age in joyful praise to God. We are uniting our praise on earth with all the host in heaven also singing their praise to God. Paul encourages believers to sing and make music in our hearts to the Lord. (Eph. 5:19, Col 3:16).

We are reminded however, that our worship to the Lord is to be *"in the beauty of holiness."* Words offered in praise amount to nothing if one is living in sin. Their words will never reach the portals of heaven. There is no substitute for holy living. Your church membership, your monetary giving, your partaking of the Lord's Supper, your reciting prayers from the prayer book and your singing of the hymns can never compensate for a holy life. These things can be done through habit, a tedious performance Sunday after Sunday without the beauty of holiness of life.

The lord knows our hearts. Nothing is hidden from Him. Putting on a pious face may fool the crowd, but it won't fool God. It is not the voice of the singer that pleases the Lord but the sincerity within the heart from which that song is sung. *Man looks on the outward appearance, but the Lord looks on the heart'* (1 Sam 16:7). *"Be holy for I am holy"* for *"without holiness no one can see God"*. (1 Peter 1:16). That alone is the only worship acceptable to the Lord.

> *"O worship the Lord in the beauty of holiness*
> *Bow down before Him, His glory proclaims.*
> *With gold of obedience and incense of lowliness,*
> *Kneel and adore Him: The Lord is His Name."*

John S. B. Monsell (1811-1875)

> *"That, cleansed from stain of sin,*
> *I may my meek and homage give,*
> *And, pure in heart, behold*
> *Thy beauty while I live.*
> *Clean hands in holy worship raise,*
> *And Thee, O Christ, my Saviour praise".*

Gregory Nazianzen (c 329-389)

ANGER

Ephesians 4:26

"If you are angry, do not let anger lead you into sin; do not let the sunset find you still nursing it; leave no loophole for the devil."

"*If you get angry*". That "*if*" implies there are times when we do get angry. We can react angrily toward someone who has upset us by something they may have said or done to us. That anger may not necessarily make itself known verbally in an out bust of self-fence but by an inward flare-up of our emotions. There might arise in the mind angry, vindictive or vengeful feelings that need to quickly be rejected before they take root and give the devil a foothold in your life causing you to sin.

There is a world of difference between righteous anger and an anger that resides in a hateful heart. Righteous anger is what Jesus had toward the Pharisees and the Sadducees who were hard unpromising critics void of any compassion toward the ordinary people. Jesus was angry at the hard-heartedness of the Pharisees when He healed the man with the injured hand (Mark 3:1-6). He revealed His righteous anger when He cleansed the Temple. He saw how the merchants who were profiting from the pilgrims had turned God's house into a den of thieves. (Matt. 21:12-13; Mark 11:15-17).

We feel righteous anger when we hear of the mistreatment of others, particularly the very young and the elderly. There would be something radically wrong if we did not feel a righteous anger at some of the things that are happening around us today.

If you are angry against someone who has offended you, you forgive them before the sun sets. Don't take it to bed with you. Don't nurse it. Even righteous anger can smoulder within robbing you of sleep. It also gives the devil a loophole into playing havoc with your mind. Turn your mind upon the Lord. Count His blessings and His peace will flood your soul.

> *"Lord, You will keep him in perfect peace.*
> *Lord, You will keep him in perfect peace.*
> *Lord, You will keep him in perfect peace.*
> *Whose mind is stayed on You."*

Scripture in Song 1972

FORGETTING THE PAST
Philippians. 3:13-14

"I do not consider myself yet to have taken hold of it. But one thing I do: Forgetting what is behind and straining toward what is ahead, I press on toward the goal to win the prize for which God has called me heavenward in Christ Jesus".

I do not consider myself yet to have taken hold of it. Paul is giving us a glimpse into his own personal life by revealing his heart's desire to win the prize for which God had called him heavenward in Christ Jesus. Spiritual giant though he was, Paul did not consider himself to have attained perfection. I am still not all that I should be. He did not believe in spiritual perfectionism because he knew that the work of the Holy Spirit is continually carried on day after day throughout his whole life.

"Forgetting those things which are behind", Paul refused to let past failures or regrets hold him back from moving forward. Instead of being chained by past mistakes, relationships, memories, defeats, temptations he focussed all his attention on finishing the race set before him.

I press toward the goal to win the prize for which God has called us heavenward in Christ Jesus". He knew God had taken hold of his life to conform him into the image of Jesus. And Paul wanted, above everything else, to see the nature of Jesus in himself (Rom.8:29). That was the prize he so coveted. To be like Jesus.

We all have things in our past that we regret, and which we need to forget. But to hold on to bitterness or unforgiveness will lock you into your past where you will be unable to forget. Don't let the weight of your past failures or regrets hold you back from moving forward. Jesus has forgiven all past sins. Forgive yourself so that you can press ahead in your high calling of God in the race set before you. The prize ahead is your complete transformation into the image of His Son, Jesus. This is God's ultimate intention for you.

> "Yesterday is history and history being miles away
> So, leave it all behind you
> But let it always remind you of the day
> The day that love made history
> You know you can't stay right where you fell
> The hardest part is forgiving yourself
> But let's take a walk into today
> And don't let your past get in the way"
>
> Mathew West (1977-)

CLAY POTS
2 Corinthians 4:7

"But we have this treasure in pots of clay to show that this all-surpassing power is from God and not from us." (Wey trans)

Paul likens our human body to a clay pot. You may be a fat clay pot, a skinny clay pot, a tall clay pot or a short clay pot. You may be a white clay pot, a black clay pot, an old and chipped clay pot or even a broken and cast aside clay pot. But if you have Jesus Christ as your Saviour there is within you the greatest treasure you can ever possess, nor ever lose.

Ancient kings use clay pots to store their treasures of gold, silver, precious stones and other valuables. They were made in all shapes and sizes. Some ornamental and others just plain. However beautiful a pot the value was not in the pot but what was inside.

The treasure you have within is of far greater value than your body of fragile clay. You have a use-by-date stamped upon you that when reached will return your clay pot to dust and ash. But the treasure within you *"is the light of the knowledge of the glory of God"*. v.6. Another way of defining this treasure is *"Christ in you, the hope of glory"* (Col 1:27).

You have this treasure in you to *"show that this all-surpassing power is from God and not from us."* There is no room for boasting. God wants to use us in fulfilling His will on earth, but we must be ready to acknowledge that we are a mere clay pot, and it is the Treasure within that has all the glory.

> *"Have Your own way, Lord! Have Your own way!*
> *You are the potter; I am the clay.*
> *Mould me and make me, after Your will,*
> *While I am waiting, yielded and still."*

Adelaide A. Pollard (1862-1934)

MY GOD! WHY?

Job 1:1

'Job, a man that was perfect and upright, and one that feared God and hated evil.'

In the land of Uz, (modern day Siria or Jordon) there lived a man who feared God and shunned evil. He was a wealthy family man with ten children and was the greatest man among the people of the East. His name was Job. He was pious, rich, loyal, and he loved God

There came the time when the angels and Satan presented themselves before the Lord. (1:6-12). The Lord God had told Satan how Job lived a blameless and upright life. *"It's only because you are so good to him"*, Satan replied. If I put him through a test, you would quickly see how weak his loyalty is to you. Then test him, said God, *"everything he has is in your hands, but on Job himself do not lay a finger."*

The first test was to take away all of Job's animals, kill his servants and then kill all of Job's sons and daughters. The second test was to afflict sores all over Job's body. The third test came via three of Job's friends, Eliphaz, Bildad and Zophar accused him of not being a good man because of the bad things that were happening to him. Job's own wife told him to curse God, but Job refused. Satan had failed in his attempt to make Job blame God for all his afflictions.

If ever a man had a right to ask, 'My God! Why?' it would have been Job. He lost his health, his family, his wealth, his livelihood and his reputation as being, the greatest man among the people of the East. And this happened to a man of integrity, a man who hated evil and loved God. But God allowed Job to be tested so his true character could be revealed. Job had lost everything but had not lost himself. *"Though he slays me, yet will I hope in him; I will surely defend my ways to his face"* (Job. 13:15).

James writes: *'Consider yourselves fortunate when all kinds of trials come your way, for you know that when your faith succeeds in facing such trials, the result is the ability to endure.'* (James 1:2-3). The trials we face in life bring to the surface what we are really like and how strong is our faith. They test the sincerity of our faith and love for God. And the trials and tribulations we do face are used by God to build up our Christian character.

> "Fear not, I am with you; O be not dismayed;
> For I am your God and will still give you aid;
> I'll strengthen you, help you, and cause you to stand,
> Upheld by My righteous omnipotent hand.
>
> When through the deep waters I call you to go,
> the rivers of woe shall not you overflow;
> For I will be with you, your troubles to bless,
> and sanctify to you your deepest distress".

John Rippon (1751-1836)
Often attributed to George Keith

THE POWER OF FORGIVENESS
2 Corinthians 2:10

"If you forgive anyone, I also forgive him. And what I have forgiven – if there was anything to forgive -- I have forgiven in the sight of Christ for your sake."

Upon hearing of sexual immorality occurring in the Corinthian Church, Paul immediately asks for the discipline of the offender. The guilty man had sinned in an incestuous affair. He lived immorally with his stepmother. He was put under church discipline and apparently repented but the Corinthian Christians would not receive him back. Paul tells them to not be too severe, and to restore the repentant man back into the fellowship. (1 Cor. Ch. 5).

In the past someone who fell into gross sin after their baptism and public profession of faith were never restored back into the fellowship of the church. No matter how sincere their repentance this hard line of discipline was enforced by reformed churches. It is this hard spirit that Paul cautions against. The devil gets an advantage when church discipline is turned into oppression. Satan gains a victory when he can get a fallen Christian separated from his church and its congregation. One commentator put it this way, *"we don't want Satan to have any victory here --*

Paul's argument is that since the believer in the Corinthian Church has shown true repentance over his sin, he ought to be forgiven and received back into the fellowship. The devil works overtime in the heart and mind of a fallen believer. He implies their sin is too serious to forgive, even insinuating it was the unpardonably sin. The devil's continuous attacks drive the repentant sinner deeper and deeper into the Slough of Despondency from which they find it increasingly difficult to extricate themselves.

Just as Christ forgave us, we ought to forgive repentant believers who have fallen. In doing so we are showing them they are not rejected but loved and accepted. In doing so we deny Satan a victory over their lives.

> "Forgiveness, forgiveness
>
> Forgiveness, forgiveness
> Show me how to love the unlovable
> Show me how to reach the unreachable
> Help me now to do the impossible
> Forgiveness, forgiveness
> Help me now to do the impossible
> Forgiveness"
>
> Mathew West (1977-)

STAND STILL ... BE STILL

Exodus 14:13, Psalm 46:10-11

"Fear not, stand still, and see the salvation of the Lord"
"Be still and know that I am God"

"*Stand still and see the salvation of the Lord*". For over 400 years the Israelites were slaves in Egypt. They were forced to build the cities of Pithom with brick and mortar under hard labour. The Egyptians treated them ruthlessly. God heard their cry and sent Moses to lead about 9,000,000 Israelites out of their Egyptian slavery. They began their long trek towards the promised Land of Canaan. Pharaoh, however, was furious. He took his vast army and six hundred of his best chariots and pursued the Israelites trapping them between his army and the Red Sea. They were unable to go forward nor backward.

What do we do? they cried. Moses replied, *"Fear not, stand still, and see the salvation of the Lord"*. Moses then stretched out his hand over the Sea; and the Lord caused the waters to divide allowing the Israelites to escape on dry land.

There is a comparison between the saving of the Israelites from their slavery to the Egyptians and being saved by Jesus from the slavery of sin. (John 8:34; Rom.7:14). The Israelites could not free themselves from their slavery. They needed help, and God sent them Moses. We cannot free ourselves from our slavery to sin. We need help, and God sent us Jesus. The Israelites were freed from their slavery. They gained new life. Those who are freed from sin. They gain eternal life.

"Be still and know that I am God"' The Psalms are primarily written for the people of God. Psalm 46 was written in a time of war when God's people faced enormous conflicts from surrounding nations intent upon their destruction. As Christians we also shall face our conflicts in life.

In his classic story of "Pilgrims Progress" John Bunyan (1628-1688), mentions four giants that Pilgrim faced on his journey to the Celestial City. Giant Discouragement, Giant Difficulty, Giant Despair and Giant Doubt. Just as they tested the faith of Pilgrim, they will also test the faith of present-day believers on their own pilgrimage to heaven

> *"Be still, my soul: your God will undertake*
> *To guide the future as he has the past.*
> *Your hope, your confidence let nothing shake*
> *All now mysterious shall be clear at last.*
> *Be still, my soul: the tempests still obey*
> *His voice, who ruled them once on Galilee."*

Katharina von Schlegel (1697- ?)

SPIRITUAL SLUGGARDS

Proverbs 24:30-34

'A little extra sleep, a little more slumber, a little folding of the hands to rest, means that poverty will come upon you like a bandit'

King Solomon was out walking one day when he happened to pass a rundown garden overgrown with weeds and thistles. Even its stone wall was a shambles. He looked, took note, and then wrote the above.

This run-down garden could well reflect the spiritual state of some Christians who week after week go to church, sit in the same seat and wait to be fed. Being 'food fed' is detrimental to your spiritual life. You can become spiritually lazy that can lead you into becoming a spiritual sluggard. To avoid becoming a spiritual sluggard you need to 'self-feed' yourself.

You need your Bible, you need a place, and you need a time. Your Bible is God's Word through which He conveys to you on a personal level the way He wants you to live your life. He doesn't just want you to hear it read to you from a pulpit. He wants you to read it for yourself so that you begin to 'self-feed' yourself. You will find it nourishment to your soul.

Choose a place and a time where you can be alone and have time with God. Call it your 'God Time' where you can meditate on His Word and reach out to Him in silent prayer.

> *"It's the voice of the sluggard; I heard him complain,*
> *You have waked me too soon; I must slumber again"*

Isaac Watts (1674-1748)

> *"Henceforth let no profane delight*
> *Divide this consecrated soul.*
> *Possess it Thou, who has the right*
> *As Lord and Master of the whole."*

C. Wesley (1707-1788)

COMPLETE IN CHRIST

Colossians. 2:9-10

"For in Him all the fullness of Deity dwells in bodily form, and in Him you have been made complete"

I well remember attending a prayer meeting years ago when one member of the group made this request to the Lord. 'O Lord, I need more power. I need more love. I need more holiness'. I couldn't help thinking he was asking for something he had already received. When Jesus takes up residence in your heart, He comes in His fulness, and in doing so you are made complete in Him. His divine attributes such as power, love and holiness do not come to us later in separate packages. They are not sent to us from heaven like a parcel post!

Jesus cannot be separated from His attributes no more than we can be separated from ours, whatever they may be. His attributes are who He is. Avoid looking upon your spiritual life like a battery that needs charging up every now and again. Think more of your spiritual life as a light bulb. A light bulb can only show its light when connected to its source of power. Break its source, and there is no light.

Jesus is the Source of your power; Jesus is the Source of your love. Jesus is the Source of your holiness. Jesus said, *"Remain in me, and I will remain in you. No branch can bear fruit of itself; it must remain in the* vine. Neither can you bear fruit unless you remain in me. I am the vine; you are the branches. If a man remains in me and I in him, he will; bear much fruit; apart from me you can do nothing." (John 15:4-5). Let your petition be: 'Lord, above all other things, I want to constantly remain in union with You.

Stop asking and start thanking Him for what He has done for you. In faith believe that you are complete in Him. You already have His power, His love and His holiness by remaining in union with Him, by abiding in Him. Live your life for Him, and you will grow in the knowledge of what it means to be complete in Him.

> 'Love beyond measure, mercy so free.
> Your endless resources given to me'.

Christina Rossetti (1830-94)

> "Thine in whom I live and move'
> Thine, Lord, the work, the praise is Thine.
> Thou art wisdom, power, and love,
> And all Thou art is mine"

Charles Wesley (1707-88)

TO DIE OR NOT TO DIE
2 Corinthians 5:8

"We are confident, I say, and would prefer to be away from the body and at home with the Lord."

The pronoun "we" obviously includes other Christians like-minded. Paul was getting old and tired. At the time of writing his letter to the Corinthian Church he was about 60 years and had served the Lord for about 30 years. During this time, he was a travelling missionary who knew his ministry was to preach the gospel to the Gentiles. He was always in danger of being robbed or killed on his travels. He faced severe opposition in his endeavours to preach Christ to the Gentiles. Paul was flogged and stoned by Jewish mobs, criticised by fellow Jews, and fellow Christians, and finally he was made a prisoner of the Romans. On his way to Rome his ship was shipwrecked of the coast of Malta where he had to spend 3 months during its cold winter. Upon his arrival in Rome, he was thrown into a Roman prison. (2 Cor. 11:23-27).

"I would prefer to be away from the body and at home with the Lord." For some life is too good to repeat those words of Paul. A wealthy friend of Samuel Johnson, (1709-1784), the renowned English writer and poet, was showing Johnson around his stately manor. As they strolled through his beautiful estate the wealthy friend said, *"Ah, Samuel, these are the*

things that make it hard to die." Beware of making yourself so comfortable that you are reluctant to leave what you have accumulated over your lifetime.

For many Christians daily life has become such a burden that their petition is *Oh! for the wings of a dove to fly away and to be at rest in the Lord".* (Psalm 55:6). They are weary of this world of violence, sin, greed, hate and corruption. Tired of the weakness of their own body subject to sickness and weakness. Without any hesitation they will say along with Paul, *"I'd rather be absent from the body and at home with the Lord."*

> *"So, when my latest breath,*
> *Shall end all earthly pain;*
> *By death I shall escape from death,*
> *And life eternal gain.*
>
> *Knowing as I am known,*
> *How shall I love that word;*
> *And oft repeat before the throne:*
> *Forever with the Lord."*

James Montgomery (1771-1854)

PRAYER WITHOUT WORDS
Matthew 6:7

"And when you pray, do not keep on babbling like the Gentiles, for they think they will be heard because of their many words."

Jesus denounces the use of mindless repetitious prayer. When the Gentiles prayed, they believed they would be heard for their much speaking to manipulate their gods to get what they wanted. Their prayers were full of meaningless repetition as they babbled on and on thinking at least one of the many gods they worshiped might hear them.

Jesus said, you've no need to repeat yourself to be heard. *"God already knows your needs"*. This raises the question: If God already knows our needs, What's the purpose of prayer? Its purpose is the opening of our hearts to God, inviting Him into our lives. Prayer pushes us to depend on God and deepens our relationship with Him. We pray in faith for God to act according to our requests.

Solomon writes, *"Stand in awe of God. Do not be quick with your mouth, do not be hasty with your heart to utter anything before God. Go near to listen. God is in heaven, and you are on earth, so let your words be few.* (Ecc.5:1-3). Before entering our time of private prayer, we need to remind ourselves who God is: He is our Creator in heaven, and we are His people on earth. He is omnipotent having unlimited power having created the Universe. There is nothing that He cannot do. He is omniscient who knows everything. He knows the future, the present and the past. He is omnipresent with the ability to be everywhere at once. Before such a God we should humbly bow the knee in deep adoration.

It is much easier to pray silently from the heart than with spoken words. He knows the desires of our hearts and He want us to express them in loving fellowship with Him. True prayer is expressed in the words of the following:

> *"Prayer is the soul's sincere desire,*
> *Uttered or unexpressed.*
> *The motion of a hidden fire,*
> *That trembles in the breast.*
>
> *Prayer is the burden of a sigh,*
> *The falling of a tear.*
> *The upward glancing of an eye,*
> *When none but God is near."*
>
> James Montgomery (1771-1854)

THE SOURCE OF DEFILEMENT
Matthew 15:11

"What goes into someone's mouth does not defile them, but what comes out of their heart, that is what defiles them."

In obedience to their tradition, Jews never ate without first washing their hands. The washing of hands, however, had nothing to do with hygiene. Their procedure was to pour water from a jug first twice over the right hand and then twice over the left hand. Care had to be taken that the unwashed hands did not touch the water used for washing. The hands are then dried with a towel before eating the meal. They believed that those who ate food without this traditional washing of the hands rendered both the food, and the partaker defiled.

"Why don't your disciples live according to the tradition of the elders instead of eating food with defiled hands?" (Mark 7:5). Calling the crowd, Jesus said, 'Listen to me and understand this: *"What goes into someone's mouth does not defile them, but what comes out of their mouth, that is what defiles them"*. Jesus tells the crowd that defilement is not what they put into their mouth but what comes out of the mouth, and what comes out reveals the wicked state of the heart. *"Evil thoughts, murder, adultery, sexual immorality, theft, false testimony, slander."* (Jer.17:9; Matt15:19-20).

There is nothing outside a person that can defile that person. There are substances such as smoking, alcohol and drugs that destroy the body. But they don't touch the soul. The *source* of defilement is internal not external. It is about who we really are. *"Create in me a pure heart, O God, and renew a steadfast spirit within me."* (Psalm 52:10).

> *"I am evil, born in sin.*
> *You desire truth within.*
> *You alone my Saviour are,*
> *Teach Your wisdom to my heart.*
> *Make me pure, your grace bestow,*
> *Wash me whiter than the snow"*

C. Kocher (1786-1872)

SECURE IN GOD'S RIGHT HAND

John 10:29-30

"My Father, who has given them to me, is greater than all, no one can snatch them out of my Father's hand. I and the Father are one"

Many years ago, I was out walking with my toddler son when we passed a low wall upon which he wanted to walk along its top. Lifting him up he tightly gripped my hand and took a few wobbly steps before I loosened his grip on me and took his hand in mine. What a change. He now wanted to run, skip and jump along the rest of that wall. What changed? He was no longer holding onto me. I was holding onto him. He trusted me and knew I would never let him go.

There is nowhere in the entire Universe that we can ever get beyond God's reach of love and protection over us. No power on earth or in the depths of hell can ever snatch us out of the security of God's right hand. It is His grip on us, not ours on Him that enables us to boldly trust Him to protect us and hold onto us. When that truth becomes fixed in our hearts there comes with it a sense of boldness and security in our walk with Him.

You may feel insecure in your relationship with God when you have no need to be. God said, *I will go before you and will be with you; I will never leave you nor forsake. Do not be afraid; do not be discouraged.* (Deut. 31:8; Heb. 13:5). There is no safer a place than to be held fast in the right hand of God.

> "Simply trusting every day,
> Trusting through a stormy way;
> Even when my faith is small,
> Trusting Jesus, that is all.
>
> Trusting as the moments fly,
> Trusting as the days go by;
> Trusting Him whate'er befall,
> Trusting Jesus, that is all."

Edgar P. Stites (1836-1921)

DON'T LOSE YOUR REWARD
John 15:1-2

"Jesus said, I am the true vine, and my Father is the Vinedresser. He cuts off every branch in me that bears no fruit, while every branch that does bear fruit, he trims clean so that it will be even more fruitful"

The bearing of fruit in a believer is always shown to be the result of a close and intimate relationship with Jesus Christ. The vine and the branches emphasize our complete dependence and the need of constant connection. The Father, as the Vinedresser, only prunes the branches that are already bearing fruit. Although it pleases Him that we are bearing fruit He knows we have the potential of bearing even more fruit for His glory.

Trimming or cleaning is done through the reading of the Word of God. It condemns sin, it inspires holiness, it promotes growth, and it reveals power for victory. (Eph. 5:26). The disciples of Jesus underwent a pruning process as Jesus applied the words of God that removed evil from them and conditioned them for further service. God does the same with us. He prunes and cleanses us from everything that impedes spiritual growth.

"If anyone does not remain in me, he is like a branch that is thrown away and withers; such branches are picked up, thrown into the fire and burnt". (v.6). These words have raised questions in the minds of many Christians. Am I going to be "cut off" and lose my salvation if I don't produce fruit? Will I be thrown into the fires of hell?

The branches that are thrown away were never properly abiding in the vine, demonstrated by the fact that they did *not bear fruit*. There are no true disciples who do not abide. But though a true Christian can never lose their salvation, they can lose their reward. (Matt. 6: 5-6; 2 John 8). We can do nothing of worth for the glory God apart from abiding in Jesus. Only by maintaining our close union with Him can we bear fruit for His glory. In Christ you are eternally secure. (John 10:28-29

> "Abiding, this will Satan's strength disarm,
> In fellowship, the world will lose its charm,
> Abiding, we sin's power need not fear,
> In fellowship, the self will disappear."

Adapted

"IF"

2 Corinthians. 1:20

"For no matter how many promises God has made, they are "Yes" in Christ".

Some years ago, I was in a Christian bookshop and noticed a small box that contained the "Promises of God" written on small cards. This small and decorated box was obviously made to be a gift to encourage the receiver to take out a promise each day of the year to cheer them up. What I did not see were the conditions attached to those promises.

God is not obliged to keep His promises if we do not first meet His conditions. God's promises come with a tag attached to them and on each tag is written the word "**IF**". "*If*' you forgive others the wrongs they have done you, your Father in heaven will also forgive you.' (Matt. 6:14-15). '*If*' we confess our sins, He is faithful and just to forgive our sins' (1 John 1:9). 'No good thing does He withhold from those '*if*' their life is blameless' (Ps. 84:11). According to one estimate there are about 3,365 promises in the Bible. All of God's promises are sure and steadfast '*if*' we fulfil His conditions attached to them.

There is one promise, however, that is often claimed by some who do so from out of its context. *"You may ask me for anything in my name, and I will do it"* (John 14:13). The disciples were about to embark as missionaries into the world in obedience to Jesus' "Great Commission" in making disciple of all nations. That promise was made in line with the will of God. His disciples could ask for anything that would assist them in their ministry of preaching the gospel of Christ.

Some believe they can ask for whatever they want in the name of Jesus and get it. Selfish requests will always remain unanswered. Those asked in accordance with the will of God will be answered.

> *"Standing on the promises that cannot fail,*
> *When the howling storms of doubt and fear assail,*
> *By the living word of God, I shall prevail,*
> *Standing on the promises of God."*

R. K. Carter (1849-1928)

"I HAVE CHOSEN YOU"
John 15:16

"You have not chosen me; I have chosen you to go and bear fruit – fruit that will last".

In New Testament times, it was customary among the Jews for pupils to choose their own Rabbi as their teacher. Jesus reverses this custom by saying to His disciples: *"You have not chosen me; I have chosen you."* It was His choice of them, not their choice of Him. Jesus knew the level of commitment each had toward Him. He knew their hearts and saw the potential they had in *"bearing fruit, fruit that will last."* He was not choosing these men from the sea of unsaved humanity to salvation and eternal life. He was appointing those who had already believed on His name to become more fruitful and productive in His service.

Jesus chose them and they in turn chose Him to be their leader and teacher. Theirs was a wholehearted commitment to Him. They world follow Him to the very end. Church history reveals that, apart from the Apostle John, they all died a martyr's death in fulfilling the Great Commission of Jesus had given them. (Matt. 28:16-20). They were fruitful in their individual lives and fruitful in their ministry. They followed Him to the end.

Look around the world and you will see Cathedrals, churches, hospitals, universities, colleges, schools and many organizations that bear the names of those whom Jesus chose so long ago to be His disciples. Their impact upon preaching the gospel of Christ was felt worldwide.

Don't disqualify yourself from being chosen by Jesus for a more fruitful and productive life in serving Him. He has already chosen you to bear fruit. (Gal. 5:22-26). Also, be open to His calling you to a wider and fruitful ministry in being involved in helping fulfil His Great Commission.

> *"My Lord, I did not choose You*
> *for that could never be.*
> *My heart would still refuse You*
> *had you not chosen me.*
>
> *My heart knows none above You.*
> *for You I long, I thirst,*
> *And know that, if I love You,*
> *Lord, you have loved me first."*

Josiah Conder (1789-1855)

OLD AGE

Psalm 71:9,18

"Do not cast me away when I am old; do not forsake me when my strength is gone. Even when I am old and grey, do not forsake me my God"

King David made this petition to the Lord. Perhaps he felt that his usefulness to God was coming to an end. *"Even when I am old and grey, do not forsake me, O God, till I declare your power to the next generation, Your greatness to all who are to come"*. v.18. He wanted to still be useful to God in his old age. David looked ahead wanting to declare God's power to the next generation, and to all who are to come. David wrote this Psalm that continues to bless and encourage the elderly people of God.

Old age can be a blessing to some, and a curse to others. The fact is we shall be in our old age what we are today. If we are not a person of faith now, we will not be a person of faith in our old age. If we are ill-tempered now, we will not be a cheerful person in our old age. If we are not developing a walk with God now, we won't have one in old age.

God's way to grow old is to develop a walk with Him now. I have visited many aged nursing homes as part of my ministry where we always sang the old hymns they knew and loved. Some residents would stay mute with long faces while others with wide smiles and joy sing heartedly to the Lord. They had walked with Jesus through life and knew He would not forsake them now that they were old, grey-haired and in the twilight years of their lives. As their physical strength slowly embed away, they are strengthened in their inner most being still able to praise their Lord. Though weak in body they were strong in faith.

My faith is strong, my body weak,
As I grow old in years.
Before me lies Your glory,
Behind me; toil and tears.

O free me from my weakness,
My spirit release like a bird.
To soar into Your presence,
Where only Your praises are heard.

Lord, grant me a peaceful ending,
As I close my eyes in death.
A happy passage from this world,
Into my eternal rest.

Peter C. Horrell (1936-

WHAT'S IN A NAME?

Philippians. 2:10

"At the name of Jesus every knee shall bow, in heaven and on earth and under the earth."

What's in a name? Much in many ways. 'The name of Herod stands for cruelty: the name of Alexander the Great stands for conquest; the name of Demosthenes stands for eloquence; the name of Beethoven stands for music; the name of Milton stands for poetry; the name of Judas stands for treachery; the names of Hitler, Mussolini and Stalin stand for barbarity, bestiality and atheism'. Yes, there is so much in a name.

There is so much in the name of Jesus. '*O Plato, Plato*' cried Socrates, '*I know God can forgive sins, but I do not know how*'. Jesus is the *how* for His name speaks of Saviour, Redeemer and Deliverer who forgives sin. A sign over a welding shop reads: *"we mend everything except a broken heart and the break of day"*. The name of Jesus stands for Physician who heals the broken hearted.

'Man is born to trouble as surely as the sparks fly upward' (Job 5:7). During these troubles, the name of Jesus stands for Friend who will never leave nor forsake you.

> *'I've found a friend, O such a friend!*
> *He loved me ere I knew Him.*
> *He drew me with the cords of love,*
> *And thus, He bound me to Him'*

James Grindlay Small (1817-1888)

The name of Jesus speaks of His omnipotence for by Him all things were created (Eph. 3:9). His name stands for authority for at His name every knee shall bow (Phil.2:10). His name speaks of eternal life for He is the Author of Life (Acts 3:15). And, His name speaks of peace, for He is the Prince of Peace (Is.9:6). Yes, there is so much in *that Name!*

> "*How sweet the name of Jesus sounds,*
> *In a believer's ear!*
> *It soothes his sorrows, heals his wounds,*
> *And drives away his fear*".

John Newton (1725-1807)

FRANCIS RIDLEY HAVERGAL

Psalm 116:15

"Precious in the sight of the LORD is the death of his faithful servants."

Shortly before passing into the presence of her Saviour, Francis Ridley Havergal, the 19th century hymnwriter whose beautiful hymns continue to inspire worship throughout the Christian community, said to those gathered around her deathbed that her sickness and pain simply meant that she would be in heaven sooner. *"It seemed too good to be true"* she told them.

Such a calm and confident testimony was the result of a life wholly consecrated to Jesus Christ. She had no fear as she faced death. With a clear conscience, a strong faith, and the peace of Christ in her heart, her biographer wrote: '*she folded her hands on her breast, sighed with relief and was gone.*' Her death was precious in the sight of the Lord. At last Jesus met his *"faithful servant"* whose hymns are sung by Christians around the world in praise to glory His Name.

During my Christian ministry, I have held the hands of dying Christians and non-Christians alike in seeking to bring comfort to them in their final hours. I admit to having fumbled to find words of encouragement for non-Christians who have shown no interest in God throughout their entire lives. I could only pray that before they slipped into unconsciousness, they would make their peace with God.

Sitting beside the deathbeds of dying Christians, I would read passages from the Bible that speak of the blessings awaiting them in heaven. Many times, I have left their bedsides, having been ministered to by their courage and faith. To see the serene smile on the face of a Christian about to pass into eternity is something I can never forget. I am convinced, that around the deathbed of every true Christian there stands an angel of the Lord, waiting to convey their spirit into the presence of their Saviour (Luke 16:20-25).

Thomas â Kempis (1380-1471) wrote: *"Grant me a good end, grant me a happy passage out of this world. Be mindful of me, my God, and direct me in the right way to Thy kingdom"*. Such was the end for Francis Ridley Havergal. She had a happy passage out of this world. May each of us experience the same when our own time comes to leave this world.

> *"Take my life and let it be*
> *Consecrated, Lord to Thee.*
> *Take my moments and my days;*
> *Let them flow in ceaseless praise".*
>
> Francis Ridley Havergal (1836-1879)

TWO ASPECTS OF GOD'S WILL
1 Peter 1:15; Hebrews 12:14; 1 Thessalonians 4:3;
Romans 8:29; 2 Timothy 2:20-21)

There are two aspects to God's will for every Christian. First, what God wants to do <u>*in us*</u>. Secondly, what God wants to do <u>*through us*</u>. The first is to make us holy. The second is to make us <u>*useful.*</u>

1. <u>What God Wants to do in us.</u>

Peter writes, "*As he who has called you is holy, you also be holy in all your conduct*". (1 Peter 1:15). Those who God calls; He calls to be holy. God's ultimate intention for His people is holiness of life. He wants to sanctify us heart, soul and mind that we be holy as He is holy. "*Without holiness no man can see God*" (Matt. 5:8; Heb. 12:14). There is no alternative for holiness. "*This is God's will for you: He wants you to be holy and completely free from immorality.*" (1 Thess. 4:3).

Our hearts must be focused upon letting God fulfil His will in our lives. Our love for Christ must be such that we long to be like Him. As we grow in Christ and draw closer to Him in love and fellowship, we will begin to loath the sin within us. We shall hate it and long to be free from it. This is the only measure by which we can gauge our spiritual growth. Do we hate our sin and long to be like Christ? Before the beginning of time, God had appointed those that belong to Him to be conformed to the image of His Son. (Rom. 8:29).

2. What God Wants to do Through us.

Paul writes: *"Now in a large house there are not only gold and silver vessels, but also vessels of wood and earthenware, and some to honour and some to dishonour. Therefore, if a man cleanses himself, he will be a vessel for honour, sanctified, <u>useful</u> to the Master, prepared for every good work"* (2 Tim. 2:20-21). Only *"vessels of honour"* can be useful to God. He ignores the rest. It is His choice to choose whom He will because He knows they will be the most effective in serving Him.

No matter how many natural gifts a person may possess or how many diplomas they have behind their name they are ineligible to be chosen as a useful vessel if they are not living a holy life. Holiness leads to usefulness. God chooses the holy and the humble above the exalted and the proud. He chooses a vessel that is clean and sanctified, and prepared for every good work."

> *"O use me, Lord, use even me,*
> *Just as Thou wilt, and when, and where,*
> *Until Thy blessed face I see,*
> *Thy rest, thy joy, thy glory share."*
>
> Francis R. Havergal (1836-1879)

TRUST—DELIGHT—COMMIT —REST

Psalm 37:1-7

TRUST in the Lord. v. 3. David wondered why evildoers prospered so well. Why the wicked often experienced so much prosperity. Do not be envious of them, he writes, what they possess is transient and in time these evildoers will *soon die* and their short-lived wealth will perish with them.

Struggling Christians may find it difficult not to feel a little envious when they see the wealth of non-believers. But Jesus said, *"Store up for yourselves treasures in heaven, where moth and rust do not destroy, and where thieves do not break in and steal"* (Matt.6:19-20). This is where our lasting treasure awaits us. ***I shall trust in the Lord".***

DELIGHT in the Lord. V. 3. *"He will give you the desires of your heart".* To delight in the Lord is the key to a happy, satisfied life. Our hearts desires steadily align with God's own desires. We begin to desire what God desires for us. We become one with Him in His purpose for our lives.

We have so much to give Him thanks for what He has done for us. Let us delight in Him for reconciling us to God. Delight in the knowledge

| 133

that we have been saved and have eternal life. Delight in anticipation of looking forward to our new home in heaven. Delight in the fact He is our close and faithful friend who will never leave us nor forsake us. ***I shall delight in the Lord.***

COMMIT your way to the Lord. v. 5-6. David committed himself unreservedly to the Lord because he trusted the Lord. To commit oneself to the Lord means to know peace, protection, and lasting satisfaction in life.

We live in perilous times. Millions fear about the future, not just for themselves but for their children and grandchildren. Christians should not allow themselves to be apprehensive with thoughts about future events. Commit all your ways before the Lord and trust Him. ***I shall commit my way to the Lord.***

REST in the Lord. v. 7. David trusted the Lord. He delighted in the Lord. He committed his way to the Lord. There was nothing more he could do now, but to rest patiently in the Lord. Because the Lord has promised to take care of those who put their trust in Him, they can rest assured He will take care of them. Instead of fretting and fearing about the future they can rest and wait for His promised help. ***I shall rest in the Lord.***

> *"But we never can prove,*
> *The delights of His love,*
> *Until all on the altar we lay;*
> *For the favour he shows,*
> *And the joy He bestows,*
> *Are for them who will trust and obey".*

John H. Sammis (1846-1919)

THE CHRISTIAN'S HOPE
1 Corinthians, chapter 15

The resurrection of Jesus is the most essential doctrine in the Christian faith. It is the very foundation upon which the Church stands. No doctrine has come under such fierce attack as the resurrection of Jesus. The belief that someone who had died and was raised again from the dead, has many sceptics both within and outside of the Church. There have been, and continues to be, numerous attempts to explain away Christ's bodily resurrection.

Those who stand upon the authority of the Bible as God's Word have no difficulty in accepting His resurrection. There is also overwhelming evidence that support Jesus rose from the dead. The growth of the church. Thousands of Christians were ready to die in the arenas of the Roman Empire rather than renounce their faith in Christ such was their faith in a living Christ. Listen to the testimonies of converted alcoholics, drug addicts, prostitutes and criminals, whose lives have changed dramatically through the power of the risen Christ. They speak of God's love, His forgiveness, and of the peace of God they have in their hearts.

This world is one vast graveyard. Everything in it dies, plants, animals and humans. The ashes of every human being born into this world are still somewhere on this planet. There is only one solitary figure in the history of the world whose mortal remains are not buried anywhere on earth. Jesus of Nazareth. Jesus predicted both his death and his resurrection (John 10:17-18). Jesus rose from the dead to give His followers the assurance that they also will be raised from the dead on the Dayu of Judgment.

Because Jesus lives, so His people will live. Jesus said: *"I am the resurrection and the life. Whoever believes in me will live, even though he dies"* (John 11:25).

"Jesus is Alive", and ...

> *"Because He lives, I can face tomorrow,*
> *Because He lives all fear is gone;*
> *Because I know He holds the future,*
> *And life is worth the living, because He lives".*

Gloria & William J. Gaither (?)

> *"When from the dead He raised His Son,*
> *And called Him to the sky,*
> *He gave our souls a lively hope*
> *That they should never die."*

Isaac Watts (1674-1748)

OUR UNSEEN GUARDIANS
Psalm 34:7

"The angel of the Lord encamps around those who fear Him, and rescues them"

The word *"fear"* implies a deep respect and reverence for the Lord. It is not a cringing fear. This passage gives support to the thought of a *guardian angel* encamping around and protecting the people of the Lord. The writer to the Hebrews tells us, *"Angels are ministering spirits sent and commissioned by God to serve those who are to inherit salvation"*. (Heb.1:14).

We are in a spiritual warfare. Paul reminds us that the enemy we are up against *"is not against flesh and blood, but against the rulers, against the powers, against the world forces of this darkness, against forces of wickedness in heavenly places"* (Eph. 6:12). It's against these spiritual forces of wickedness that we need protection.

The angel of the Lord assigned to protect us has more to do with our spiritual security rather than our physical. Their service to us is primarily on the spiritual level. They protect our souls from the onslaughts of these demonic forces. The devil and his legions of demons seek to weaken our faith, tempt us into sin and disrupt our lives in every way possible.

The angel of the Lord has been assigned to rescue the Lord's people from the unseen forces of evil in the world. Only when we leave this world and enter into heaven shall we know just how much evil the angel of the Lord protected from. They will continue to rescue us up to the day of our death, and their mission will finish when they convey our souls into the safety of heaven. (Luke 16:22).

<u>**Footnote:**</u>
There are some Christians who ask, Can I talk to Angels? Can I pray to Angels? Absolutely not! Praying to an angel is specifically forbidden in Scripture. The book of Revelation, for example, depicts John bowing down before his angelic guide to worship him. The angel forbids him to do so. (Rev.22:9). Even Satan can masquerade as an angel of light. (2 Cor.11:14).

> "Angels are the dispensers and administrators
> of the divine beneficence towards us. They
> regard our safety, undertake our defence, direct
> our ways, and exercise a constant solicitude
> that no evil befalls us."
>
> John Calvin (1509-1564)
> *Institutes of the Christian Religion*

LORD OF OUR CIRCUMSTANCES
Romans 8:28

"And we know that in all things God works for the good of those who love him, who have been called according to his purpose".

Christians go to this verse to find comfort, hope and meaning in their lives. And rightly so. But it is not a promise for everyone. It is limited to those who love God and are called according to His plan for them. It is a promise for Christians, for those who have trusted in Jesus alone for salvation. This promise affirms that things are working together for good amid suffering and that God is working even in our suffering for our good.

Someone said, 'God allows what he hates to accomplish what he loves.' God does not consider our suffering in and of itself to be good. God hates to see His people suffer yet He can work *all* things, not just some things for our good. He manages the affairs of our life because we are called according to His purpose. Everything that happens in our lives is ultimately used for our good and for the glory of God. God's sovereignty and ability to manage every aspect of our lives is demonstrated in the fact that He uses all things for our good.

The Lord is Lord of our circumstances. Nothing that happens to us takes God by surprise. He is working for our good. Paul has a word of encouragement: *"The sufferings of this present time are not worthy to be compared to the glory that will be revealed to us"*. (Rom. 8:18-25). *"If you suffer with Christ, you shall reign with Him"* (2 Tim. 2:12).

> *"Ye fearful saints, fresh courage take,*
> *The clouds ye so much dread;*
> *Are big with mercy, and shall break,*
> *In blessings on your head".*

William Cowper (1731-1800)

WHY DOES GOD ALLOW IT?

That question is often asked by Christians and non-Christians. Why does a kind and loving God allow such catastrophes to occur in many parts of the world with such enormous loss of life? Theologians have grappled for centuries over that question and still have no satisfactory answer.

Christianity has always proclaimed God as loving and compassionate. But how do you tell that to a grieving mother who has lost her children? Or to a father who has seen his home and family swept away in a tsunami? Or to a child left an orphan? Words are meaningless and the less spoken the better unless uttered in silent prayer for the victim.

I believe, however, that God is neither indifferent, nor inactive to the suffering of humankind. I see Him involved in alleviating the anguish of victims in these stricken countries. I see His compassion revealed in the lives of doctors and nurses treating the injured and the dying. I see God's love manifested in the lives of women comforting frightened children. I see a compassionate and weeping God in the tears shed by people reaching out to help those traumatized in their loss.

Love and compassion are divine attributes sown within the heart of humanity. These attributes reveal the uniqueness and nobleness of humans. God does care. He is involved in the lives of an army of international volunteers, who hasten to help those emotionally and physically scarred by these terrible events. Not by words but by deeds of kindness.

Why God chooses not to intervene to prevent such catastrophes is beyond our understanding. But, whenever and wherever a disaster occurs in some part of the world, we shall continue to see God's love and compassion revealed through the lives of ordinary men and women who labour to bring help, healing and hope to those affected by these tragedies.

> *"From Thee all skill and science flow*
> *All pity, care, and love,*
> *All calm and courage, faith and hope*
> *O pour them from above".*

Charles Kingsley (1819-1875)

(A copy of the letter I sent to a local newspaper in response to the 2004 Boxing Day tsunami in Indonesia with the loss of more than 230,000 lives) PCH

CHASING THE WIND

Ecclesiastes 6:9

"It is better to be satisfied with what is before your eyes than give reign to desire; this too is emptiness and chasing the wind"

"*Vanity of vanities, said the Preacher, vanity of vanities; all is vanity*". A modern translation puts it this way: "*Emptiness, emptiness, says the speaker, emptiness, all is empty*" (Eccl. 1:2). Solomon, the son of King David, was looking back over his life, and despite his enormous wealth wrote, "*emptiness, emptiness, all is empty*".

Most of the wealthiest people on earth live lives without a sense of deep and lasting satisfaction. They are rich but always discontented. Many live in fear of losing their wealth. Wealth gives them a feeling of security, self-confidence and superiority. The wealthy all have one thing in common; they have an insatiable craving for wanting more wealth, and the more they make the more they want. The word "enough" is not found in their vocabulary.

Wealth can never satisfy the deepest needs of the soul. Many who do not have wealth think that having it will solve all their problems. Jesus knows we need money to meet our daily needs. Money is not evil. It's the love of it that we are warned to avoid. Paul warned his readers against the *love money, for is a root of all kinds of evil. Some people, eager for* money, have wandered from the faith and pierced themselves with many griefs" (1 Tim. 6:10).

Dreaming of possessing wealth is meaningless. It is nothing more than chasing the wind. Nothing this world has to offer can ever fulfil the needs of the soul. We are spiritual beings that can only find true satisfaction in what God can give us. This He has already done by sending His Son, Jesus, to save us, and in doing so, He satisfies the deepest longings of the soul.

> "Keep your lives free from the love of money and be content with what you have, because God has said, "Never will I leave you; never will I forsake you."
>
> (Heb. 11:5)

> "For riches cannot satisfy,
> Nor gold nor silver can,
> 'Tis only Jesus satisfies,
> And fills the heart of man.
>
> The altogether lovely One,
> O won't you taste, and see?
> For Jesus ever satisfies,
> He satisfies me."
>
> (Author unknown)

SELF-DENIAL

Matthew 16:24

"Then Jesus said to his disciples, "Whoever wants to be my disciple must deny themselves and take up their cross and follow me."

Jesus had just predicted his death telling His disciples how he must suffer, be killed, and on the third day be raised to life again. His death would be by crucifixion. (Matt. 16:21-22). He then told them that, *"Whoever wants to be my disciple must deny themselves and take up their cross and follow me."* Those words would have shocked and filled them with revulsion. Death on the cross wasn't just simply cruel neither just simply shameful, both publicly and socially. It also had a theological significance in Judaism. Death of the cross was a sign of being cursed of God. It is written, *"Cursed is everyone who is hanged on a tree."* (Deut. 21:22-23; Gal. 3:13). This was the curse that Jesus was about to suffer in His own body for the sins of the world.

"Whoever wants to be my disciple must deny themselves and take up their cross and follow me." To deny yourself is not the giving up of things but the giving up of yourself wholly and completely to Jesus Christ. To deny yourself and take up your cross has nothing to do with the daily burdens you carry or problems you may have to face. It is to live for Christ and to be ready to identify with every aspect of His rejection, shame, suffering,

and death. If self-denial is a hard lesson, it is no more than what Jesus Himself did to save us.

Whoever wants to be a disciple of Jesus, can only be so on His terms. He is speaking candidly to His disciples by laying down the conditions of discipleship. As He spoke to His disciples so long ago, so He speaks to us today. *"Whoever wants to be my disciple must deny themselves and take up their cross and follow me."* (Matt.16:21-24).

> *Take up the cross, and follow Christ,*
> *Nor think till death to lay it down.*
> *For only he who bears the cross*
> *May hope to win the glorious crown."*

Charles W. Everest (1814-1877)

THE GREATEST COMMANDMENT
Matthew 22:38

This is the first and greatest commandment. And the second is like it, "Love the Lord your God with all your heart, and with all your soul, and with all your mind. Love your neighbour as yourself."

A Pharisee came to Jesus and asked, *"Teacher, which is the greatest commandment in the Law? Jesus replied, "Love the Lord your God with all your heart, and with all your soul, and with all your mind"*. (Matt. 22:34-40). To love God with all our heart, soul and mind is to have our affections on Him more strongly than anything else. Our love for Him cannot be half-hearted. It implies being ready to give up, do, or suffer anything to please and glorify His name.

We are able to love Him because He is our heavenly Father. He has our welfare at heart and wants us to have a close relationship with Him. He loved us so much that He sent His only Son to die on a cross to save us from our sins. Our heavenly Father is holy, faithful and loving. Never, ever will He forsake us.

Choosing to follow God with all our heart is loving God with all our heart. It is with purity of heart that enables us to see God, trust God, fear God and love God. If Jesus is our Saviour, we shall have no difficulty in loving His Father. Our love for Him stems from what He has done for us in Christ. *"Jesus died for us while we were yet sinners"* (Rom. 5:8). Our love for Him can only be revealed by our obedience to Him.

"THIS IS THE FIRST AND GREATEST COMMANDMENT" AND THE SECOND IS LIKE IT "LOVE YOUR NEIGHBOUR AS YOURSELF"

This is to practice justice towards our fellow human beings. We don't love others just by feeling kind or affectionate towards them. We love them through our interactions with them. In many cases we must deny ourselves for the good of others, to regard another as more important than ourselves.

> *"If ye love me, keep my commandments". "If a man loves me, he will keep my words: and my Father will love him, and we will come unto him, and make our abode with him,* (John 14:15, 23)

> *"Lord it is my chief complaint*
> *That my love is weak and faint:*
> *Yet I love You and adore.*
> *O for grace to love You more."*
>
> William Cowper (1731-1800)

"AMAZING GRACE"
Ephesians 2:8

"For by grace are you saved through faith; and that not of yourselves, it is the gift of God."

The best-loved song concerning God's grace, is John Newton's beautiful, and soul touching hymn, "Amazing Grace." This "Amazing Grace" was the favourite doctrine of the apostle Paul. God has given an amazing gift, the gift of salvation to all who are willing to accept it. This gift is salvation of the soul. It was secured through the shedding of Christ's blood in payment for the sins of the whole world – *for by grace you have been saved through faith; and not of yourselves, it is the gift of God"*.

O what a glorious gift! To be raised from spiritual death to new and everlasting life in Christ. What joy it is to know your sins have been forgiven; to enjoy peace with God, are part of the family of God and have heaven as your future home. All this, and much more, is a gift of God. *"By grace we have been saved through grace.".*

Our part is to believe what Jesus did on our behalf. Faith means to stop any attempt to save yourselves by your own good works. To work means to merit, or to earn. You can't earn a gift. You don't pay for a gift. It's free. You can only receive it with gratitude. If someone gives you a gift, you do not ask "How much do I owe you?" What a gift God has given to us! *"It was nothing we could or did achieve -- it was God's gift of grace" (Phi)* Our only response should be: Thank You Lord. Thank You.

> *"Grace, 'tis a charming sound,*
> *Harmonious to my ear.*
> *Heav'n with the echo shall resound,*
> *And all the earth shall hear.*
> *Grace first contrived a way,*
> *To save rebellious man.*
> *And all the steps that grace display,*
> *Which drew the wondrous plan."*
>
> Phillip Doddridge (1702-1751)

THE BATTLE FOR THE MIND
2 Corinthians 10:5

"We demolish arguments and every pretension that sets itself up against the knowledge of God, and we take captive every thought to make it obedient to Christ"

Paul is defending his ministry by refuting the arguments of those preventing people from gaining any knowledge of the true God. His opponents, possibly the philosophers of Athens. had their own philosophical arguments refuting Paul's witness about Christ. Perhaps they suggested some of the philosophies of man as alternatives that could replace the teachings of Christ. When they heard about Christ's resurrection some sneered but others believed. (Acts 17:16-34).

The devil has built strongholds in the minds of hundreds of millions of the world's populations. They act like fortresses to stop them from coming to a saving knowledge of Christ. Unknown to the vast majority they are in a spiritual warfare against an enemy whose goal is to have blind their eyes to the truth. Like any cult leader who has succeeded in brain-washing his followers, he manipulates those over whom he has enslaved. Millions are held captive under false religions, man's philosophies and many other falsehoods contrary to the teachings of the true God.

Paul writes about *"taking every thought captive"* otherwise we could be ensnared and led away into untruths. We are in a spiritual warfare. The battlefield is for the mind.

The Christians only safeguard is to maintain a close union with Christ in prayer and obedience to His Word.

"As man thinks, so is he"

Proverbs 23:7

THE JUDGMENT SEAT OF CHRIST

2 Corinthians. 5:10

"For we must all appear before the judgment seat of Christ, so that each of us may receive what is due us for the things done while in the body, whether good or bad."

There are two judgments mention in the New Testament. The "Judgment Seat of Christ" (2 Cor. 5:10), and the "Great White Throne Judgment." (Rev. 20:11-15). The first is mentioned by Paul in his letter to the Corinthians, the second by John in Revelation. Are both Paul and John writing about the same event? Paul calls it the "Judgment Seat of Christ" whilst John refers it as the "Great White Throne." Could it be that Paul and John just chose to focus on different aspects of the same event. Whether they take place together or not, the main point is that both the saved and the unsaved will be judged for how they lived their lives on earth.

The appearance of believers before the *"judgment seat of Christ"* is to evaluate the worth of their lives when they lived on earth, whether for good or for bad. Christians are secure in Christ, but they must still appear before Christ to have their lives assessed by Him. (Rom.8:1). This judgment is a time of disclosure, accountability and evaluation. If a

Christian has lived only for their own gain, they shall suffer loss. If they have lived and laboured for Christ, they shall be rewarded. Everything about us will be revealed before the judgment seat of Christ. When we stand before Christ it will be too late for regrets. Today is the time to prepare for our inevitable appearance before His judgment seat by asking ourselves: Am I truly living my life fully committed to Christ and to His mission on earth?

> "Search me, O God, and know my heart today,
> Try me, O Savior, know my thoughts, I pray;
> See if there be some wicked way in me,
> Cleanse me from every sin, and set me free.
>
> Lord, take my life, and make it wholly Thine,
> Fill my poor heart with Thy great love divine;
> Take all my will, my passion, self and pride,
> I now surrender, Lord, in me abide."
>
> James Edwin Orr (1912-1987

THE SINS OF PRESUMPTION
Psalm 19:13

Keep back your servant also from presumptuous sins; let them not have dominion over me; then shall I be upright, and I shall be innocent from any great transgression."

The reason King David refers to presumptuous sins as plural is because he was aware there is more than one sin that would be a presumptuous sin. "*A sin that is committed wilfully against manifest light and knowledge is a presumptuous sin,*" i.e., it despises and rejects Christ with a fixed will and resolution. (Spurgeon (1834-1892). This presumptuous sin inevitably leads to committing the *'great transgression:* the unpardonable sin. To presume upon God's mercy is a presumptuous sin. To add to or take away anything from God's Word is a presumptuous sin. (Rev.22:18-19). To declare you are speaking in God's stead is a presumptuous sin.

There is a proneness in all of us to be over-confident that can cause us to fall unintentionally into presumptuous sin. Peter said he would never deny Jesus but did so three times before the rooster crowed. He went outside and wept bitterly for what he had done. (Matt. 26:75). He was overconfident in himself. He trusted in his own heart. Presumptuous sins arise from carelessness with God and his word and being careless with the needs of others. It is the result of pride and over-weening self-confidence.

The prayer of David was he might have a proper distrust of himself and not be led by an improper reliance on his own power that would lead to sin. Perhaps it was this very experience that led David to offer this petition. His earnest and humble prayer teaches us that even the saintliest of the Lord's people need to this prayer:

> *"Thy righteous judgments whilst we see,*
> *On Sloth and on Simplicity.*
> *And whilst Presumption's fate we trace,*
> *Preserve us, Jesus, by Thy grace."*

Rev. Thomas Smith. (author unknown)
From 'Original hymns: illustrative of the Pilgrim's Progress" 1831.)

HIDE AND SEEK

Jeremiah 29:13

"You will seek me and find me when you seek me with all your heart".

"Hide and Seek" is played by children all over the world. The hider would find the best place to hide so as not to be found. The seeker would not stop looking until the hider was found. Is God playing "Hide and Seek" with us? Has He hidden Himself to make it difficult for us to find Him? Unlike the game where the hider does not want to be found, God *wants* to be found. He said, *"You will seek me and find me when you seek me with all your heart".*

There are many people who have no intention of seeking God. They are too caught up in the pursuit of their own interests. But those who seek God with all their heart will find Him. The half-hearted will not find Him. The double-hearted will not find Him. The faint in heart will not find Him. Only those who seek Him whole-heartedly calling upon Him in truth will find Him. Like the father of the prodigal who ran to embrace and kiss his lost son, God, in love and compassion is waiting to embrace those who seek Him with all their heart. (Luke 15:11-32).

Why is it that so many seek but do not find God? Because they are seeking God in places he cannot be found. God cannot be found in the philosophies of man. He cannot be found in Eastern religions or any other of the false religions in the world. God has already revealed to the world the only way in which He can be found. He sent His Son, Jesus, into the world to save the world. (John 3:16). Jesus said, *"I am the way, the truth and the life. No one can come to the Father but by me"* (John 14:6-11).

"Thou art the Way: to Thee alone
From sin and death, we flee.
And he who would the Father seek
Must seek Him, Lord, by Thee"

Bishop George W. Doane (1799-1859)

THINKING AS GOD THINKS
Mark 8:33-38

"But Jesus turned around, and, looking at His disciples, rebuked Peter. 'Away with you, Satan', He said; 'you think as man thinks, not as God thinks.'

Jesus had just told His disciples how *"the Son of Man must suffer many things and be rejected by the elders, chief priests and teachers of the law, and that he must be killed and after three days rise again"*. Peter immediately took Jesus aside and began to rebuke Him. In doing so he was unwittingly used of Satan. Peter was confident that he was right and that Jesus was wrong. Though His outburst of concern for Jesus was natural, he was unknowingly taking the part of Satan in opposing God's eternal plan in Jesus dying on a Cross. Satan – via Peter – again tempts Jesus to save the world with a short-cut. (Matt.4:8-10). *Get behind Me, Satan!* Jesus said. This was a very strong rebuke to Peter.

Jesus knew Satan's purpose was to discourage Him from fulfilling God's will by going to the cross. Peter had no idea that what Jesus had said about having to *"suffer and die and after three days rise again"* was God's way of salvation for the whole world. (Isaiah 53; John 3:16). Like the other disciples, Peter's thinking was earth-bound. He believed Jesus would become a political leader who would set up His kingdom on earth and rid the Romans from their land. But it was not in God's plan that Jesus become an earthly king.

"You think as man thinks, not as God thinks," said Jesus. Peter was looking at things in the light of mere human wisdom and not from the perspective of the will of God. To think as God thinks is to see things from God's perspective. It is to look ahead into eternity. God has set His eternal plan and that plan is revolving around Jesus Christ. It began with Him; it continues with Him and will find its completion in Him.

> *"At the Name of Jesus, every knee shall bow,*
> *Every tongue confesses Him, King of glory now.*
> *Tis the Father's pleasure, we should call Him Lord,*
> *Who from the beginning, was the mighty Word."*

Caroline M. Noel (1817-1877)

LOST IN ADAM – RESTORED IN CHRIST

Genesis 1:26

"Then God said, let us make mankind in our image, in our likeness, so that they may rule over the fish in the sea and the birds in the sky, over the livestock and all the wild animals, and over all the creatures that move along the ground.

When God said, *"let us make mankind in our image"*, some have taught that the reference *us* refers to God speaking to angels. This is a popular interpretation among some Jews. But this does not fit with the rest of Scripture. Angels are created beings, not co-creators with God. Though not explicitly stated in this verse, the implied nature of the Trinity is evident.

Humans did not evolve from lower forms of life. We were created in the image and likeness of God. Our likeness with God is not a physical resemblance. Our likeness to God is the capacity for moral, intellectual and spiritual choices. God made us as a triune being with spirit, soul and body and in that order of importance. Spirit and soul distances us from every other creature on earth.

When God created Adam in His own image there was nothing impure, unjust, evil, mean or vile in Adam. Adam was created in the image of God that consisted of wisdom, righteousness, true holiness, knowledge, reason, creativity, moral consciousness and free choice. He was created by God so that he could have fellowship with God.

From the moment Satan succeeded in causing Adam to disobey the command of God, God's image in Adam was ruined. We are not blamed for Adam and Eve's disobedience. We have, however, inherited a sinful nature. It is like inheriting a rogue gene that has been passed down to us through each generation. No longer do we have access to God. (Eph.2:2).

But a new opportunity to regain what Adam had lost has been opened to us. *"But just as death came to us through Adam, through one man, Jesus Christ, came life"* (Rom. 5:12-21). Jesus is the image of God and His image is what God wants to see in us. (Eph.4:22-28). We should never forget that it is God's ultimate intention that the image of His Son, Jesus, be fully restored in those whom He has called.

> "O to be like You! blessed Redeemer;
> This my constant longing and prayer;
> Gladly I'll forfeit all earth's treasures,
> Jesus, Your perfect likeness wear"
>
> Thomas O. Chisholm (1866-1960)

DEATH BETTER THAN BIRTH

Ecclesiastes 7:1

"The day of death is better than the day of birth"

What was going through the mind of King Solomon when he wrote these words? Solomon had it all. He was the son of King David and known for his wisdom, his wealth, and his writings. He became ruler in approximately 967 B.C. and his kingdom extended from the Euphrates River in the north to Egypt in the south. He accumulated enormous wealth. Old Testament 1 Kings states that he owned 12,000 horses with horsemen and 1,400 chariots. He strengthened his kingdom through marital alliances, and his crowning achievement was the building of the Temple in Jerusalem (2 Chronicles 3).

So why would Solomon, born into such wealth and privilege write: *"The day of death is better than the day of birth"*? Job gives us the answer: '*man is born to trouble as surely as sparks fly upward*' (Job 5:7). Like the rest of humanity, Solomon was '*born to trouble*' despite his innate wisdom and immense wealth.

The birth of a newborn brings much joy to its parents. As they look upon the face of their little bundle of joy their hearts are filled with love and gratitude for its safe and healthy arrival. Their precious bundle, however, has just been born into a war zone. Their infant has come into a world of war, hatred, corruption, crime, and death. What lies ahead for that child on a personal level is heartache, grief, pain and death. No human being is immune from these troubles associated with living in this world.

For multitudes of people the thought of death fills their hearts with fear. Solomon, a righteous man who feared and served God, did not fear death. Solomon saw it as the day he would be set free from all the troubles of life. *"The day of death is better than the day of birth"*. Just as physical birth launched him into a life of trouble, his physical death would usher him into a life of peace, love, joy and everlasting life.

That applies to all the followers of Christ. Their day of death will be better than their day of birth because it ushers them into their eternal rest with Jesus. They will be forever free from all the troubles of life, the infirmities of the body, and the sinful nature that has hounded them through life. The best is yet to come.

> *"Precious in the sight of the Lord is the death of His saints".* (Psalm 116:15).

> *"There is a land of pure delight,*
> *Where saint's immortal reign:*
> *Infinite day excludes the night,*
> *And pleasures banish pain".*

Isaac Watts (1674-1748)

A LIGHT ON MY PATH

Psalm 119:105

"Your word is a lamp for my feet, a light on my path".

'There were no fixed lamps in Eastern towns, so each person carried a lamp to avoid stumbling over obstacles or wandering off into paths which would lead into danger'. King David guided his own steps by a lamp and could see the dangers ahead by its light. The King, however, had another lamp used for a different purpose. *"Your word is a lamp for my feet, a light on my path"*. God's word acted as a lamp, a light that revealed the way he should walk before God.

Jesus said, *"Search the Scriptures for they testify of Me"*. The Pharisees, to whom Jesus spoke these words, diligently searched the Scriptures, but they searched them the wrong way. They treated the Scriptures as a book of rules. Of the 613 laws found in their Old Testament, the Pharisees reckoned there were 365 negative laws – *'you shall not'*, and 248 positive laws – *'you shall'*. Upon these "negatives" and "positives" they developed their own system of rules that became their traditions, but in doing so, made God's Word invalid. (Mark 7:13).

If the approach to reading the Bible is the same way as the Pharisees, you will miss its main message. But to read the Bible with an open heart and mind, and a sincere desire to know its truths is to discover that from the

Book of Genesis to Revelation it testifies of Jesus. As a light on our path, it reveals to us the way we should live our lives. It protects us from error, it leads us into all truth, it encourages us in times of doubts and difficulties, it keeps us from sin and comforts us in times of fear and distress.

C. H. Spurgeon (1834-1892) *"There are times when solitude is better than society, and silence is wiser than speech. We should be better Christians if we were more alone, waiting upon God, and gathering through meditation on His Word spiritual strength for labour in His service. Why is it that some Christians, although they hear many sermons, make but slow advances in the divine life? Because they neglect their closets, and do not thoughtfully meditate on God's Word.*

"O send Thy Spirit, Lord,
Now unto me,
That He may touch my eyes,
And make me see:
Show me the truth concealed
Within Your Word,
And in Your Book revealed
I see the Lord".

Mary A. Lathbury (1841-1913)

STRUGGLING WITH SIN

Romans 7: 7-25

*"For I know that good itself does not dwell in me,
that is, in my sinful nature. For I have the desire
to do what is good, but I cannot carry it out".*
"I have the intention and urge to do what is right,
but no power to carry it out"

When we were born again by the Spirit an inner conflict begins to place within our lives. Up to that time there was no conflict because we were under the one power of our sinful nature. There were no rivals. But once the Spirit has taken up residency within our lives a conflict takes place between the power of our sinful nature and the power of the indwelling Holy Spirit. Our new relationship with Christ does not eradicate our sinful nature. It remains active and very much alive within us. The conflict between our sinful nature and our new nature are rivals each seeking supremacy over the other.

C.H. Spurgeon (1834-1892). "Oh, how often have men, who have been struggling after holiness, had to use these words of the apostle! The more holy they become, the more they realize that there is still something better beyond them, after which they struggle, but to which they cannot yet attain; so still, they cry, "The good that we would we do not: but the evil which we would not, that we do." Oh! this accursed indwelling sin! Would

God it was driven out. We do not say this to excuse ourselves—God forbid—but to blame ourselves that we permit this sin to dwell within us. Yet must we rejoice in God that we are born again, and that this new "I" the true "I," will not yield to sin, but fights against it".

Christians are a divided person. An old Indian Christian was explaining to a missionary that the battle inside him was like a black dog fighting a white dog. *"Which dog wins?"* asked the missionary. *"The one I feed the most,"* replied the Indian. Paul wrote, *Set your minds on things above, not on earthly things.* Feed your mind on the truth of God's Word. (Col.3:2).

> *"Yield not to temptation,*
> *For yielding is sin.*
> *Each victory will help you*
> *Some other to win.*
> *Fight manfully onward,*
> *Dark passions subdue*
> *Look ever to Jesus:*
> *He will carry you through".*
>
> Horatio R. Palmer (1834-1907)

THE CHRISTIAN'S THOUGHT LIFE

Philippians 4:8

"Finally, brothers and sisters, whatever is true, whatever is noble, whatever is right, whatever is pure, whatever is lovely, whatever is admirable --if anything is excellent or praiseworthy—think about such things".

Right thinking leads to right living. We must be as careful what we feed into our minds as to what we feed into our bodies. In his book, *"Disciplines of a Godly Man"*, Kent Hughes (1942-) writes, *"It is impossible for any Christian who spends the bulk of his evenings, month after month, week upon week, day in and day out watching the major TV networks or contemporary videos to have a Christian mind"*. With so much violence, obscenity and just plain rubbish on TV, Christians need to be on their guard as to what they watch.

Paul urges us to think upon *"whatever is true, whatever is noble, whatever is right, whatever is pure, whatever is lovely and whatever is admirable."* Our mind is the starting point for our behaviour. When the devil seeks to entice us to sin, he injects unclean thoughts into our minds seeking to tempt us to disobey God in some way. The choice is ours. We either reject his "fiery darts" or fall victim to them.

"As you begin to hide God's Word in your heart, it will slowly but surely "change your mind."
"If you focus on the truth, you will speak the truth.
If you look on noble things, nobility will mark your life.
If you seek out lovely things, your life will be lovely to others.
It you dwell on which is right, that which is wrong will have no attraction to you. It you think on pure things, you will become pure.
If you look for virtue, you will find it.
If you search for higher things, you will elevate your own life".

Ray Pritchard "Keep Believing Ministries"

"May the mind of Christ my Saviour
Live in me from day to day,
By His love and power controlling
All I do and say".

Katie B. Wilkinson (1859-1928)

THE ANOINTED CHRISTIAN
1 John 2:27

"As for you, the anointing you received from him remains in you, and you do not need anyone to teach you. But as his anointing teaches you about all things and as that anointing is real, not counterfeit—just as it has taught you, remain in him"

As a new Christian in the early 60's I wanted to know more about the beliefs and practices of other Christian denominations. A small group from our Baptist Church would visit these churches to "try-them-out". They were mostly Pentecostal and Charismatic with their emphasis upon the gifts of the Spirit, especially the necessity of speaking in tongues. 'If you don't speak in tongues', they said, 'you are not saved.' Even though I was young in the faith, I felt a check within my spirit that something about that statement as not quite right although I could not put my finger upon the reason why.

Shortly afterwards in one of my private devotions I read these words from 1 John's letter; *"As for you, the anointing you received from him remains in you, and you do not need anyone to teach you"*. The words seemed to leap out me. Instantly I knew I had no need of any so-called spiritual extras. The anointing I had received and remains in me was the fulness of Holy Spirit received at the time of my new birth. I knew without a shadow of doubt that I had received my fulness in Christ.

To say "*we do not need anyone to teach you*" does not mean we no longer have need of any Bible teachers. John is not saying, forget all human teachers. It means we don't need them as much as in our former days when we were young in our faith. Through the anointing of the Holy Spirit and our spiritual growth we are enabled to understand divine truth for ourselves. As we grow stronger in faith, we ought to become more capable of steering our own course as God's Spirit teaches us. We should never reject the wise counsel of godly teachers given to us by God. They are God's gifts to His Church to minister and encourage His people.

> Let the Holy Spirit guide;
> Let Him teach us what is true.
> He will testify of Christ,
> Light our minds with heaven's view.

Penelope Moody Allen (1939-

THE FOLLY OF WEALTH

Psalm 49:16-17

"Do not envy a man when he grows rich, when the wealth of his family increases; for he will take nothing when he dies, and his wealth will not go with him"

It is not folly to have wealth; it is folly to love wealth. Wealthy people spend much of their wealth on building elaborate homes, filling them with the best furnishings, owning elegant cars, dine at the top restaurants, drink the finest vintages, travel first class and stay at five-star hotels. The prosperity of non-believers can tend to shake the faith of some Christians who are going through hard times. It could lead to some harbouring thoughts of envy.

"Do not envy a man when he grows rich, for he will take nothing with him when he dies". (1 Tim. 6:7). C. H. Spurgeon said: *"Through the river of death man must pass naked. Not a rag of all his raiment, not a coin of all his treasure, not a joy of all his honour, can the dying worldling carry with him"*. Do not be bothered when you see the rich proper. Covetousness can lurk in the heart of even the best of Christians. We are warned to be on our guard against being envious of another's wealth. Temporal prosperity is not worth fretting about.

In olden days they used a shroud to bury the dead. A shroud was a burial garment without pockets to remind the living they take nothing with them into the next world. Now-a-days you can be buried in your best suit, but the pockets are still empty. *"We brought nothing into this world, and it is certain we can carry nothing out"*. (1 Tim. 6:7). Everything we invest in will soon be gone. Be rich toward God and your reward awaits you in heaven.

Lord, if I am tempted to envy those, who
have much more than me,
To have such envy in my heart, then, Lord deliver me;
Remind me, Lord, of what I have, secure in heaven above,
A treasure beyond all worldly worth, a token of your love.

Peter C. Horrell (1936-)

THE WHOLE AMOUR OF GOD
Ephesians 6:11-17

"Put on the whole armour of God... belt of truth ...breastplate of righteousness ... footwear as a ready messenger of the gospel ... shield of faith ... helmet of salvation ... sword of the Spirit ... and the weapon of prayer.

Paul reminds us that our battle is not against flesh and blood but against the invisible forces of evil. For this reason, he commands us to take up the whole amour of God to be able to resist and overcome these malignant forces of the evil. The armour God has provided us with is of a spiritual nature. We are in a spiritual warfare and are urged to put on the whole armour of God for our protection and our victory over the devil and his demons.

The **belt of truth** means to be truthful in all our dealings with others. A Christian who is untruthful opens a chink in their armour allowing the devil a foothold in their life. Truth should surround us like a belt.

The **breastplate of righteousness** protects our heart. The righteousness of a Christian speaks of integrity and holy living. Such a life is above the accusations of the devil. To be righteous is to live in obedience to God's commands.

The ***footwear*** means a preparation to be eager in sharing the good news of the Gospel with others when opportunity arises.

The **shield of faith** protects our minds from the fiery accusations and lies of the devil. One of the devil's tactics is to try and make us doubt our salvation. When faith is strong it is impossible for the devil to break through this shield of faith. Faith is to believe that God will do what He has promised. To have an unshakeable assurance of salvation will act as our *helmet* to ward off all doubts.

The ***sword of the Spirit is the Word of God.*** Jesus used the Word of God to defeat Satan. He quoted scripture three times (Matt. 4:1-10). *'The Word of God is living and powerful, and keener than any two-edged sword, piercing even to the severance of soul from spirit exposing the very thoughts and motives of the heart'* (Heb. 5:12).

Prayer is the most effective weapon in the arsenal of God. A prayerless Christian is a powerless Christian, and therefore vulnerable to fail in resisting the devil. Prayer and Bible study are the most powerful tools for opposing the devil.

> *"Soldiers of Christ! Arise*
> *And put your armour on!*
> *Strong in the strength which God supplies,*
> *Through His Eternal Son"*

> Charles Wesley (1707-1788)

GOD'S CO-WORKERS
Acts 8:29-31

"The Spirit told Philip, Go to that chariot and stay near it. Then Philip ran up to the chariot and heard the man reading Isaiah the prophet. Do you understand what you are reading? Philip asked. How can I, he said unless someone explains it to me? So, he invited Philip to come up and sit with him"

We know little about Philip. We do not know his age, his nationality, or where he came from. All we know about Philip is that he was a Christian, and one of the seven deacons chosen to serve in the church in Jerusalem (Acts 6:5). Because of his evangelistic gifts he became known as Philip the Evangelist in the early church. As he preached the gospel of Christ in the city of Samaria, crowds flocked to listen to what he had to say. It was a spiritual revival in Samaria with signs and wonders taking place in the Name of Christ. Men and women in great numbers believed and were baptized. (Acts 8:4-12).

When the angel of the Lord appeared and told him to leave his successful evangelistic ministry in Samaria and go south into a desert place, Philip immediately obeyed (Acts 8:26). The first lesson we learn from Philip was his obedience in leaving his fruitful ministry in Samaria and going into the desert where few people lived. Obedience and faith are the key to being a useful vessel in God's hands. He was a **Man of God,**

Along the desert road Philip caught sight of a high Ethiopian official in the service of the Queen of Ethiopia sitting in a carriage reading aloud the prophet Isaiah. He had been to Jerusalem on a pilgrimage and was on his way home. The Spirit said to Philip, *'go and join the carriage"*, and Philip immediately did so. Here is another lesson we can learn. Philip was sensitive to the Spirit's leading. He was sensitive to the **Spirit of God.** (1 Kings 19:12).

Sitting beside the Ethiopian, Philip asked, *'Do you understand what you are reading? How can I except someone help me'*. Philip then began to explain the prophecy related to Jesus the Messiah. *"All of us, like sheep, have strayed away. We have left God's paths to follow our own. Yet the LORD laid on him the sins of us all"* (Isaiah 53:6). Here we find another lesson from Philip. He could show the Ethiopian through the Scriptures that Jesus was the Messiah. He was acquainted with the **Word of God**

> "Lord, I make a full surrender, All I have I give to Thee.
> For Thy love so great and tender, Asks the gift of me"

Charles W. L. Christien (1839-1926)

PRISONER OF THE LORD

Ephesians 4:1

"As a prisoner for the Lord, then, I urge you to live a life worthy of the calling you have received"

Charges of sedition were levelled against Paul by the Jewish leaders. They wanted him dead. The Romans, however, were obliged to protect him because he was a Roman citizen born in the city of Tarsus under Roman protection. His case was too complicated and so the Roman authorities sent him to Caesarea, where he was questioned by the Jewish Sanhedrin, the Roman governors Felix and Festus, and before King Agrippa. Using his right as a Roman citizen, he appealed to Caesar to hear his case in Rome.

When he arrived in Rome, he remained under house arrest waiting for his case to be heard. (Acts 14:1-7; 16:19-40; Ch. 23-27). Prisoners were free to move about during the day, but at night were chained to a Roman soldier to prevent him from escaping. In literal terms, Paul was a prisoner of Rome, yet he saw himself as a prisoner of the Lord.

Centuries later. another prisoner declared herself a prisoner of the Lord. Her name was Madame Guyon, a French mystic who advocated Quietism (a form of Christian mysticism) considered to be heretical by the Roman Catholic Church. She was imprisoned by order of Louis X1V, and held in the infamous Bastille, from 1695 to 1703. From her cell, she wrote on many different subjects relating to prayer, union with Christ, a commentary on the Song of Solomon, her prison autobiography, and poems. Her writings became well known and continue to challenge and bless present day Christians. Though a prisoner of the King, she considered herself a prisoner of Christ.

It is a challenge to ask ourselves, Am I a prisoner of Jesus Christ? Does He have such a control over my life that I love being under His authority and quick to obey His commands? There is no greater joy in the Christian life than to know you have been imprisoned by the embrace of Christ's love for you. As His willing prisoner He will never let you go.

> "Thy beautiful, sweet will, my God,
> Holds fast in its sublime embrace
> My captive will, a gladsome bird,
> Prisoned in such a realm of grace"

Madame Guyon (1648-1717)

> "Make me a captive Lord, and then I shall be free.
> Force me to render up my sword, And I shall conqueror be,
> I sink in life's alarms, when by myself I stand.
> Imprison me within Thine arms, and strong will be my hand"

George Matheson (1842-1906)

THE RETURN OF A BACKSLIDER
Hebrews 11:8

"By faith Abraham, when he was called, obeyed by going out to a place which he was to receive as an inheritance, and he went out, not knowing where he was going"

A Forward Step

At the grand old age of 75 Abraham took a step of faith trekking 650 kms from the city of Ur, southward toward the land of Canaan. God had promised him a three-fold blessing. He promised Abraham the land of Canaan, He promised him a seed, referring to Jesus and promised He would make Abraham a world-wide blessing (Gen. 12:1-4). Upon his arrival in Canaan, the first thing he did was to build an altar and call upon the Name of the Lord (Gen. 12:8). Imagine his disappointment when he discovered there was a famine on the land. He had travelled such a long, hazardous journey, only to find the land that God had promised him was short of food.

A Downward Step.

Abraham then decided to take matters into his own hands. He left Canaan, and the altar he had built and took a step towards Egypt. In Egypt things began to go horribly wrong. Afraid for his life he told Pharaoh that Sara, his wife, was his sister. (Gen.12:10-20). In leaning to his own understanding, Abraham had put himself way out of God's will. *"Trust in the LORD with all your heart and lean not on your own understanding"* (Prov.3:5). He was not where he should have been.

A furious Pharaoh, having been deceived by Abraham concerning his sister, ordered Abraham, and his family to be escorted out of Egypt. When Abraham reached the border of Egypt, he was faced with another big decision: About 2000 kilometres north-east was his city of Ur, while directly north was the land of Canaan. Ur was where he was born, a city of comfort, friends, and plenty of food. In Canaan, there was a severe famine.

An Upward Step

Genesis 13 tells us the story. Abraham turned his back on Ur and took a step towards Canaan. The first thing he did was to return to the altar he had built where he had called on the Name of the Lord. We can imagine this old man kneeling and confessing that he had been a fool. God took care of the famine in Canaan, and it became known as the land of 'milk and honey'. God never gives up on those whom He has called. It is never too late for a back-sliding Christian to return to Jesus Christ. Jesus is only a prayer away.

> *"Backsliding souls return to God,*
> *your faithful God is gracious still,*
> *Leave the false way you long have trod,*
> *And He will all backslidings heal"*

Joseph Hart (1712-1768)

LASTING IMPRESSIONS

Psalm 42:7

"Deep calls unto Deep"

During more than 50 years of Christian service in different parts of the world, I have had the privilege of having had fellowship with hundreds of Christians. I am now old in years, frail in body, strong in spirit and waiting for God's call. I now have plenty of time to think back over my life. One of the questions I ask myself is; Of the countless Christians I have ever met; how many have left the most lasting impression upon my life? I thought back over the years and counted six who stood out from the hundreds I have met.

It is difficult to put into words how their lives left such an impact upon my life. I can't remember much about what we talked about, and their faces are just a blur in my mind. It was not what they said but who they were that I remember. It had to do with the depth of their spirituality. It seemed as if their own spirit was silently communicating with my spirit in close and deep fellowship.

"Deep calls to deep" is a call to a deeper intimacy with God. One deep is the heart of a searching Christian and the other deep is the heart of God each reaching out to one another. "Deep calls to deep" is a believer who is seeking and thirsting after God in the same way deer pants for water.

"As the deer pants for the water brook, so pants my soul for you, O God. My soul thirsts for God, for the living God". (Ps. 42:1-2).

We all leave behind an impression of ourselves upon others, either for good or otherwise. One of our most powerful testimonies is to leave behind the impression of a Christ-like life.

> *"Make me a blessing, make me a blessing,*
> *Out of my life may Jesus' shine.*
> *Make me a blessing, O Saviour, I pray,*
> *Make me a blessing to someone today."*

Ira Bishop Wilson (1880-1950)

THE GREAT LIBERATOR
John 8:36

"If the Son sets you free, you will indeed be free"

Freedom of speech, freedom of assembly, freedom to worship, freedom of movement, freedom to travel is just some of the basic rights and privileges that people enjoy in Western countries. But there is one freedom many do not enjoy. It is freedom from sins power, and from sins condemnation. Jesus said, *"everyone who sins is a slave to sin."* (John 8:34). The person who lives in habitual sin is a slave to sin. They are chained and held fast in the worst form of slavery on earth, and there is no power on earth that can free them from this form of slavery.

The slaves of sin are held by the impulses and the instincts of their lower nature. They are in bondage to sin and cannot free themselves. The power of sin has so strong a grip that it is impossible for them to break loose from their miserable state of slavery. It needs a greater power outside of themselves to set them free.

When a person turns to Christ, they have a new Master more powerful than the power of inherited sin. While sin enslaves true freedom comes in our relationship to Jesus Christ, through abiding in His Word, and being His disciple. *"If the Son sets you free, you will indeed be free."* Jesus sets us free from sins power. He sets us free from sins penalty of death. (Rom. 6:23). He sets us free from a guilty conscience and a guilt of shame. And in its place, He gives us peace with God.

> "Jesus! the name that charms our fears,
> that bids our sorrows cease;
> such music in the sinner's ears
> is life, and health, and peace.
>
> "He breaks the power of cancelled sin,
> he sets the prisoner free;
> His blood can make the foulest clean,
> His blood availed for me".
>
> Charles Wesley (1707-1788)

A GRAND EPITAPH

2 Timothy 4:7

"I have fought the good fight, I have finished the race, I have kept the faith"

When Paul wrote these words, he was in sight of his own death. From his prison cell in Rome, he knew his life was to end with the swift stroke from a Roman sword. He had no regrets. He once said, *"I would prefer to be away from the body and at home with the Lord"* (2 Cor.5:8). Now his time had finally come to go home with the Lord.

When Paul first encountered the resurrected Jesus on the Damascus Road, he did not know that he had been chosen to carry the name of Jesus before the Gentiles and their kings. In doing so he would have to endure great sufferings. (Acts 9:15-16). And suffer he did. During his missionary work for Christ he was flogged, stoned, shipwrecked, rejected and threated with death by fellow Jews. He was criticised by fellow Christians, imprisoned and constantly in danger of his own life. (Acts 27-28; 2 Cor. 11:16-33).

In this, his last letter, he tells Timothy of his approaching death and wrote his own epitaph: *"I have fought the good fight, I have finished the race, I have kept the faith."* The Christian life is represented as a race to be won. *"Run in such a way as to get the prize* (1 Cor. 9:24). Starting well is relatively easy, finishing well is a different matter! This is a challenge to every believer who have put their hand to the plough. (Luke 9:62). How do you want to be remembered? What do you hope people will say about you after you have crossed the finishing line? Something better I'm sure than the man whose epitaph is:

> "Here lies a man who did no good,
> And if he'd lived, he never would;
> Where he'd gone, how he fares,
> Nobody knows and nobody cares"

(Author unknown)

Prayer

O Lord, grant to me the perseverance to finish the race you have set before me that I may be able to say:

> *"I have fought the good fight, I have finished the race, I have kept the faith"*

And Your response to me, dear Lord, will be:

> *'Well done, good and faithful servant!*
> *Come and share your Lord's happiness!'*

(Matt.25:23)

"HE ABIDES IN US"

1 John 3:24

"Whoever keeps His commandments abides in God, and God in him. And by this we know that He abides in us, by the Spirit whom He has given us"

There are many church attendees who believe they are Christians because their parents were Christians, or because they attend church every Sunday, take the Eucharist, give their offering, or are involved in doing charitable work in their home church. Others call themselves Christians because they were born in a Christian country!

So, what evidence are there of being a true Christian according to the Bible. Jesus said, *"By their fruits you shall know them"* (Matt. 7:15-20; Gal. 5:22-23). Where there is no spiritual fruit implies there is no spiritual life. Evidence of being a true Christian comes from the abiding Spirit within, *"The Spirit Himself bears witness with our spirit that we are children of God"* (Rom. 8:16). *"And by this we know that He abides in us"*. To abide in Jesus, is to have a vital connection to the source of all eternal life and joy through the Spirit.

Those that abide in Jesus know they are abiding in Jesus, because of the assurance of His witness within. This assurance comes through a mutual intimacy enjoyed between the true Christian and the Holy Spirit. You can't be abiding in Jesus and not know it though you may be attacked with doubt from time to time.

Paul wrote, *If anyone does not have the Spirit of Christ, he does not belong to Christ"* (Rom. 8:9). It cannot get clearer than that. The only true Christian is the one who has the Spirit of Christ within them.

> "He lives, He lives, Christ Jesus lives today!
> He walks with me and talks with me along life's narrow way.
> He lives, He lives, salvation to impart!
> You ask me how I know He lives? He lives with my heart".
>
> Alfred Henry Ackley (1887-1960)

SLEEP WILL BE SWEET

Proverbs 3:24

"When you lie down, you will not be afraid; when you lie down, your sleep will be sweet".

Not all sleep problems are due to insomnia, sleep apnoea or other physical ailments. Many people go to bed at night with a guilty conscience that has chased them through the day and continues to haunt them through the night. Guilt, fear and anxieties are a major disruption to a good night's sleep. Wicked men can never sleep well at night. Lying in bed their minds are *"like the tossing sea, which cannot rest, whose waves cast up mire and mud. There is no rest for the wicked"* (Isa. 57:21). Wicked men are unable to enjoy peace and rest at night because of the pervading fear they have of their adversaries who out to kill them.

There are other bad bed companions that will disrupt your sleep such as fear of death, God's judgment, fear of the future with all it looming unknowns' and uncertainties. These should never rob a Christian of their sleep. C. H. Spurgeon said, *"Those who lie down under the protection of the Lord are as secure as kings and queens in their palaces, and a great deal more so. Ill dreams shall be banished, or even if they come, we shall wipe out the impression of them, knowing that they are only dreams.*

To have sweet sleep we must have sweet lives, sweet tempers, sweet meditations, and sweet love".

Paul has some good advice for Christians who look forward to a good night's sleep. *"Do not let the sun go down while you are still angry ...it will give the devil a foothold in your life* (Eph. 4:27). Even righteous anger, if allowed to fester, can turn to sin. It can stir the emotions and play havoc with one's thoughts at night. Confession and forgiveness before sleep leads to a good night sleep. *"The Lord grants sleep to the ones He loves"* (Psalm 127:2).

There are times, however, when we do have sleepless nights. This can be due to some physical ailment. Should that occur, ask the Lord:

> *"If in the night I sleepless lie,*
> *My mind with heavenly thoughts supply.*
> *Let no dark dreams disturb my rest,*
> *No powers of evil me molest."*

Thomas Ken (1637-1711)

A VOICE IN THE NIGHT

1 Samuel. 3:9

"Speak, Lord, for Thy servant hears Thee"

It was only after three successive calls that convinced the high priest Eli, that it was God who was speaking to twelve-year-old Samuel. When Samuel first heard a voice, he thought it was Eli who was calling him. Eventually, Eli realized it was the voice of God speaking to Samuel and so instructed the boy on how to respond. "Go lie down, and it shall be if He calls you again, you shall say, *"Speak, Lord, for Thy servant hears Thee"*. Samuel listened as the Lord told him he was going to judge Eli and his family because of their wickedness and Eli's refusal to punishment them. Eli's descendants, instead of enjoying a lasting service in the priesthood would suffer punishment, shame, poverty and eventually an early death.

We don't know how the Lord spoke to Samuel. Many would like to hear God speak to them in an audible voice. Peter, James and John heard the audible voice of God from the cloud when Jesus was transfigured before them. *"This is my Son, whom I love; with Him I am well pleased. Listen to Him!* (Matt. 17:5). On another occasion a large crowd heard God's audible voice came from heaven as Jesus was speaking to them. (John 12:28-31).

Although we do not know how the Lord spoke to Samuel, we do know how He speaks to us today. He speaks to us through His written Word, the Bible. Before meditating on His Word let your petition be, *"Speak Lord. for Thy servant hears Thee."* The Lord also speaks to us in a *"still small voice"* more often as words you feel than hear. (1 Kings 19:12-13). In times of grief and suffering God's inner voice is accompanied with an overwhelming sense of peace that passes all understanding.

> *"O give me Samuel's ear,*
> *The open ear, O Lord,*
> *Alive and quick to hear*
> *Each whisper of Your Word.*
> *Like him to answer at Your call,*
> *And to obey You first of all".*

James Drummond Burns (1823-1864)

FAITH OVER FEAR

2 Timothy 1:7

"For God did not give us a spirit of fear, but a spirit of power, of love and of self-control"

There are times when we may feel timid or afraid. When we face personal anxieties about health, security and relationships that can often leave us feeling weak and apprehensive. Having to speak in front of others can make some nervous. There are those who fear confrontation. Others are fearful of being made to look foolish and others fearful of rejection. Some fear death.

From his prison cell in Rome, Paul was able to encourage Timothy by reminding him that *"God did not give us a spirit of fear, but a spirit of power, of love and of self-control."* This is the same power that came upon the disciples enabling them to become fearless witnesses for Christ in Jerusalem, Judea and Samaria. (Acts 1:8). It empowered them to face the harshest persecution, and in the end, death as martyrs for the sake of Christ.

The Spirit of power enables us to live a holy life. (Eph.3:16). It empowers us to exercise self-control thus keeping the devil from gaining a foothold in our lives. We have been given the ability by the power of the Spirit in not letting our emotions get the better of us that could result in saying hurtful things that upset others. Self-control is one of the fruits of the Spirit. (Gal. 5:22-23).

Why fear death when our death is precious in the sight of the Lord. (Psalm 116:15). Why fear the future when God holds the future. We are the apple of His eye (Psalm 127:8). Why should we fear when the only fear we need to fear is to fear the Lord. Fear Him and it drives out all other fears.

> *"Fear Him, you saints, and you will then*
> *Have nothing else to fear.*
> *O make His service your delight,*
> *Your wants shall be His care".*

Nahum Tate (1652-1715)
Nicholas Brady (1659-1726)

GAIN THROUGH LOSS

Philippians 3:8

What is more, I consider everything a loss because of the surpassing worth of knowing Christ Jesus my Lord, for whose sake I have lost all things. I consider them garbage, that I may gain Christ"

If ever a man could have gone to heaven without Christ it was Paul of Tarsus. *"Circumcised on the eighth day of the people of Israel, of the tribe of Benjamin, a Hebrew of Hebrews; regarding the law, a Pharisee; as for zeal, persecuting the church, as for righteousness based on the law, faultless"* (Phil. 3:4-6). When Paul wrote this letter, he had been serving Christ for about thirty years. He had already abandoned all confidence in his pedigree privileges and his ceremonial righteousness as a Jew. He found that by losing his Jewish privileges, he gained much more in Christ.

"Yes, all things I once thought were so important are gone from my life. Compared to the high privilege of knowing Christ Jesus as my Master, firsthand, everything I once thought I had going for me is insignificant - dog dung. I've dumped it all in the trash so that I could embrace Christ." (The Message). For Paul, nothing else mattered in compassion to know Jesus Christ. He considered that everything that life had to offer as garbage in comparison to the surpassing value of knowing Jesus.

This is a challenge for each of us who name the Name of Christ. What value do we put on honour, reputation, popularity, our achievements, our talents, our education, our bank balance? Do we consider it as garbage in comparison to knowing Jesus? Paul was writing about losing something to gain something. In Christ he found much more than he lost. He found a justifying righteousness, peace with God, pardon for sin, eternal life and future glory.

> *"The world has great rewards to give*
> *And counts achievements high,*
> *But all the honours and delights*
> *Can never satisfy.*

Christopher Idle (1938-

THE LORD IS LEADING
Genesis 24:27

"I have been guided by the Lord"

Abraham asks his most trusted servant, Eliezer to travel to his former homeland to find a wife for his son Isaac. He was the oldest of Abraham's servants who was responsible for all that Abraham possessed. He was dependable, trustworthy, and obedient who prayed to God for guidance and success on his mission. After travelling about 800 km from Hebron to Haran God revealed to him that it was a lady named Rebekah who was to be the wife for Isaac. Upon the success of his mission, he looked back over his journey and said, *"I have been guided by the Lord"*.

"The steps of a good man are established by the Lord, who delights in His way". (Psalm. 37:23). These words were written by King David more than 1000 years after the death of Abraham. David was aware of his own descent dating back to Abraham and would have read the history about Abrahams faithful and righteous servant Eliezer. David's emphasis is upon a _good_ man, who _delights_ in the Lord's way. The Lord guides the steps of those who have put their trust fully in Him.

We can rest assured that our steps are being ordered by the Lord. It is often only in hindsight that we see how He guided our steps unbeknown to us at the time. In His wisdom and foresight, He overrules events in our lives, thus ordering our steps to keep us on the straight and narrow.

When we finally enter the portals of Heaven, like Eliezer we shall proclaim:

"I HAVE BEEN GUIDED BY THE LORD"

> *"When my spirit, clothed immortal,*
> *Wings its flight to realms of day,*
> *This my song through endless ages-*
> *Jesus led me all the way"*

Fanny J. Crosby (1820-1915)

FAITH AND DOUBT

Mark 9:24

"I have faith ... help me to believe more!

Jesus, and three of His disciples, Peter, James and John, climbed a high mountain where Jesus was transfigured before them. The appearance of Jesus' changed. His clothes became whiter than any earthly bleaching could make them. This wasn't a light coming on Jesus from the outside. It was a change on the outside that came from the inside. The rays of glory and brightness shone through His body and through His clothes that made Him look as bright as the light of the sun. And there appeared with Him Elijah and Moses, talking to Him about His approaching death in Jerusalem. Jesus gave Peter, James and John orders not to tell anyone of what they had seen until after His resurrection.

When they came off the mountain, they were met by a large crowd who were arguing with His other disciples. What are you arguing about? A man in the crowd answered *"Teacher, I brought my son who has epilepsy to be healed but your disciples couldn't heal him"*. Bring him to me, said Jesus. When He saw the boy in convulsions, He asked the father how long had been like this. From childhood, the father replied, *"but if you can do anything, take pity on us and help us"*. Jesus replied, *"Everything is possible for one who has faith"*. Immediately the boy's father cried out, *"I have faith, help me to believe more!*

Just as the boy's father was challenged about the level of his faith, so we as Christ's followers will be challenged about the level of our own. The father found his faith very weak and desired that he might be helped to be strong in faith. *"I have faith, help me to believe more!* We all pass through the storms of life that at times tests the level our faith. It will be necessary to make the same petition, because faith is imperfect in this life, and often weak and defective in its exercise. Like the boy's father, let the weak in faith cry out to the Lord, *"I have faith"*, *help me to believe more!*

> *"I'm so glad I learned to trust You,*
> *Precious Jesus, Saviour, Friend.*
> *And I know that You are with me,*
> *Will be with me to the end.*
>
> *Jesus, Jesus, How I trust Him!*
> *How I've proved Him o'er and o'er*
> *Jesus, Jesus, precious Jesus!*
> *O for grace to trust You more!"*

Louisa M. R. Stead (1850-1917)

"BE HOLY, BECAUSE I AM HOLY"

1 Peter 1:16

"He who has called you is holy, so be holy in all that you do; for it is written: Be holy, because I am holy"

This command was first spoken by Moses who was instructed by God to tell the Israelites, *"Be holy because I, the Lord your God, am holy"*. (Lev.19:2). God had set His people Israel apart for Himself. Nearly 1,400 years later, Peter quoted these words of Moses. He is writing to New Testament Christians telling them: It is written: *"Be holy, because I am holy"*. The main idea behind holiness is *"being apart."* Those whom God has called He has set apart for Himself.

When applied to God, it points to His perfection, that He is above and beyond His creation in such a way as to be separate from it. God's purity is such that He is totally isolated from all sin. When God calls us to holiness, it means that we are to be set apart from the world to become like Him, separate from sin. It means living our lives differently to those of the world. We are called to live as part of God's family rejecting the evil of this world. In doing so our lives will reflect that our lifestyle is different to that of the world.

Christians are commanded, *"Do not love the world or anything in the world. If anyone loves the world, the love of the Father is not in him."* (1

John 2:15). There can be no fence-sitting in the way we live our lives. We cannot have a love for the world and a love for God at the same time. It is one or the other. *"Be holy because I, the Lord your God, am holy"*. True worship comes from those who have been set apart from God and are living their lives separate from sin.

> *"Worship the Lord*
> *In the beauty of holiness,*
> *Bow down before Him*
> *His glory proclaims:*
> *Gold of obedience*
> *And incense of lowliness*
> *Bring and adore Him.*
> *The Lord is His Name"*
>
> John S. B. Monsell (1811-1875)

GRIEVE NOT THE SPIRIT
Ephesians 4:30-32

"Do not grieve the Holy Spirit, by whom you were marked with a seal for the Day of redemption"

Paul is not addressing a group of rowdy hooligans in some tavern or bar. He is writing to a Christian church in the city of Ephesus in which the congregation had some real issues they had to deal with. Within its congregation there are hints of falsehood, anger, stealing and unwholesome talk. Paul held nothing back. *"Get rid of all bitterness, anger, brawling, slander, and every form of malice"*. And all of this was occurring in a Christian church! He urges them to *"be kind and compassionate to one another, forgiving each other, just as in Christ God forgave you."*

In his first letter to the Church in Thessalonica, Paul urges them *"not to quench the Holy Spirit."* (1 Thess.5:19). It means not to stifle the sanctifying work of the Spirit in your life. To the Ephesians congregation he urges them *"not to grieve the Holy Spirit."* Throughout the New Testament, the Holy Spirit is referred to as a person (John 6:63; 14:26; Rom. 8:11, 16, 26; 1 John 5:6). He is a personal being, a "He." He has feelings. He can speak (Acts 8:29). He can be grieved (Eph. 4:30). He can be resisted (Acts 7:5). He can be blasphemed. (Matt. 12:31). He has a mind (Rom. 8:27).

The Holy Spirit was grieved by the disunity in the church and the lack of love in the Church. Did the Ephesian Church take heed to this letter of Paul? Apparently not. Forty years later the apostle John wrote about the Ephesian Church. Jesus had to rebuke them their lack of love toward each other. (Rev.2:1-7). Whatever grieves the Holy Spirit ought to grieve us too. Let us walk sensitive to the Spirit's promptings so we neither quench nor grieve Him in any way.

> *"Grieve not the Holy Spirit of God,*
> *in whom you were sealed for the day of redemption.*
> *Let all bitterness and wrath and anger and bawling and slander*
> *be put away from you, with all malice;*
> *and be ye kind one to another, tender-*
> *hearted, forgiving one another,*
> *as God in Christ forgave you."*
>
> Ephesians 4:30-32

HEART BURN
Luke 24:32

"They asked each other, "Were not our hearts burning within us while he talked with us on the road and opened the Scriptures to us?"

They had no idea who the stranger was that approached them on the road to Emmaus. The stranger asked them what they were discussing and why they looked so sad. The one called Cleopas, answered, *"Are you the only one visiting Jerusalem who does not know the things that have happened there in the last few days?"* As so Cleopas explained to the stranger. *"The chief priests and our rulers handed Jesus over to be sentenced to death, and they crucified Him. But we had hoped that He was the one who was going to redeem Israel. And what is more, it is the third day since all this took place. In addition, some of our women amazed us. They went to the tomb early this morning but did not find His body. They came and told us that they had seen a vision of angels, who said he was alive. Then some of our companions went to the tomb and found it just as the women had said, but they did not see Jesus"* (Luke 24:19-24).

"How dull you are", the stranger said. From the writings of Moses and all the prophets, He began to open up the passages which referred to Himself in the Scriptures" (John 5:39). But the two disciples still did not recognize who the stranger was.

Upon reaching the village to which they were going, the stranger acted as if to continue His journey, but they invited Him to stay the night. When He sat down with them over a meal, He took bread, gave thanks, broke the bread, and offered it to them. In a flash, their eyes were opened, and they recognized Him. (Matt. 26:26-28) Jesus then vanished from their sight. Then they asked each other, *"Were not our hearts burning within us while he talked with us on the road and opened the Scriptures to us?"*

> You walked with two lone travellers, along the Emmaus Road,
> Sad, they were, and grieving, they carried a heavy load.
> Their hope was in their Leader, who
> would have been their Guide,
> But the chief priests and the rulers had Him crucified.
>
> You opened up the Scriptures, to encourage and inspire,
> The flame of truth took hold and set their hearts afire.
> So, as You walked with them, O Lord, also walk with me,
> Open-up my eyes O Lord, that I might wiser be.
>
> O Lord, O Lord, speak to me, illuminate my mind,
> And as you speak to me, O Lord, enflame this heart of mine.

Peter C. Horrell (1936-

A CHANGE OF MIND

Romans. 12:2

"Do not be conformed to the pattern of this world, but let God transform your mind within, to find and follow God's will, that is, what is good, well-pleasing to Him, and perfect."

Paul is urging his readers not to adopt the customs of this world. Don't live according to the fashions of the times. Do not let the world squeeze you into its mould. The world's corrupt system can be summed up in three evils: the lust of the eyes, the lust of the flesh, and the pride of life. The lust of the eyes speaks of covetousness. The lust of the flesh is illicit sexual conduct, and the pride of life is a craving for honour and applause.

Paul is urging believers to be transformed by renewing their mind. He is saying we can become different people by changing our thinking. The change will be like that of a 'caterpillar into a butterfly'. (Eph. 4:23-24; Col. 3:9-10). We do this by reading God's Word and applying what It says to our own lives. Allowing oneself to be conformed to the pattern of the world or being transformed into the image of Christ determines your usefulness to the Lord.

By prayerfully reading His Word and being obedient to its message a new pattern of thinking will gradually transform our thinking to think only as God thinks. Allowing God to transform our minds we shall *"follow God's will, that is, what is good, well pleasing to Him, and perfect"*.

> *"May the mind of Christ my Saviour*
> *Live in me from day to day,*
> *By His love and power controlling*
> *All I do and say.*
>
> *May the Word of God enrich me*
> *With His truth from hour to hour,*
> *So that all may see I triumph*
> *Only through His power"*

Katie B. Wilkinson (1859-1928)

A BOTTOMLESS ABYSS
Jeremiah 17:9

"The heart is the most deceitful of all things, desperately wicked; who can know it?"

Who could deny there is something inherently wicked in the world. Man's inhumanity to man, greed, corruption, war, aggression reveal there is show there is something wrong mankind. Jeremiah points to the problem. The heart is deceitful and desperately wicked. *Who can know it?* It is like a bottomless abyss. Much in our own hearts remain unknown to us. But God sees it. Jesus sees it. He revealed its contents to the self-righteous Pharisees. For *"out of the heart come evil thoughts, murder, adultery, sexual immorality, theft, false testimony and slander"* (Matt. 15:19).

Ever since the Fall, our hearts have been polluted with sin. We are prone to sin and to disobey God. We cannot trust our hearts. Solomon wrote, *"He who trusts in his own heart is a fool"* (Prov.28:26). And then comes his advice, *"Trust in the Lord with all your heart; and lean not to your own understanding"*. (Pro.3:5-6). As we grow in grace and our knowledge of Christ, we become more and more aware of the sinfulness of our own heart. The closer our relationship with a holy God the more aware we shall become of our own sinfulness.

Jesus said, *"Blessed are the pure in heart, for they will see God"* (Matt. 5:8). To be pure in heart involves having a singleness of heart toward God. A pure heart has no hypocrisy, no guile, no hidden motives. The pure heart is marked by transparency and an uncompromising desire to please God in all things. With King David let us ask,

> **"CREATE IN ME A PURE HEART, O GOD, AND RENEW A STEADFAST SPIRIT WITHIN ME"**
>
> (Psalm 51:10)

> *"My stony heart to flesh convert,*
> *my inbred sin from me remove.*
> *Apply Your blood to all my heart*
> *and melt it by Your dying love.*
> *This rebel heart by love subdue,*
> *O make it soft and make it new."*
>
> Charles Wesley (1707-1788)

FANNING THE FLAME

2 Timothy 1:6

*"For this reason, I remind you to fan
into flame the gift of God,
which is in you through the laying on of my hands"*

This is Paul's second and last letter to Timothy in which he urges him to *"fan into flame the gift of God, which is in you"*. The gift is the gift of the Holy Spirit. Timothy received this gift when hands were laid upon him commissioning him for ministry. This is not the only way God gives gifts, but it is a way that we should not neglect.

Each one should use whatever gift he has received to serve others, faithfully administering God's grace in its various forms." (1 Peter 4:10). The seven gifts of the Holy Spirit are wisdom, understanding, counsel, fortitude, knowledge, piety, and fear of the Lord. Other gifts are prophesy, serving, teaching, encouraging, giving and mercy. (1 Cor.12; Eph.4:11; Rom.12:6-8). No born-again Christian is without a gift of the Spirit to be used for the mutual benefit of the Church. Every believer has a gift in which to serve others for the glory of God. We were saved to serve.

God does not work His gifts through us as if we were robots. He needs our cooperation and our desire in using the gift we already have. He wants to use us, but He needs the cooperation of our will, of our desire and drive to do so. The idea of fanning the flame is to keep it burning bright and strong. Left to itself it will always burn out. We shall all give an account of ourselves before the judgment seat of Christ on what we did and how we lived when on earth on Judgment Day. (2 Cor.5:9-11).

"I remind you now to fan into flame,
The gift that God has bestowed,
When my hands were laid upon you,
the gift of the Spirit of God.

The gift that God has given to us,
Is no cowardly spirit at all.
But one that is strong and loving and wise
The gift of the Spirit of God"

John M. Talbot (1954-

CONFIDENCE TOWARD GOD

1 John 3:21

"If our conscience does not condemn us, then we have confidence toward God"

The Bible mentions there is a good conscience (1 Peter 3:16), a clear conscience (Acts 24:16), a defiled conscience (Titus 1:5) a weak conscience (1 Cor.8:7) a seared conscience (1 Tim 4:2) and an evil conscience (Heb.10:22-24). Every human being is born with a moral conscience. It's that inner voice that identifies right and wrong. If we do wrong our conscious will condemn us. Through conscience, the intuitive knowledge of God reveals what God requires of us. Every human being has a conscience. The Gentiles who had no knowledge of the scriptures knew the difference between what was right and what was wrong. (Rom.2:14-15).

"If our conscience does not condemn us, then we have confidence toward God." The believer who has *"confidence toward God"* is free and unrestricted in his fellowship with God. They can have confidence in their prayers and petitions knowing that God hears them. Their conscience does not trouble them. When they are aligned with God's will, their conscience will confirm they are on the same page with God. If we are in line with God's will for our lives, we have the confidence toward God knowing He will listen to our requests and respond to our needs.

C.H. Spurgeon said, *"Other people may condemn us, but that does not matter; they may impute to us wrong motives, and misrepresent us, but that is no concern of ours so long as we have confidence toward God"*. Blessed are the ones who know the testimony of a good conscience. Blessed indeed is the Christian who has peace, rest, joy, and confidence toward God.

> *"If God and conscience both approve your way.*
> *Be undismayed, let all accuse who may.*
> *If God and conscience does your way upbraid,*
> *Then truly you have cause to be afraid".*

Author unknown

THE DIVINE WHISPER

Psalm 85:8

"I will listen to what the Lord says to me"

Thomas Á Kempis (1379-1471). *"Give no heed to the voices of the world. Place little confidence in the words of others. Trust little the whisperings of your own heart. Many voices from within and without seek to grab our attention"*. We need to distinguish the Lord's voice from the avalanche of other voices that clamber for our attention.

The Psalmist wrote, *"I will listen to what the Lord says to me"*. It is up to us to give Him the chance to do so. He wants to hear our petitions and is always there to help us. But as He listens to us, He in turn wants us to listen to Him. A listening ear is of far more value than a talkative tongue when we approach the throne of grace in prayer. He already knows our needs. To hear the Lord's voice, we must be free from any anxieties that cause turbulence in our soul.

Our first petition; Lord, quiet my heart and mind that I might be able to hear what you want to say to me. We must have peace within. Our hearts are a holy sanctum that God claims for His own. It is here where we can hear His 'still small voice', a whisper, speaking to us. It is our own private world where we commune with God and He communes with us.

He teaches us His truths inwardly by His Spirit. He writes them upon our hearts, truths that can never to be forgotten. When in His presence let your thoughts flow out to Him in love. Quietly meditate upon His love and mercy and think on all that He has done for you. Thank Him. Thank Him. Thank Him. And His peace will flood your soul in joy and thanksgiving.

Let the Psalmists petition be yours too:

"I will listen to what the Lord says to me"

Lord, I want to listen
My heart is open to You;
O Lord I want to know You more,
And a closer walk with You.

Peter C. Horrell (1936-

CHRISTIAN SUFFERING

Romans 8:18

"I consider that our present suffering is not worth comparing with the glory that will be revealed in us"

Since the foundation of the church in the first century up to the present-day hundreds of thousands of Christians have been put to death for their faith in Christ. Early believers died as martyry's by order of various Roman Caesars for refusing to acknowledge that Caesar was divine. That he was God. In some countries like Afghanistan, North Korea, Somalia, Libya, China and Yemen to become a Christian will result in a death sentence.

Paul, however, is not just referring to the sufferings caused by open persecution. He includes everyday difficulties we face living in this world. *"Man is absolutely going to, (on account of sin either their own or the sins of others) experience trouble as surely as sparks fly upward."* (Job 5:7)

Paul writes that our present *suffering is not worth comparing with the glory that will be revealed in us",* The Christian life would be foolish and tragic without the prospect of heaven. (1 Cor. 15:19,32). This coming glory will not only be revealed *to* us but revealed *in us*. God has already put his glory into us here on earth, but in heaven it will be revealed for all to see.

If there had been any other way for man's salvation than having to pass through suffering, Jesus would have shown it to us. But our spiritual advancement does not come through sweetness of life, but through tribulations and afflictions. *"Through many tribulations we must enter the kingdom of God"* (Acts 14:22).

> "Be still, my soul: your God will undertake
> to guide the future as He has the past.
> Your hope, your confidence let nothing shake;
> all now mysterious shall be bright at last.
> Be still, my soul: the waves and winds still know
> His voice who calmed them while He dwelt below"
>
> Katharina von Schlegel (1697-1768)

"GIVE ME NEITHER POVERTY NOR RICHES"

Proverbs 30:8-9

"Keep falsehood and lies far from me; give me neither poverty nor riches but give me only my daily bread. Otherwise, I may have too much and disown you and say, 'Who is the Lord?' Or I may become poor and steal, and so dishonour the name of my God"

The identity of Ague, the author of this Psalm is uncertain. Whoever he was he had valuable insights into the wisdom and fear of the Lord. He asks two requests from God. *"Keep falsehood and lies far from me, and 'Give me neither poverty not riches.* Lies and falsehood are among the most serious sins a person can commit. It breaks trust and ruins relationships. There are six things the Lord hates, two of which are *'a lying tongue'* and a *'false witness'*. (Pro. 6:16-19). Telling lies gets a person on a slippery downward slope that is difficult to get back up.

His second request is, *'Give me neither poverty nor riches.* His request is to have just enough for his daily bread. He asks he won't be so poor that he cannot afford to buy bread and be tempted to steal. He begged for a moderate income.

And neither did he want riches. Ague feared wealth as much as poverty. He saw the potential danger in having riches. It could lead to greed when enough is never enough. Wealth can also make you forget God. It can make a wealthy person so self-dependent that they see no need for God in their lives.

"The heart of man is restless till it finds its rest in You". The pursuit of riches and satisfaction to satisfy the restless heart is like chasing the wind. 'We are not physical beings having a spiritual experience; we are spiritual beings having a physical experience'. We were created by God for God. Only His Son, Jesus Christ can give peace to the restless heart. The desire for satisfaction and peace of heart is a spiritual one though many do not know it.

> *"Give me neither poverty nor riches,*
> *Give me just the sustenance I need,*
> *Lest I become rich, I would forget you,*
> *Lest I become poor, then I would steal*
>
> *Give me just Your sovereign hand to guide me,*
> *Give me strength to walk where you will lead,*
> *Let me rest beneath Your strong protection,*
> *You are my provision and my shield"*

I have done my best to discover the identity of the song without success. Whoever you are, Thank You.
Ghost Ship.
DMCA Agent
ML Genius Holdings, LC
1222 6th St.
Santa Monica CA 90401.

"NEVER NURSE A GRUDGE"

Ephesians 4:26

"In your anger do not sin": Never go to bed angry"

The world in which we live is full of anger residing in the hearts of men. It is expressed in two ways. There is a righteous anger acceptable to the Lord and a sinful anger unacceptable to the Lord. Sinful anger is expressed in explosive out bursts of anger due to some altercation with someone else. It remains smouldering within the heart of a bitter person ready to get even against anyone that offends them. Those who have this kind of anger are controlled by their anger.

Righteous anger is not sinful. There are two recorded incidents when Jesus was angry. When He cleared the Temple. He said, *"It is written my house will be a house of prayer; but you have made it a den of robbers"*. He then made a whip out of cords and drove them from the Temple area. (Mat. 21:12-13). His was a righteous anger against the Pharisees who showed no sympathy for the man He had just healed in the temple. They threatened to kill Jesus for doing so. (Mark 3:5).

Righteous anger can flare up when we see the poor and the vulnerable being taken advantage of by scrupulous individuals. It comes to the surface when we hear of child neglect, abuse of women or animal cruelty. But even righteous anger must be laid aside before sunset.

Then there is an anger directed at someone else. Flaring up with an inner anger against someone who has criticized you leaving you angry and upset. This makes an awful bed companion and is sure to rob you of your sleep. *'Do not nudge a grudge in bed'*. Forgive where forgiveness is needed. Deal with it before bedtime. Do not allow it to take up permanent residence in your heart otherwise it will breed bitterness in your spirit. Leave it in God's hands. Let it pass. To allow it to churn around inside you will give the devil a foot-hold in your life that he will use for his own wicked purposes. (Eph. 4:26-27).

A PRAYER

Calm my restless heart, O Lord, whisper peace within,
That I might know Your rest, dear Lord, free from any sin
Remove the anger and the hurt, the bitter taste in me,
That as I rest in bed tonight, from that I shall be free.

Thank You for the promised rest, as I sleep tonight,
With Your presence and your peace, I'll have a restful night.
So, when I wake at dawn, free from guilt and shame
I'll walk again with You, O Lord, to praise Your holy name.

Peter C. Horrell (1936-

THIS SIDE OF THE VALLEY

Psalm 23:4

"Even though I walk through the valley of the shadow of death, I will fear no evil"

Psalm 23 is the favoured Psalm to be read at the deathbed of dying saints. For many, they are the last words they hear as they pass through this Valley into the presence and protection of Christ.

"The Lord is my Shepherd". Just as a shepherd used his shepherd's staff and rod to rule, guide, and protect his flock, so the Lord has corrected, protected, and guided us through life that we would not go astray. We are often unaware how the Lord has guided and protected us until in hindsight we look back and see how He worked out that which was good for us. Otherwise, like sheep we would have gone astray.

Many will fear as they approach this Valley of the shadow of death. If they have not walked righteously in life, they will not walk fearlessly through this Valley. They will have no guide to lead them, no comforter to reassure them and no hope to sustain them. For them it will a Valley of fear, solitude, and regret.

Not so for the Christian. As Jesus walked with us through life, He will also walk with us through the Valley of our death. He knows this Valley for He Himself passed through it. He will never abandon us. He could no more abandon us than His own Father could abandon Him, by leaving Him in the grave.

THE OTHER SIDE OF THE VALLEY

The Valley was behind me, I'd passed through my valley of death,
My earthly pilgrimage had ended when I took my final breath.
I was never alone in the Valley, for Jesus my Saviour was there,
He walked me through the Valley, secure in His loving care.

There was no fear of evil, no dread disturbed my peace,
His Presence ever with me, His love had never ceased.
We walked and talked together, oh! what joy His face to see,
And the glory of His Kingdom, He had prepared for me.

Oh! Christian friend, do not fear, you'll never walk alone,
Jesus, your Guide and Shepherd, will lead you safely home.
He'll guide you through the Valley, the Valley of your death,
And lead you to the place, of your eternal happiness.

Peter C. Horrell (1936-

THE WINGS OF A DOVE
Psalm 55:6

***"Oh, that I had the wings of a dove! I
would fly away and be at rest"***

Many Christians would wish they had the *wings of a dove* to fly away from all the troubles they face in their daily lives (Job 14:7). King David, the writer of this Psalm, had more than his share of them. He writes *'I cried my eyes out; I feel hollow inside; my life is consumed by anguish'* (Psalm 31:10).

The dove, doubtless the rock pigeon, is remarkable for the swiftness of its flight to some inaccessible cliff far from the haunts of men to be at rest. David wished he had the wings of a dove to escape from all his troubles and to be at rest.

A life *'consumed by anguish'* is surely the most extreme torment one can experience. It affects the mind, the emotions, and the physical wellbeing of its victim. To be consumed by anguish is nearly always caused by a family member as in the case of King David. No one can cause more grief in the heart of another than from someone they are close to and deeply love.

Suffering grief over the death of a loved one can often heal in time. But grief caused by someone loved and cared for over the years can last a lifetime. Some children can be very cruel to their aged parents. The abuse that results in emotional and mental anguish comes in various forms. Verbal abuse. Being left alone and forgotten in a nursing home. Grandparents denied access to their grandchildren. Aged parents coerced into parting with assets/money, etc, etc.

Their emotional and mental suffering is intense because it is caused by someone they have raised from childbirth. It could leave a Christian victim so distraught they entertain a death wish, not against the one who has hurt them, but for themselves. Their silent petition: "*Oh, that I had the wings of a dove, I would fly away and be at rest*" with my Saviour.

God feels the pain of those whose lives are consumed by anguish. He also gives us the key on how to replace our anguish with His peace. It is found in FORGIVENESS. Forgive those who have hurt you. Pray for them. In doing so you will find God's grace will sustain you.

> *My life's consumed by sorrow, I'm overcome with grief,*
> *The anguish, pain and suffering, I pray for some relief,*
> *Betrayed by a loved one, for whom I cared and loved,*
>
> *I still reach out in love to him, a love from heaven above.*
> *Lord, hold it not against him, forgive as I have done.*
> *Reveal to him your mercy, reveal to him your love. Refresh*
> *me by Your grace and let my sorrows cease, Sustain me*
> *with your grace and grant to me inward peace.*

Peter C. Horrell (1936-

GROW IN GRACE

2 Peter 3:18

"But grow in the grace and knowledge of our Lord and Saviour Jesus Christ. To him be glory both now and forever! Amen".

These are the last words of an old man, written down as his legacy for us. Peter nears the end of his life, writing to congregations whom he is not likely to see or write to again. His final doxology pays homage to Jesus Christ as true God. His martyrdom is near and his injunction to us is: *"Grow! grow in grace, and in the knowledge of our Lord and Saviour Jesus Christ"*.

As we grow in grace, we become increasingly aware of God's holiness, justice, and sovereignty. This is evidenced by a growing sense of our own selfishness and pride. Martyn Lloyd-Jones (1899-1981). *"Personally, I can be certain I am growing in grace if I have an increasing sense of my own sinfulness and my own unworthiness; and if I see more and more the blackness of my own heart."*

We cannot grow in grace apart from Jesus Christ. Without our abiding in Him we will remain spiritually stunted in our Christian life. This growth in grace is gradual. We may not discern change from week to week, but over the long haul, we should be able to detect change in ourselves. Our love for Him is greater. our hate for sin is stronger, and our desire for a closer walk with Him becomes a constant yearning of our soul.

When Peter wrote, *"grow in the grace and knowledge of our Lord and Saviour Jesus Christ."* Peter wanted his readers to know Jesus personally and to become more acquainted with Him. That is only achieved by spending solitary time with Him in fellowship and prayer. As we walk with Him as our constant Companion, talk with Him as our Friend, and trust Him as our Guide we shall inevitably grow in our *"knowledge of our Lord and Saviour Jesus Christ. To him be glory both now and forever! Amen"*.

I long my Lord, oh how I long,
to know You more each day,
To grow in grace and knowledge,
for this my Lord, I pray.

You are my Saviour and my God,
whom heaven and earth adore,
To You be all the glory,
both now and evermore.

Peter C. Horrell (1936-

THE GROWING CHRISTIAN

KEEP KNOWING   Ephesians 3:19. *'to know the love of Christ Jesus"*

If we could travel to the farthest regions of the universe, we would still be within the reach of God's love. His love has no perimeters. It knows no height nor depth. *'Nothing in all creation can separate us from the love of God which is ours through Christ Jesus our Lord'*. (Rom. 8:38-39). To know this; to feel this; to have a lively sense of it, is one of the highest privileges of the Christian.

> *"O love that will not let me go; I rest my weary soul in Thee.*
> *I give Thee back the life I owe, that in Your ocean*
> *depth its flow may richer, fuller be".*
>
> George Matheson (1842-1906)

KEEP GROWING   2 Peter 3:18 *'to grow in grace ... and in knowledge'*

Christians who continue to love and obey Christ will grow in grace and continually increase in the knowledge of Him. They will long become more like Jesus as they spend time with Him in prayer and close fellowship. Charles Wesley (1707-1708) *"The end and design of grace being purchased and bestowed on us, is to destroy the image of the earthy, and restore us to that of the heavenly"* (Col. 1:10; 2 Cor. 3:18).

> "O Jesus Christ grow Thou in me, and all things else recede.
> My heart be daily nearer Thee from sin, be daily freed".
>
> Johann Caspar Lavater (1741-1801)

KEEP SHOWING 1 Peter 2:9 *'show forth the praises of Christ'* (KJV)

That you should show forth the praises of "virtues". The one great object for which we were redeemed, is that we might proclaim the glory of God. This we do, by showing forth by our behaviour the virtues of mercy, wisdom, power, goodness, and love, to a world of darkness, ignorance, error, sin and hopelessness.

KEEP GLOWING Matt. 5:16 *'let your light shine before men'*

Jesus said, *'You are the light of the world ... let your light shine before men, so that others will see the good that you do and will praise your Father in heaven'* (Matt 5:14-16). The followers of Jesus are as lights in the world. They ought to live in a way that attracts others to also turn to Jesus.

> "In this world of sin and care, this shall ever be my prayer:
> "Savior, wheresoever I be, may the Christ-life shine in me."
>
> Johnson Oatman, Jr. (1856–1922)

THREE DIFFERENT LEVELS OF LIVING

1 Corinthians. 2:14-3:4. (KJV)

1. LIFE ON THE LOWEST LEVEL. *The Natural Man* 1 Cor. 2:14

"But the natural man receives not the things of the Spirit of God: for they are foolishness unto him: neither can he know them, because they spiritually reject them"

Life lived on this level refers to the person living a life separate from God. They live their lives as though God does not exist. Their goal is the pursuit of wealth and pleasure. According to Paul, *'the natural man'* is someone to whom the things of God appear to be nonsense. They are spiritually blind. They are unable to see what God wants to do for them in Christ. They cannot see nor appreciate the value of the gospel, the Good News.

They may have fame and fortune, be in positions of power and privilege and yet are living their lives on the lowest level because they have shut God out of their lives. Life lived on this lowest level may appear to be normal, but in God's eyes it is an ***abnormal level.***

2. LIFE ON THE MIDDLE LEVEL.   *The Carnal Man* 1 Cor. 3:3

> *"You are still carnal. For where there are envy, strife, and divisions among you, are you not carnal and behaving like mere men?"*

Life lived on this level refers to a Christian whose commitment to Christ is half-hearted. They are *'neither hot nor cold'*, but *'lukewarm'* in their commitment to Jesus (Rev. 3:15-16). Christians who live on this level want the best of two worlds. Christ is not the sole occupier of their hearts. Other idols lurk within, known only to them and to God.

Paul is writing to Christians, not to non-Christians. He is admonishing Christians in the local church who are content to be hearers of the Word, but not doers of the Word. He refers to them as the *'carnal'* man. They are missing out on all the fullness that God had intended for them in Christ. In God's eyes, they are living their spiritual lives on a **subnormal level.**

3. LIFE ON THE HIGHEST LEVEL.   *The Spiritual Man* 1 Cor. 3:1.

> *"And I, brethren, could not speak unto you as unto spiritual, but as unto carnal, even as unto babes in Christ."*

Life lived on this level refers to the Christian whose commitment to Christ is 100%. Upon this level God wants all His people to live their lives. Only then can the Christian grow in their understanding of God's truths and grow into spiritual maturity. Only upon this highest spiritual level of commitment to Christ can they enjoy the closest fellowship with Him. Those who live on this level are called the *'spiritual man'*, or the spiritual people who are living the **normal level** *life* that God had intended for them.

TWO ASPECTS OF GOD'S PEACE

(Romans 5:1; Colossians 3:15)

1 PEACE WITH GOD

"Therefore, having been justified by faith, we have peace with God through our Lord Jesus Christ". (Rom. 5:1). Until this takes place *"Our hearts are restless till they find their rest in Thee"* (Augustine (354-430 AD). There exists a state of enmity between God and man because of sin. God made the first move of reconciliation between Himself and sinful humankind by sending His Son, Jesus, into the world (John 3:16).

Man can never achieve peace with God through his own efforts. It can never be earned by belonging to a local church or by doing good works, singing hymns, or reciting prayers from a Prayer Book. Paul writes: *'For it is by God's grace that you have been saved, through faith. It is not your own doing, but God's gift. There is nothing here to boast of since it is not the result of your own efforts'* (Eph. 2:8-9).

There is but one way to find peace with God, and that way is through Christ. It is freely offered to all repentant sinners by faith alone. Finding peace with God is based solely upon the death of Christ. There is no other way to God but through Christ. Jesus said: *"I am the way, the truth and the life, no one comes to the Father but by me"* (John 14:6).

Peace with God—all sins forgiven!

> *Peace with God—all guilt removed!*
> *Peace with God—foretaste of heaven!*
> *Peace with God—His mercy proved!"*

2 PEACE OF GOD

"*And let the peace of God rule in your hearts …*" (Col. 3:15). Paul is writing to Christians who have already made their peace with God. They must now allow that peace to '*rule in their hearts*'. Every Christian at some time can feel that their "*peace with God*" *takes* flight, like a bird. Their hearts seem to be in a state of turbulence. Many things can rob us of our peace. Misunderstanding with fellow Christians, disagreements in the local church, family disputes, financial pressures, sickness, and grief. In the case of the Colossian Christians, it was the threat of persecution from the Roman authorities.

The secret of letting the '*peace of God rule in our hearts*' *is* to take everything to Him in prayer. Let the peace of Christ act as umpire when anger, envy, and such passions arise; and restrain them. His peace will calm down every agitated element of the heart. Trust Him, and you will be amazed how He works it out for your good and for His glory. Learn to leave your anxieties in the Hands of God and allow His peace to rule your heart.

> '*Peace, perfect peace, our future all unknown?*
> *Jesus, we know, and He is on the throne'.*

FOUR WAYS TO KNOW CHRIST

1. CHRIST OUR SAVIOUR – *"COME TO ME,"* said Jesus

"*Come to me, all of you who are tired from carrying your heavy loads, and I will give you rest"* (Matt.11:28). This speaks of **SALVATION**. Not to know Jesus as Saviour is not to know Him at all. Those weighed down with guilt and shame, who carry a heavy load of sin will find forgiveness and salvation in Jesus. His invitation is open to all who confess themselves sinners and who seek forgiveness and rest from their burden.

2. CHRIST AS OUR TEACHER – *"LEARN FROM ME,"* said Jesus.

"*Take my yoke, and put it on you, and learn from me, for I am gentle and humble in spirit"* (Matt. 11:29). This speaks of **INSTRUCTION**. A motto in Latin over the entrance of a college read: "Enter to Learn". Christ as our Saviour also becomes our Teacher. He teaches us how to pray, He instructs us in how to live, and He guides us into all truth. There is no better Teacher than Jesus Christ. It means, however, spending time with Him in His Word so He can teach us.

> *"Learn of Jesus Christ to pray.*
> *Learn of Christ to bear the cross.*
> *Learn of Jesus Christ to die".*
>
> James Montgomery (1771-1854)

3. <u>CHRIST AS OUR LORD</u> – ***"FOLLOW ME,"*** said Jesus.

"Follow me, and I will teach you to catch men" (Matt. 4:19). This speaks of **<u>SUBMISSION</u>** to His Lordship. Jesus said, *"Whoever does not carry his own cross and come after me, cannot be my disciple"* (Luke 14:27). To follow Christ, is a call to discipleship. It means submission to His will, regardless of cost. There is only one throne in our hearts, and Jesus wants sole occupancy of that throne. If He is not the Lord of our heart, He is not Lord of our lives.

> *"The dearest idol I have known,*
> *Whatever that idol be.*
> *Help me to tear it from Thy throne,*
> *And worship only Thee".*

W. Cowper (1731-1800)

4. <u>CHRIST AS OUR LIFE</u> - ***"ABIDE IN ME,"*** *said* Jesus.

"<u>Abide in me</u>, and I will remain in union with you … I am the vine … unless you abide in me you cannot bear fruit …" (John 15:4-5). This speaks of **<u>FRUITFULNESS.</u>** Only the branch attached to the vine can bear fruit. Only in union with Christ can we bear the fruit of the Spirit and live a life of holiness. (Gal. 5:22-23)

> *"And every virtue we possess, and every victory won,*
> *and every thought of holiness is His alone"*

Harriet Auber (1773-1862)

FOUR WAYS GOD SPEAKS TO US

1) GOD SPEAKS TO US THROUGH **CREATION**   Psalm 19:1-6

The Psalmist wrote: *"The heavens declare the glory of God; the skies proclaim the work of his hands"*. *"Without a sound or a word, silent in the skies, their message reaches out to the entire world"*. John Calvin (1509-1564) writes, *"when a man, from beholding and contemplating the heavens, has been brought to acknowledge God, he will learn also to reflect upon, and to admire His wisdom and power"*.

> *"Heav'n above is softer blue*
> *Earth around is sweeter green,*
> *Something lives in every hue*
> *Christless eyes have never seen."*
>
> George Robinson (1838-1877)

2) GOD SPEAKS TO US THROUGH **CONSCIENCE**   Romans 2:14-16

Concerning the Gentiles' ignorance of Jewish Law, Paul wrote, *"the Law's commands are written in their hearts ... their consciences sometimes accusing them or sometimes defending them"*. Immanuel Kant, the 18th cent. German philosopher said there are two things that fill me with awe: *"The starry heavens above me, and the moral law within me"*.

Conscience is that innate faculty in a man's spirit that attaches itself to the highest the man knows. A healthy conscience commands and obligates him to do what is right and abstain from doing what is wrong. The moral law within was written by the Great Lawmaker: God Himself.

> *"What Conscience dictates to be done,*
> *Or warns me not to do.*
> *This teaches me more than Hell to shun,*
> *That more than Heav'n pursue."*
>
> Pope (1688-1744) *Universal Prayer*

3) GOD SPEAKS TO US THROUGH THE **SCRIPTURES**.   2 Tim 3:16-17３

The purpose of the Bible is to instruct its readers *'for salvation'*. This indicates that Scripture has a practical purpose, and that purpose is moral rather than intellectual. It contains all things necessary for salvation. James I. Packer (1926-2020). *"The Scriptures are acknowledged to be, so to speak, God's mould for shaping our whole lives. Peoples from every nation, culture, race, and tongue, have testified to its influence for good upon their lives"*.

> *"What glory gilds the sacred page,*
> *Majestic like the sun!*
> *It gives a light to every age,*
> *It gives, but borrows none"*
>
> W. Cowper (1731-1800)

Four Ways God Speaks To Us

4) GOD SPEAKS TO US THROUGH **CHRIST**.   Hebrews 1:1-4

"In the past God spoke to our ancestors many times and in many ways through the prophets, but in these last days He has spoken to us through His Son." Andrew Murray (1828-1917) wrote *"The ministry of angels and prophets was only to prepare the way; it never could satisfy the heart of either God nor man; the real power of the life of God, the full experience of His nearness, the true deliverance from sin, the shedding abroad of the love in the heart; this could not be communicated by the ministry of creatures. The Son Himself had to come as the Word of God to us, the bearer of the life and love of the Father. The Son Himself had come to bring us into living contact with the Divine Being."*

> *"God has spoken by Christ Jesus,*
> *Christ, the everlasting Son.*
> *Brightness of the Father's glory,*
> *With the Father, ever one:*
> *Spoken by the Word incarnate,*
> *God, before all-time began,*
> *Light of light, to earth descending,*
> *Man, revealing God to man"*

G. W. Briggs (1875-1959)

"Speak, Lord, in the stillness,
While I wait on Thee;
Hushed my heart to listen,
In expectancy.
Speak, O blessed Master,
In this quiet hour;
Let me see Thy face, Lord,
Feel Thy touch of power.
Speak Thy servant heareth,
Be not silent Lord;
Waits my soul upon Thee,
For Thy quickening word".

E. May Grimes (1868-1927)

WHAT JESUS TOOK TO HIMSELF

1. JESUS TOOK A LOAF - that speaks of **SUPPLY**   (Matthew 14:13-21)

You would hardly think it worth bringing a small loaf to the notice of Jesus when faced with feeding about 5000 people. There is, however, a spiritual lesson to be learned from this small loaf of bread. Before it could be used by Jesus, it first had to be in the hands of Jesus. When in His hands He was able to bless and use it. The lesson is clear: He can only use and bless that which is given to Him. If our lives are in the hands of Jesus, He will use us to meet the needs of others.

2. JESUS TOOK A CHILD – that speaks of **SIMPLICITY**   (Matthew 18:1-6)

His disciples asked, *who is the greatest in the Kingdom of Heaven?* In answering Jesus took a child, and said, whoever humbles himself and becomes like a child, is the greatest in the Kingdom of Heaven. The eyes of a small child reveal trust and innocence. You see a soul untainted by sin. They are the personification of humility and purity. They are quick to respond to love, and quick to return it. The greatest in the Kingdom of heaven are those who possess these child-like virtues.

3. JESUS TOOK A TOWEL – that speaks of **SERVICE**.   (John 13:1-11)

"At the name of Jesus every knee shall bow" (Phil 2:10-11), and yet, on the night of His betrayal the Lord of heaven and earth bends His own knee to wash the feet of His disciples thus giving us all an example of humble service. A servant mentality is highly prized by God. Service to others, however small that service may appear, will never go unrewarded on the Last Day. It will ultimately receive heaven's best accolade: *"Well done good and faithful servant"*. (Matt. 25:21).

> *"When Jesus took a servant's towel –*
> *His honour set aside.*
> *He humbly showed us how to serve,*
> *And how to conquer pride"*

4. JESUS TOOK A CROSS – that speaks of **SACRIFICE**   (John 19:17-18)

A.W. Tozer (1897-1963) wrote, *"Now among the plastic saints of our time, Jesus must do all the dying and all we want is to hear another sermon about His dying. Jesus does all the sorrowing, and we want to be happy"*. When Jesus said, *'take up your cross'* it was a call to share in His sufferings. Jesus never promised an easy life for His followers. The only path that leads to blessing, is the same path Jesus Himself walked when He took up His own cross to Calvary. Taking up the cross means to put aside one's own selfish desires and follow Christ as Lord and Master of our life.

> *"Take up thy cross, the Saviour said*
> *If thou wouldst My disciple be.*
> *Take up thy cross, with willing heart,*
> *And humbly follow Me."*

Charles W. Everest (1814-1877)

A PORTRAIT OF AN IDEAL CHRISTIAN

1 Tim. 6: 11-16 (KJV)

A CHRISTIAN THAT FLEES v.11.

There are things every Christian should avoid if they wish to grow in faith and live a life pleasing to God. In his letter to Timothy, Paul mentions some of which he urges him to flee. Flee from: *"false doctrines, controversies, jealousy, malicious talk, insults, evil suspicions and being in constant friction with men of warped minds"* propagated by false teachers (1 Tim. 6:1-10; 2 Tim. 2:21-24). Christian's ought to flee from becoming embroiled in debating over erroneous teachings that lead to friction which often ends in heated arguments.

A CHRISTIAN THAT FOLLOWS v.11

Set your heart upon the following: *"righteousness, godliness, faith, love, endurance and gentleness"*, in contrast to the perverse behaviour of false teachers. That same warning is current for present day Christians. The pursuit of these divine virtues should be the supreme goal of every Christian who wish the blessings of God upon their lives. The priorities of the world are to pursue wealth and fame, power, and prestige. Such pursuits should never ever be of interest to any Christian.

A CHRISTIAN THAT FIGHTS v.12

"Fight the good fight of faith". The Christian's life is a spiritual warfare. We are called to be soldiers for there are many spiritual enemies we must contend with. The devil and his demons will never let up in their onslaught against us. (Eph. 6:10-20). We shall continually face opposition on our pilgrimage through this world to our Celestial City, but Jesus will never leave us nor forsake us. He will give us the encouragement and the strength to see us through to the very end.

A CHRISTIAN THAT FURNISHES 2 Tim. 3:16-17

All Scripture is God-breathed, and is useful for teaching, rebuking, correcting, and training in righteousness, so that the man of God may be thoroughly equipped for every good work". The Bible provides us with spiritual guidance which is "profitable" for matters relating to our conduct and beliefs. The KJV version puts it this way: *'That the man of God is thoroughly <u>furnished</u>'* or well equipped to be useful in the hands of God. A *"furnished"* Christian is well equipped in knowing their Bible and able to assist younger Christians to grow in their faith.

SACRIFICES TO GOD

THE SACRIFICE OF PRAISE   Hebrews. 13:15

'*Let us continually offer up a <u>sacrifice of praise</u> to God*'. There is so much for which we can praise God. Praise Him for His love and mercy. Praise and thank Him for sending His Son to save us from sin's condemnation. Praise Him for our salvation. Praise Him for the hope of heaven. Praise Him for eternal life. Praise Him for His presence with us. To offer these sacrifices when we are passing through difficult times wilt test our faith. But to be able to do so is well pleasing to the Lord.

THE SACRIFICE OF GOOD WORKS   Hebrews. 13:16.

'Do not neglect <u>doing good; with such sacrifices</u> God is pleased'. He is delighted when we turn to do good for others. To share with the needy and the poor are sacrifices that every follower of Christ is called to do. Doing good will involve effort, time, and money. Visiting the lonely, the sick, and the aged. These are good works that Jesus recognizes and rewards. In serving others, He said, *"you served me"*. (Matt. 25:31-40).

THE SACRIFICE OF TEMPORAL THINGS   Philippians. 4:18.

'I have received what you sent, an acceptable <u>sacrifice</u> ...' Paul was supported by gifts from the church in Philippi. They were not a wealthy congregation, yet they gave sacrificially so he could continue his missionary work. Probably the gift did not come to very much, if estimated in Roman coinage; but takes time to write a letter of thanks to the congregation in Philippi. Like the *'poor widow'*, they gave all they could give (Mark 12:43). This reveals an important principle regarding giving. There is more joy in giving than receiving.

THE SACRIFICE OF OUR BODIES   Romans. 12:1-2.

'Present your <u>bodies a living holy sacrifice</u> to God'. In contrast to the dead sacrifice of the Old Testament, a Christian is called to be a living sacrifice that God can sanctify and use for His glory. The Christian ought to always remember that their body is the temple of God in which His Spirit dwells. Our bodies are to be upon as holy and must not be defiled (1 Cor. 3:16-17). The presenting of our bodies to God implies that we no longer have any claim on ourselves. We belong to God

THE SACRIFICE OF A HOLY LIFE   1 Peter 2:5.

'You are living stones ... a holy priesthood to offer up spiritual <u>sacrifices</u> to God'. Holy means to be set apart by God, and for God just as the priests under law were set apart and sanctified for that office. All Christians are priests who have been set apart, to live and serve and live holy lives (1 Peter 2:5). Though surrounded by immorality in the world, we are to remember that we belong to a holy priesthood and must live a life pleasing in the sight of God (1 Peter 1:16).

FIVE CHRISTIAN PRIORITIES

1. Watch your **DEVOTION**.   Reading: Luke. 10:38-42.

Martha became so caught up in her service for Christ that, unlike her sister Mary, she neglected to sit at the feet of Christ. We need to beware of falling into the same trap as Martha. There is no substitute for sitting at the feet of Jesus in silent prayer. It enables us to hear the *'still small voice'* of God within. Service for Christ, yes; but not at the cost of neglecting one's devotion to Christ. Bishop J. C. Ryle (1816-1900). *"Prayer is the most important subject in practical religion. All other subjects are second to it. Reading the Bible, keeping the Sabbath, hearing sermons, attending public worship, going to the Lord's Table – all these are very weighty matters. But none of them are so important as private prayer"*.

> *"O Thou! by whom we come to God,*
> *The life, the truth, the way.*
> *The path of prayer thyself has trod:*
> *Lord, teach us how to pray".*

James Montgomery (1771-1854)

2. Watch your **DIRECTION**.   Readings: Hebrews. 12:1-2; Philippians. 3:13-14

The writer of Hebrews compares the Christian life to a race. Christians are described as runners competing for a prize and are urged to run with perseverance the course set before them. There are obstacles to overcome and giants to contend with in our contest. Like Christian in Bunyan's "Pilgrim's Progress", the followers of Christ will face their own trials and temptations. In times such as these we shall need patience and perseverance to keep looking ahead with our attention fixed upon Christ. Our calling is not a stroll or a saunter through a park but to a race. The prize is nothing less than the crown of life.

> *"Turn your eyes upon Jesus*
> *Look full in His wonderful face*
> *And the things of earth will grow strangely dim*
> *In the light of His glory and grace."*
>
> Helen H. Lemmel (1863-1961)

3. Watch your **DIET.**   Readings: 2 Timothy. 3:16-17.

As a young Christian in the early sixties, a Christian businessman gave me this advice: *'Peter, if you ever get too busy to read your Bible you are far busier than God ever intended you to be'*. His words hit home. There can be little if any spiritual progress without reading the Bible. Spiritual life needs spiritual nourishment which leads to spiritual growth and maturity. Next to prayer there is nothing so important as Bible-reading. John W. Stott (1921-2011). *"God's word is as essential to us spiritually as food is to us physically. Both life and health are - quite literally – impossible without it. It is by His word that God implants spiritual life within us. It is by the same word that He instructs, reforms, nourishes, encourages, and* strengthens us. It is truly by His word alone that the man of God grows into maturity'".

> "O send Thy Spirit, Lord, Now unto me,
> That He may touch my eyes, and make me see:
> Show me the truth concealed, within Thy Word,
> And in Thy Book revealed I see the Lord".

Mary A. Lathbury (1841-1913)

4. Watch your **DRESS**.   Reading: Hebrews. 12:1-3

Runners strip down to the lightest clothing when competing in a race. They know the less weight they carry the more chance of winning the contest. The Christian runner must also rid themselves of any weight that hinders their progress. The apostle writes: *'Throw off every encumbrance and the sin which so easily entangles us.'* There may be habits, pleasures, self-indulgences, and associations that hold a Christian back. We must shed them as the athlete sheds his tracksuit when he goes to the starting mark. Henry Matthew (1662-1714) wrote *"all inordinate affection and concern for the body and the present life or fondness for it, is a dead weight upon the soul that pulls it down when it should ascend upwards"*.

> "Run the straight race through God's good grace'
> Lift your eyes and seek His face.
> Life with its way before you lies'
> Christ is the path, and Christ the prize".

John S. B. Monsell (1811-75)

5. Watch your **DISCIPLINE**.   Reading: 1 Corinthians. 9:24-27

Paul was always fascinated by the picture of an athlete competing in the Isthmian games held in the city of Corinth. He knew that an athlete must train with intensity to win the contest and be crowned with the coveted laurel wreath. Self-denial and self-mastery are required. Comparing himself to an athlete in training he writes: '*I keep the appetites of my body under complete control ... lest I should be disqualified.*' The Christian's life is not one of ease and self-indulgence. It entails discipline in keeping the physical appetites of the body and the lusts of the flesh under control. Only by walking in the Spirit can a Christian exercise self-control over the weakest areas of their lives. Anything that is doubtful they should ask: "What would Christ do in this situation?"

> *"Holy Spirit, breath on me,*
> *My stubborn will subdues.*
> *Teach me in words of living flame*
> *What Christ would have me do".*
>
> Edwin Hatch (1835-1889)

Five Christian Priorities

A FOURFOLD DESCRIPTION OF THE CHRISTIAN

A SOLDIER

As a soldier, the Christian is called to be at the forefront of the battle. This implies conflict, hardship, and danger. Paul reminds Christ's followers that they are *'not fighting against human beings, but against wicked spiritual forces in the spirit world'.*, He writes, *'put on the whole armour of God'* (2 Tim.2:3-4; Eph. 6:11-20). We are in a spiritual warfare and singled out by the unseen forces of evil intent on seeking to spiritually destroy us.

> "Sure, I must fight if I would reign.
> Increase my courage, Lord.
> I'll bear the toil, endure the pain,
> Supported by Thy word"

Isaac Watts (1674-1748)

A SERVANT

Jesus said the greatest among His followers are those who serve others. (Mk 10:43-45). When we help those less fortunate than ourselves, we are serving Christ. Jesus said: *"I was hungry, and you gave me something to eat; I was thirsty, and you gave me drink; I was a stranger, and you invited Me in; naked, and you clothed Me; I was sick, and you visited Me; I was in prison, and you came to Me"* (Matt 25:35-36). No theology there! Just plain practical Christianity.

> *"Brother, let me be your servant,*
> *Let me be as Christ to you.*
> *Pray that I may have the grace*
> *To let you be my servant,* too"
>
> Richard Gillard

A STUDENT

Whatever literature the Christian may read and enjoy, they should first read the most valuable Book of all, the Bible. Paul wrote, *"All Scripture is inspired by God* and *useful for teaching the truth, rebuking error, correcting faults, and giving instruction for right living"* (2 Tim 3:16). Herein is its immeasurable value: *'It makes us wise unto salvation'*. Christian's ought to be fervent students in knowing their Bibles.

A SAINT

Every born-again believer has been *'sanctified'*, set aside, *"in Christ Jesus and called to be a saint'* (1 Cor. 1:2). God's ultimate intention for each of us is to be transformed into the image of His Son, Jesus. This is top priority for without this spiritual transformation we shall fall short in what God had had planned for us.

> "A heart in every thought renewed, And full of love divine.
> Perfect and right, and pure, and good: A copy, Lord, of Thine".
>
> Charles Wesley (1707-88)

MILK OR MEAT?

1 Corinthians 3:2

"I gave you milk, not solid food, for you were not ready for it. Indeed, you are still not ready for it"

Paul wouldn't have made many friends in the Church in Corinth when they received this letter! He called them spiritual infants, still in their baby-stage incapable of comprehending the deeper truths of Christ. *"I gave you milk, the simple and easiest doctrines of the Christian faith, but I couldn't give you solid food because you were not ready for it.*

He referred to the *'solid food'* as the deeper mysteries of God. He rebuked them and held them responsible for their own lack of spiritual growth. Like the Christians in the Church in Laodicea, the congregation in Corinth were lukewarm in their relationship with Christ. (Rev.3:14-22). He cautioned them for their lack of spiritual growth due to being indifferent towards Christ.

Paul wrote, *'I press toward the mark for the prize for which God calls us upward to heaven because of what Christ Jesus has done for us'* (Phil. 3:14-15). We are either contributing to our own spiritual growth or going backwards. There is no 'marking time' in our spiritual lives. Spiritual immaturity results from lack of interest in wanting to grow in our spiritual understanding. It will inevitably lead to spiritual apathy.

As Christians we are urged to keep growing in our understanding of the mysteries of God (2 Peter 3:18; Phil.1:9; Col. 1:9; James 1:5). There are believers in churches today who are "infants' though they have attended church for years. Each of us have our own part to play in our own spiritual growth. The Lord expects those He has adopted into His family to grow into spiritual maturity.

> *"Holy Spirit, Truth divine,*
> *Dawn upon this soul of mine;*
> *Word of God, and inward light,*
> *wake my spirit, clear my sight"*

Samuel Longfellow (1819-1892)

INVITING GOD'S SCRUTINY

Psalm. 26:2

"Test me, O Lord, and try me, examine my heart and my mind; for your love is ever before me, and I walk continually in your truth."

Self-examination is all important (Ps. 4:4), but we need God to examine us too. *'Test me, try me, examine me'*, David pleads. Because of his love for God, he sincerely wanted to know if there was anything in his heart that offended God. If so, he pleaded to reveal it to him so that he *'can walk continually in God's truth.'* David wanted nothing in his heart that would hinder his fellowship with the Lord.

Job wrote, *'mortals are born into trouble as sure as sparks fly upwards'* (Job 5:7). God has chosen not to control everything going on in the world. Our faith and our love for Christ is often tested in times of sickness, grief, financial stress, family difficulties, loneliness and misunderstandings with other people. *'Test me, try me, examine me'*, and God tests us by using our troubles to reveal the state of our own hearts. How we react to these pressures reveal something about ourselves to ourselves in how strong our faith is in God.

Job's love for God was tested. He lost everything. His home, family, health, reputation and friends. Yet he could still say, *'Though he slays me yet will I trust in him'* (Job. 13:15). Abraham's love and obedience to God was tested. He was asked to sacrifice his son, Isaac (Gen 22:1-13). He was about to do so then God provided a ram in Isaac's place.

To invite God's scrutiny to *'Test me, try me, examine me'* is an indication of our own desire to please Christ and have a closer walk with Him.

> *"Search me, O God, and know my heart today,*
> *Try me, O Saviour, know my thoughts I pray;*
> *See if there be some wicked way in me,*
> *Cleanse me from every sin, and set me free"*
>
> Francis Bottome (1823-1894)

QUICK TO LISTEN - SLOW TO SPEAK

Ecclesiastes 5:2

'Do not be quick with your mouth, do not be hasty in your heart to utter anything before God. God is in heaven, and you are on earth, so let your words be few'.

"*Guard your steps when you go to the house of God*" wrote Solomon. "*Go near to listen rather than to offer the sacrifice of fools*". Solomon's plea is, slow down, stop and think before rushing in and making a fool of yourself before God. Furthermore, Solomon advises us to carefully consider our words before opening our mouths. How often we rush into making our requests known to God without due consideration: *'do not be quick with your mouth'*. We need to compose ourselves by first turning our thoughts quietly towards God.

'God is in heaven' is a reminder of His infinite holiness and majesty and worthy of our thoughtful reverence. As we approach His Throne of Grace, we need to reminding ourselves who He is and who *'we are on earth'*. He is the Almighty God; creator of heaven and earth who made us for Himself to have fellowship with Him. *'He is the Potter we are the clay'*. (Is. 45:9). There is no room for levity when approaching His presence.

They that know God best are in awe of Him most. They will fear Him and love Him and with reverence adore Him.

'*So, let your words be few*', as were the words of the publican, '*God be merciful to me a sinner*' (Luke. 18:13 It is a comforting thought to know that He wants to hear our petitions, but there is no need to be "long-winded" about them. Jesus said, '*When you pray, do not repeat the same words over and over again who think, like pagans, that by using many words they will be heard*'. *Do not be like them, for your Father knows what you need before you ask him*' (Matt. 6:7-8). He is already aware of all our needs and ready to meet them.

> "*Prayer is the soul's sincere desire,*
> *Unuttered or expressed;*
> *The motion of a hidden fire,*
> *That trembles in the breast*".

James Montgomery (1771-1854).

QUESTION TIME!
Matthew 18:1

"Who is the greatest in the kingdom of heaven?

The disciples asked Jesus that question. They wanted to know who among them would hold the highest position. Undoubtedly, they thought of a worldly kingdom where honours would be bestowed, and positions of importance conferred on them like any worldly monarchy. Jesus could have answered the question simply by pointing to Himself as the greatest in the kingdom of heaven. But He wasn't concerned about His own importance. He didn't have to be the centre of attention.

Instead, He took a child and said, *"whoever humbles himself like this child is the greatest in the kingdom of heaven"*. It must have been a small child because Mark tells us He took him up in His arms. (Mark 9:36). Children do not try to be humble, but they are. There is no pride in a small child. They do not threaten. They are teachable at a young age. And they are not good at deceiving (Ask parents!) A child is held up as the ideal for humility and innocence.

It is not in man's nature to play second fiddle. To go for the lowest place by humbling ourselves is one of the most difficult things in the world for both saint or a sinner to do. Humility in our Western culture implies not being boastful about our own accomplishment, not calling attention to what we have achieved. The humility Jesus demands is something else entirely. It first implies bending the knee to God Almighty and acknowledge us as sinners in need of salvation.

True humility is being able to give up everything we want to do in order that God can do what He wants to do. It is to live continually under His authority as His obedient servant. In doing so we are humbling ourselves before Him. We humble ourselves when we obey His commands. We humble ourselves when we bow our hearts before Him in prayer. We humble ourselves when we beg His forgiveness for our sin. And we humble ourselves in our service for others.

> *"The saint that wears heaven's brightest crown,*
> *In deepest adoration bends;*
> *The weight of glory bows him down,*
> *Then most when most his soul ascends.*
> *Nearest the throne itself must be*
> *the footstool of humility".*

James Montgomery (1771-1854)

ASSURANCE

Romans 8:16

"The Spirit himself testifies with our spirit that we are God's children"

Over the years I have met Christians who have doubted their salvation. They have regularly attended church, joined in the worship and have taken part in the Lord's Supper. Yet they still have harboured doubts about their salvation.

How can we be sure we are saved? The answer, *"The Spirit himself testifies with our spirit that we are God's children"*. His Spirit testifies, keeps communicating to our spirit over and over that we belong in God's family. He confirms to us what is true on a deep and personal level. There is peace, a deep sense of His presence that cannot be explained in words.

There is further evidence that assures a person is saved and belongs to God. They desire to live a life that is pleasing to God. They seek a deeper relationship with Him through prayer and meditation in His Word, the Bible. Evidence of really belonging to God is a growing hatred of sin in your life, and a longing to become more Christlike. These holy desires in your heart are evidence that your heart is in tune with the heart of God. And they are the desires that God Himself has sown within the heart of those that belong to Him.

They are not the desires of an unsaved person. *"If anyone does not have the Spirit of Christ, they do not belong to Christ"* (Rom. 8:9,14). The assurance that we are saved is the *"Spirit himself testifies with our spirit that we are God's children"*

> *"Blessed assurance, Jesus is mine!*
> *Oh, what a foretaste of glory divine!*
> *Heir of salvation, purchase of God,*
> *Born of His Spirit, washed in His blood.*
> *This is my story, this is my song,*
> *Praising my Saviour all the day long,*
> *This is my story, this is my song,*
> *Praising my Saviour all the day long"*

Fanny J. Crosby (1820-1915)

THE HUMANITY AND DIVINITY OF CHRIST

John 11:35

'Jesus wept'

In the death and the resurrection of Lazarus we see the humanity and the divinity of Jesus revealed. "Jesus wept". He wept over Jerusalem (Luke 19:41). He wept in the Garden of Gethsemane and again at the tomb of Lazarus. His tears are evidence of His humanity. The fact that Jesus weeps bring context to human pain and suffering. When bad things happen, we often ask, "does God even care?" This simple statement, "Jesus wept", proves that He does.

When Jesus heard Lazarus was sick, He remained where He was a full four days before setting off to the place Lazarus was buried. Perhaps the reason why Jesus waited for four days could be due to a Jewish tradition. *"Grief reaches its height on the third day. For three days the spirit hovered about the tomb and may return to the body. But on the fourth day, when the body begins to decompose, it retires and abandons the body"*. After four days Lazarus was truly dead. No chance of resuscitation after four days.

Jesus had every intention of raising Lazarus from the dead, but it would in His own time. When Jesus said, *"Take away the stone from the entrance of the tomb"*, Martha replied, *"but by this time there is a bad stench, for he has been there four days"*. Jesus said, *"Did I not tell you that if you believed, you would see the glory of God?"* After four days in the tomb there would be no doubt in the minds of the people that Jesus raised a man who was truly dead. When Lazarus did walk away from his tomb many of the visiting Jews believed in Jesus. (John 11:45).

In raising Lazarus, Jesus revealed His Divinity. He was truly human and truly divine. From the very beginning He had the nature of God but laid it aside and took upon Himself the likeness of a man. (Phil. 2:6-8). He became truly human able to sympathise with our weaknesses and temptations (Heb. 4:15).

Jesus sees our tears and is moved by them. He shed them Himself. He knows about our grief in losing a loved one. He knows, He loves, and He cares, and will always be with us in our own loss and grief.

> *"Jesus wept! Those tears are over,*
> *But His heart is still the same;*
> *Kinsman, friend, and elder brother,*
> *Is His everlasting name.*
> *Saviour who can love like Thee,*
> *Gracious One of Bethany?*

Ralph McTell (1944-

MORE OF JESUS LESS OF ME
John 3:30

"He must become greater; I must become less".

More than 500 years had passed between the last prophet, Malachi of the Old Testament, and the appearance of the prophet John the Baptist in the New Testament. This period between the Two Testaments is known as the Silent Years. God was silent. This period is full of historical events in which we can see the preparation for the coming of Jesus Christ into the world.

John was to be the last of the prophets that God used on earth. He was a powerful preacher who attracted large crowds. People came from long distances to listen to and to be baptized by this fiery Jewish prophet. He was bold and courageous in his preaching holding nothing back. He called the Pharisees and Sadducees a *'brood of vipers.* (Matt. 3:7). He was popular with the people and the centre of attention, but this was the last thing John the Baptist wanted.

When Jesus was baptized, the Spirit come down from heaven as a dove and descended upon him. John loudly declared, *"this is the Son of God, the Lamb of God who takes away the sin of the world, whose sandals I am unworthy to untie. He must become greater; I must become less".* (John 11:27-34; 3:36). In doing so John humbled himself before the crowds and before God. He wanted Jesus to take centre stage.

"He must become greater, and I must become less". John the Baptist was the forerunner preparing the way for One far greater than himself. (Is. 40:3). Jesus was the Messiah and His work must continually be exalted. Jesus was the man that the people must follow, not John. Jesus must become greater and John less and less.

We could apply a spiritual lesson to our own lives from these words. *He must become greater; I must become less'*. We *'become less'* when we humbly put ourselves under His authority. We will become less when He is indeed Lord and Master of our lives.

> *"O Jesus Christ, grow Thou in me,*
> *And all things else recede;*
> *My heart be daily nearer Thee,*
> *From sin be daily freed.*
> *Make this poor self-grow less and less,*
> *Be Thou my life and aim,*
> *O make me daily, through Thy grace,*
> *more worthy to bear Thy name"*

Johann C. Lavater (1741-1801)

JESUS IS THE FOUNDATION

Full reading
1 Corinthians 3:10-15

'For no-one can lay any foundation other than the one already laid, which is Jesus Christ"

"*F*or we must all appear before the judgement seat of Christ, that each one may receive what is due to him for the things done while in the body, whether good or bad".(2 Cor.5:10). This is not a judgment of us but an assessment of our work whilst on earth. Evangelists, pastors and teachers will be judged according to the worth of their ministries. James writes that *"we who teach will be judged more strictly"*. (James 3:1). Having to give an account of ourselves will reveal upon what foundation our work was built upon.

Those that proclaim, *"He is the way, the truth and the life, and the only way to God"* are continuing to build their ministry on a solid foundation. The foundation is Jesus Christ, the Founder of our faith. On His account we can hope for pardon and eternal life. He is our foundation that helps us stand firm as we face the storms of life.

There are those who believe they are serving the Lord but doing so in a shameful manner. Some are TV preachers who are building their own kingdoms and profiting from doing so in the name of Jesus. When they stand before the Judgement Seat their works will evaporate like smoke from wood, hay and stubble.

We shall all have to give an account of ourselves before the Judgement Seat of Christ. It is wise for each of us to prepare ourselves for His assessment when we stand before the Supreme Judge of the world.

> *"The Church's one foundation is Jesus Christ her Lord,*
> *She is His new creation, by water and the Word:*
> *From heaven He came and sought her, to be His holy Bride;*
> *With His own blood He bought her, and for her life He died".*
>
> Samuel J. Stone (1839-1900).

BLESSED WITH A BAD MEMORY
Philippians 3:13-14

"Brothers, I do not consider myself yet to have taken hold of it. But one thing I do: Forgetting what is behind and straining towards what is ahead. I press on towards the goal to win the prize for which God has called me heavenwards in Christ Jesus".

The Christian's life is likened to a race. Spiritual giant though he was, Paul confessed that he had not yet reached the perfection he was reaching for in his own race. *'I press onward, so that I can win the prize of being called to heaven'*. (v12). *"I forget what is behind"* that will hinder me reaching my goal. He was determined to toss aside memories of his past that would hinder his progress. And Paul had lots of bad memories to get rid of. He was an accomplice to murder and a fierce persecutor of the Church. (Acts 8:1-3).

Perhaps there are things in our own past that we need to put behind us. Sins confessed should not be allowed to hinder our progress in our own race. Sins confessed are sins forgiven. (1 John 1:9). Some, however, must learn to forgive themselves too.

There is a time to remember and a time to forget. The time to remember is when we first put our faith in Jesus. We were reconciled with God through Christ and found our peace with Him. We received the assurance of our salvation and eternal life. Think upon these things. The time to forget is as we run the present race set before us. Isaiah said, *"Forget the former things; do not dwell on the past"*. (Is 43:18). Don't allow yourself to be shackled down with your past sins, regrets, and failures. Keep your eyes fixed upon Jesus the Author and Finisher of our faith.

> *Looking upward every day,*
> *Sunshine on our faces;*
> *Pressing onward every day,*
> *Toward the heavenly places".*

Mary Butler (1841-1916)

A CALL TO HOLINESS

1 Thessalonians. 5:23-24

"May God himself, the God of peace, sanctify you through and through. May your whole spirit, soul and body be kept blameless at the coming of our Lord Jesus Christ. The one who calls you is faithful, and he will do it".

Sanctification means both being set apart and being made holy in life. God sets us apart when we turn to Christ. He makes our heart His dwelling place. We have been set apart so we can be conformed into the image of Christ by His Spirit. Paul's petition for the Thessalonica Christians is *"May God Himself, the God of peace sanctify you through and through"*. God doesn't just want to sanctify part of us. He desires to have all of us, Spirit, Soul and Body, through and through.

Most people think of the three components of the human being as body, soul and spirit. Paul reverses this order giving highest priority to the spirit and the lowest to the body. God designed the human to live after the order of spirit, soul, and body. Not body, soul and spirit. Man has reversed this order and gives priority to the body and the lowest to the spirit. We do not know what binds spirit to soul or soul to spirit or both to body. That mystery is only known to God.

Paul's petition for "*through and through*" sanctification should not imply that it can be attained in this present life. Neither does it suggest sinless perfection. We are still cursed with sin that on occasions overcomes our endeavours to remain without sin. Its power over us will be weakened as we mature in faith, but it will never be eradicated.

Evidence of being made holy is a longing to become more Christlike. A love for God's word. Deep remorse over sin. A dislike of the world's corrupt system. A heart-felt desire to live a life pleasing to God.

"MAY YOUR WHOLE SPIRIT, SOUL, AND BODY BE KEPT BLAMELESS AT THE COMING OF OUR LORD JESUS CHRIST"

BENEDICTION

"Now unto Him who is able to keep you from falling, and to present you faultless before the presence of His glory with exceeding joy, To the only wise God, our Saviour, Be glory and majesty, dominion and power both now and forever, Amen,

Jude 1:24

WHAT IS YOUR GIFT?
Matthew 25:29

'For everyone who has will be given more, and he will have an abundance. Whoever does not have, even what he has will be taken from him'

A businessman leaves on a journey to a distant land and entrusts his estate to several servants to whom he also gave some talents*. He told them, *"Use this to earn more until I get back"*. He was a hard and unforgiving man hated by his people. Upon his return he called in his servants and asked them how much they had earned with the talents they had been given. The 1st servant did exceptionally well having doubled the five talents he had received. He was praised and given more. The 2nd servant didn't do as well but still did a fairly good job. He too was praised and given more. The 3rd servant comes in and he didn't even do anything with his talent but simple buried it. What he had was taken from him.

This is a parable of the Three Talents that Jesus gave to a large crowd. It's about being held accountable for what they had been entrusted with. There is a spiritual lesson for each of us from this parable. Every Christian has been entrusted with a wonderful gift of the Holy Spirit to be used in the service of others. (1 Peter 4:10-11). This gift has been given for the purpose of being used. Whoever uses their gift for the extension of God's kingdom on earth will receive more or shall be rewarded more. Use it or lose it, and the 3rd servant who did not use it lost it. In doing so he lost his reward.

There are many ways for a Christian to leave the gift they have received dormant and unused. Other interests have taken away their desire to serve Christ they once had for Christ. Like the 3rd servant they have buried their gift instead of putting it to good use. The day is coming when we shall stand before Jesus to give an account of how we used the gift that God gave to us.

> *"Jesus confirm my heart's desire,*
> *to work, and speak, and think for Thee;*
> *Still let me guard the Holy Spirit,*
> *and still stir up the gift in me"*
>
> Charles Wesley (1707-1788)

* A talent was worth several hundred pounds

FAITH – HOPE – LOVE

1 Corinthians 13:13

"But the greatest of these is love"

It appears love was lacking in the Corinthian Church. There seems to have been a division within its membership over the importance of some spiritual gifts over others. As found in some present-day churches too much emphasis was given to one or two gifts over the exclusion of others.

Paul seeks to address the problem. The Corinthians were particularly attracted to the gift of tongues. But tongues are meaningless without love. If I have faith that could move mountains, even that amount of faith, yet do not have love it is nothing. If I give away all my goods to feed the poor but have not love, it has no profit. And if I give my body to be burned as a martyr it is of no value without love.

In using such terminology Paul is telling us that love overrides all other credible things we can do in our Christian living. Without love they profit us nothing. Doing these things is not the measure of our true spiritual credentials. Love is the only measure. There is no substitute that can replace love in the Christian life.

"Faith, hope, love but the greatest is love". Paul defines love. 'Love is patient, kind and gracious. It is never jealous neither anxious to impress. It is not conceited. Never rude. Nor selfish. Not self-seeking. It bears no malice. Is never glad when others go wrong. Love delights in the truth. Is always hopeful, ever patient and endues to the end.' (1 Cor. 13:4-8).

Love is the greatest because it is an attribute of God. (1 John 4:8). When we are in heaven, we will no longer need faith nor hope. They will already have fulfilled their purpose. Love will reign supreme throughout the wide expanse of heaven.

> *"Love can always conquer,*
> *whatever discord brings;*
> *and love can also cover,*
> *a multitude of things.*
>
> *Don't you underestimate,*
> *what love can ever do;*
> *for love is God eternal,*
> *and His love renew".*

St. Titus Brandsma (1881-1942)

Titus Brandsma was a Dutch Carmelite friar, a Catholic priest who vehemently opposed Nazi ideology before the Second World War. He was imprisoned at the Dachau concentration camp where he was murdered. He was canonized as a saint on 15 May 2022 by Pope Francis.

"I CONSIDER THEM RUBBISH"

Philippians 3:8

"I consider everything a loss compared to the surpassing greatness of knowing Christ Jesus my Lord. I consider them rubbish, that I may gain Christ ...

Saul of Tarsus had much to boast about. He was an Israelite, born of the tribe of Benjamin, a true Hebrew who was circumcised when eight days old according to Jewish Law. As a Pharisee, he strictly obeyed the Law's standards of righteousness. No fault could be found in him. He was blameless. (Phil. 3:5). After his encounter with the risen Christ on the Damascus Road a radical change occurred in his life that completely changed his beliefs and his priorities.

Now, as Paul looked back over his life, he thought of what he once valued and considered it *'rubbish'*. He came to realise that the righteousness he had attained by the Law's standard was nothing more than his own self-righteous moralism. He saw that true righteousness acceptable by God came only through faith in Jesus Christ.

"I consider everything a loss compared to the surpassing greatness of knowing Christ Jesus my Lord. I consider them rubbish, that I may gain Christ". Paul was already an acknowledged leader in Judaism and the loss of leadership would include losing honour and respect. This loss, he writes

about, would also refer to financial loss. Paul sums it up by writing all my achievements are rubbish compared to knowing Jesus and the power of the resurrection.

If you were to ask people what the most important thing is, they possess in life you would get various replies. 'My home, my reputation, my career, my bank balance etc. Few would be willing to sacrifice it all for knowing Christ and the power of His resurrection. Yet there are those who are willing to do so. And like Paul they have gained far more than what they have lost. Like the Apostle they consider that what they once valued is 'rubbish' compared with enjoying a closer relationship with Christ. Nothing we have or can ever accomplish can be compared with knowing Jesus Christ.

> *"I'd rather have Jesus than silver or gold;*
> *I'd rather be His than have riches untold;*
> *I'd rather have Jesus than houses or lands;*
> *I'd rather be led by His nail-pierced hand".*
>
> Oscar C. A. Bernadotte (1859-1953)

THE SEARCH FOR SATISFACTION
Ecclesiastes 1:8

'All things are wearisome; more than one can say. The eyes never have enough of seeing, or the ear its fill of hearing'

Humankind has a greedy nature that craves more than this world has to offer. It is insatiable in its endless pursuit to find satisfaction in life. Life is meaningless and empty to most people in the world.

'The eyes never have enough of seeing'. They see much, but wish to see more, something new to gaze upon. There are those that spend hours before their television and can never see enough. They want to see more. They are never satisfied. *'The ear cannot hear enough'*. Even with music constantly blaring into it via an earphone, it wants to hear more. It is never satisfied.

In their search to find satisfaction in life people accumulate wealth and possessions only to find they still yearn for more of the same. What they have is never enough. They want more. The millionaires in this world are never satisfied. They want more. Possessing millions, they still have an emptiness in their lives that wealth can never satisfy. You can own the fastest car, the most beautiful home and have a heathy back balance and yet be one of the most miserable and unsatisfied people living on earth. Human desire is never satisfied. It is the consequence of our restless nature. Looking to material things to bring satisfaction in life is like chasing the wind.

You can never find true satisfaction in this world. You are a spiritual being created by God to live and find your fulfilment in Him. Only Jesus Christ can satisfy the deepest yearnings of your soul.

> "I'm satisfied with Jesus, whatever He may do,
> And this same satisfaction is waiting now for you;
> I'm satisfied with Jesus, we're ever I may be,
> And, while I now obey Him, He's satisfied with me"
>
> E. G. Masters (Published 1897)

WHERE IS YOUR TREASURE?
Luke 12:34

'For where your treasure is, there your heart will be also'

'If you want to know where your heart is, look where you're spending your money'. We live in a materialist culture in which most people place their value on material possessions, and the more they have the more they want. Their focus is upon accumulating wealth so they can purchase the things in life they think will make life more enjoyable.

In the 'Parable of the Rich Fool', Jesus said *'a man's life does not consist in the abundance of his possessions'*. The rich man had so much wealth he decided to retire and take life easy, *'eating, drinking and being merry'*. Jesus called him a fool. *'This very night your life will be demanded of you. Then who will get what you have prepared for yourself?* (Luke 12:13-21). The rich man had material wealth but in God's eyes he was a spiritual pauper.

Jesus refers to the deceitfulness of riches (Mark 4:19). It deceives people into believing that riches will bring them happiness. It deceives by blinding them to their own spiritual poverty. It deceives by giving a false security. It deceives as it takes control over one's life and makes them its slave. Riches often create selfishness. The rich fool who lived for himself said, 'my land', 'my barns', 'my grain', 'my goods' all belong to me. He thought only of himself.

There is nothing sinful in the pursuit of wealth. But when it becomes the love of your life it becomes your treasure. Where your treasure is, there your heart is also. Jesus said, *'Do not store up for yourselves treasures on earth where moth and rust will destroy them. But store up for yourselves treasures in heaven where neither the moth nor rust cannot destroy them'* (Matt. 6:19-20).

> *No eye has seen no ear has heard,*
> *Whatever the treasure be;*
> *To dwell in Your eternal presence,*
> *Will be enough for me.*

(Peter C. Horrell (1936-

THE LAMB OF GOD

John 1:29

"Look, the Lamb of God, who takes away the sin of the world"

The Dragon, the Eagle, the Tiger, the Bear and the Lion are symbols of the most powerful nations on earth. These wild creatures have one thing in common. They devour their victims. Their symbols depict strength and potency acting as a warning to other nations not to threaten them in war. They describe their enormous power over the world. In the sporting world teams have adopted names such as the Bulldogs, Panthers, Hawks, Eagles, Dragons, Lions and Wolves as their symbols depicting their strength and aggressiveness to the sporting world.

In stark contrast to these symbols on earth, Heaven's symbol is a Lamb, an emblem of meekness. John the Baptist was the last and greatest of God's prophets to Israel. He was chosen to announce the coming of the promised Messiah (Isaiah 53:1-12). He describes his vision of the Holy Spirit in the form of a dove descending on Jesus at His baptism. In one of his most powerful statements John announced, *'Look, the Lamb of God who takes away the sin of the world'*.

The Jewish celebration of the Passover looks back to the days when Moses saved God's people from their slavery in Egypt (Exodus 7-12). A lamb without blemish was required as a yearly sacrifice to God at the

Passover Feast. The slain lamb was chosen as a sacrifice predicting Jesus, the *'Lamb of God' who takes away the sin of the world'*. Jesus was sent into the world to save the world. He died as a sacrificial Lamb upon a cross.

> *'For God so loved the world that he gave his one*
> *and only Son, that whoever believes in him shall*
> *not perish but have eternal life'* (John 3:16).

> *To go beyond the furthest star,*
> *far past all worlds above;*
> *Though lost within the depths of*
> *space, I'm still within God's love.*
> *His love revealed on Calvary's Cross,*
> *I cannot comprehend;*
> *When Jesus died to save my soul,*
> *T' was love that knows no end.*

Peter C. Horrell (1936-)

HEAD KNOWLEDGE OR HEART KNOWLEDGE?

John 5:39-40

'You diligently study the Scriptures because you think that by them you have eternal life. These are the Scriptures that testify about me, yet you refuse to come to me to have life'

The Priests, the Pharisees and the Sadducees, were diligent in their study of the Scriptures, i.e., Bible, particularly the Law and the Prophets. They believed that possessing the written Scriptures they also had possessed eternal life. Rabbi Hille (110 BCE-10 CE), the renowned rabbi taught that by studying Jewish law they would gain for themselves eternal life in the world to come. Therefore, they memorized large portions from the Law and from the Prophets.

When King Herod called them together, he asked them where the Christ was to be born. Knowing the Scriptures they immediately replied in Bethlehem of Judea. The prophet has written: *"But you, Bethlehem, in the land of Judea, are by no means least among the rulers of Judea; for out of you will come a ruler who will be a shepherd of my people Israel"* (Micah 5:2; Matt. 2:3-6). These priests could quote from memory any of their prophets.

For centuries the Jews had waited for the coming of their Messiah. The Scriptures testified of His coming, but they missed the point of why he was coming. A little more reading from Isaiah 53 would have shown them the reason why. They relied upon their possession of the Scriptures for eternal life. They ignored the One who was to come and give them eternal life. The purpose of the Scriptures was not to give them eternal life but to point them to their Messiah who came to give eternal life. The religious leaders had a head knowledge about the Scriptures but missed its real message.

There are many homes that have an unread Bible tucked away somewhere in a drawer or cupboard. Search it out and read it with an open heart and mind. From its beginning to it end you will discover that its central message is about Jesus Christ.

"FOR GOD SO LOVED THE WORLD THAT HE GAVE HIS ONE AND ONLY SON, JESUS CHRIST, THAT WHOSOEVER BELIEVES IN HIM SHALL NOT PERISH BUT HAVE ETERNAL LIFE IN HIM"

> "His glory gilds the sacred page,
> Majestic like the sun:
> It gives a light to every age,
> It gives, but borrows none"
>
> Willian Cowper (1731-1800)

THE LORD'S PRAYER
Matthew 6:9-13

"Lord, teach us to pray ... Our Father ..."

Father. This request came from his disciples as they watched and heard Jesus praying with such passion to his Father that it moved them to ask, *'Lord, teach us pray as John taught his disciples to pray'*. (Luke 11:1). The Prayers of John's disciples were like those of the Pharisees who prayed three times a day, at the third, the sixth and ninth hour.

Jesus said, when you pray, say **'Our Father in Heaven'**. He points us to the One to whom all our requests should be made. He is the Father of humanity because he created the world and, in that sense, fathered the world. (Mal.2:10; Acts 17:28). In the early 1900s liberal European theologians began using used the term, "The Fatherhood of God and the Brotherhood of Man". They believed God is the universal Father who dwells in every human being on earth, including those who have rejected Jesus Christ and His gospel. This contradicts the teachings of Jesus and the Apostles. God is not everyone's Father, but He is everyone's God. Only a relationship with Jesus is what allows someone to call God their Father. This demonstrates a privileged relationship with Him.

The disciples of Jesus did not ask Him *how to* pray but *to pray*. No one can teach us *how to pray*. It is the Spirit of God that *prompts* us *to* pray and gives the confidence of calling God our Father. He becomes our Father when we accept His own Son as our Saviour and in doing so, we are adopted into God's family. (Gal. 4:5-7). There are many that have been denied an earthly father's love. But they can know their heavenly Fathers love by accepting His Son Jesus as their Saviour thus finding peace and reconciliation with their God and Father.

> *"Abba Father, let me be,*
> *Yours and Yours alone,*
> *may my will forever be,*
> *ever more Your own"*

Dave Bilbrough (1955-

THE LORD'S PRAYER
Matthew 6:9-13

"Lord, teach us to pray ... in Heaven"

Heaven. A short time before His death, Jesus said to His disciples, *'I go and prepare a place for you'* (John 14:2-3). Where that place is we do not know but we can be sure it is a place without borders. It will take all of eternity to discover heaven's vastness and its beauty of what Christ has prepared for His followers.

It would be a mistake to limit heaven to a geographical location somewhere in the Universe. Heaven could embrace the ever expanding and never-ending Universe. After the destruction of this world Universe will be re-formed and adapted to be the permanent residence of Christ and His people. (2 Peter 3:13; Rev 21:1).

Heaven is a place of activity. Its central object is a Throne from which commands are issued and authority exercised (Rev 4:1-11). Angels and archangels, seraphim and cherubim are in attendance in carrying out the commands of the One seated upon its central Throne. We know very little about heaven except it is a place where service is rendered by angelic beings. Those who are with Christ in heaven will also exercise their capabilities and powers of service to God. What that service involves is impossible to say, but one can be certain, there will be no idle saints in heaven!

We won't be changed into angels in heaven as some believe, but we shall be with the multitudes of angels who are in heaven. In heaven we shall talk and laugh when we meet and recognize family and friends once again. This will make Heaven even more enjoyable. But above all we shall see Jesus who made it possible for us to be with Him in the first place.

Referring to the resurrected body that we shall have in heaven, they seem to differ from one another in their gloried state. Paul wrote, *"There is one glory of the sun, and another glory of the moon, and another glory of the stars; for one star is different from another star in glory"*. (1 Cor. 15:41-44). This seems to indicate that, although all Christians will be raised with spiritual bodies there will be varying degrees of glory in our resurrected bodies, quite possibly in proportion to the measure of the godliness attained, or of service rendered when on earth.

> *"My knowledge of that life is small,*
> *the eye of faith is dim,*
> *but 'tis enough that Christ knows all,*
> *And I shall be with Him"*

Richard Baxter (1615-1691)

THE LORD'S PRAYER
Matthew 6:9-13

"Teach us to pray ... Your kingdom come ..."

Kingdom. God's kingdom is both in the present and the future. It already exists on earth and will continue to do so well into the future. The kingdoms on earth consist of certain territories or some area of land. But God's kingdom is not territorial. It is where He reigns in the hearts of His people. The Pharisees asked Jesus when the kingdom of God would come, He replied, *"The kingdom of God does not come visibly, nor will people say, 'Here it is,' or 'There it is,' because the kingdom of God is within you."* (Luke 17:20-21). The kingdom of God was among them, but the Pharisees did not realize it.

The petition *'Your kingdom come'* is asking that God's spiritual reign will extend over the whole earth. His will is that all peoples from every tribe and nation will become part of His kingdom with Jesus as their Lord and King. Prior to His ascension back to heaven, Jesus gave His disciple a mission. *"All authority in heaven and on earth has been given to me. Go, therefore, and make disciples of all nations, baptising them in the name of the Father and of the Son and of the Holy Spirit"* (Matt. 28:18-20).

The Great Commission of Jesus is still going on. As members of His kingdom, we all have a part to play in seeking to hasten Christ's return by taking the gospel to the furthermost parts of the earth. When it has reached all nations, *'then the end will come'*. (Matt. 24:14).

> *"Seek the coming of the Kingdom;*
> *Seek the souls around to win them,*
> *Seek to Jesus Christ to bring them;*
> *Seek this first, seek this first".*
>
> Georgiana M. Taylor (1848-1915)

THE LORD'S PRAYER
Matthew 6:9-13

"Teach us to pray ... Your will be done on earth as it is in heaven"

Your will. This was the ruling principle in the life of Jesus. He came into the world to do the will of God. 'If God's will is-to-be done on earth, it will be through God's people'. When we pray God's '*will be done on earth as it is in heaven*' we are asking that something will happen that has not yet happened on earth. The world is in chaos and there is a lot to be done on earth to make it equal to what is in heaven.

Yet God's will on earth is already in progress. It all began with the coming of Jesus Christ and will be consummated at His Second Coming. Prior to His arrest Jesus went to the Garden of Gethsemane to pray. Three times he asked, '*My Father, if it is possible, may this cup be taken from me*' referring to His coming suffering on a cross. Then He added, '*If it is not possible for this cup to be taken away unless I drink it, may Your will be done*' (Matt. 26:36-46). It was an act of selfless surrender to the will of God.

We all have our part to play in advancing His will on earth. We must surrender our own will so as God can bond us to His will. Jesus carried His cross to fulfill His Father's will. He asks us to take up ours. This implies putting aside our own ambitions by making God's will top priority in our lives. (Matt 7:21; Luke 9:23). What is done in heaven God wants to see done on earth. That is God's will and our prayer.

> *"When in the wonderous realms above,*
> *Our Saviour had been called upon,*
> *to save our world of sin by love, He said,*
> *"Thy will, O Lord, be done"*

Frank I. Kooyman (1880-1963)

THE LORD'S PRAYER
Matthew 6:9-13

"Teach us to pray ... Give us today our daily bread"

Daily Bread. We were not created to live independently from God. This petition, *'Give us today our daily bread'* shows how dependent we are on Him to give us our daily needs. It shows us how much we depend upon Him. Most of us in Western countries would never have to make this request for our daily bread. Strolling through a supermarket with its shelves leaden with varieties of bread, we have a choice of what variety to choose.

There are millions of people in the world who would literally need this petition for bread to be answered for themselves and for their children. It is not what bread they will have but whether they will even have bread at all. This petition should not be a selfish request. We need compassion and remember their need as we say the Lord's Prayer. Give 'us' our daily bread means thinking of others besides ourselves.

This phrase: *'our daily bread'* can refer to more than physical food. Jesus said, *"I am the bread of life, he that comes to me will never go hungry, and he who believes in me will never be thirsty"*. (John 6:35). Jesus is saying that He can satisfy the deepest need and yearnings of your soul.

Guide me, O Thou great Jehovah,
Pilgrim through this barren land;
I am weak, but Thou art mighty;
Hold me with Thy powerful hand;
Bread of heaven, Bread of heaven,
Feed me till I want no more,
Feed me till I want no more".

William Williams (1717-1791).

THE LORD'S PRAYER
Matthew 6:9-13

"Teach us to pray ... Forgive us our debts, as we have forgiven our debtors"

Our debts. There are three different versions concerning this fourth petition in the Lord's Prayer: 1. "Forgive us our debts," 2. "Forgive us our trespasses," 3. "Forgive us our sins." Most English versions have translated the Greek words to 'forgive our debts' which also means our sins. When we ask God to forgive our sins, we are asking Him to show us the same mercy we have shown in forgiving others who have offended us.

Peter asked, *"Lord, how often shall my brother offend against me, and I forgive him? till seven times?* Jesus replied, *"not seven times, but seventy times seven times.* Peter believed his seven-time standard of forgiving was sufficient. But the answer Jesus gave suggests there is no limit on forgiveness (Matt. 18:21-22). Forgiven people must continue to forgive. Don't keep count.

There is a vital link between the way we treat other people and the way God is going to treat us. Jesus said, *'Do not judge, and you will not be judged. Do not condemn, and you will not be condemned. Forgive, and you will be forgiven'* (Luke 6:37). Unforgiving people can never find forgiveness from a forgiving God.

Our forgiveness to those who have offended us must be sincere. Some find this difficult to do. *"If only you knew how much I was offended."* That may be true, but we must remember that all of us have *offended* God. When asking Him to forgive us in the same manner we have forgiven others we can be certain that God will show His mercy towards us by forgiving us.

> *"Forgive our sins as we forgive.*
> *you taught us, Lord, to pray,*
> *but you alone can grant us grace*
> *to live the words we say.*
> *How can your pardon reach and bless*
> *the unforgiving heart;*
> *That broods on wrongs and will not let*
> *old bitterness depart?*
>
> Rosamond E. Herklots (1905-1987)

THE LORD'S PRAYER
Matthew 6:9-13

"Teach us to pray ... And lead us not into temptation, but deliver us from the evil one."

Tempt**ation.** The interpretation of this controversial petition of the Lord's Prayer has been debated for centuries. God will never tempt us. It is not in His Holy nature. (James 1:13). So, if God does not tempt, why did Jesus instruct us to pray 'lead us not into temptation? Pope Francis called for a new version of the Lord's Prayer that doesn't imply that God leads us into temptation. That, he says, *"is the Devil's job"*. It should read, *"do not let us fall into temptation."*

The Lord knows the future events that can affect our lives. Our plea, *"lead us not into temptation"* is asking for His protection by leading us away from future temptations that could cause us to fall. It is a plea to our Father to _lead us away_ from such circumstances where temptation is so acute that we could not overcome it.

God does allow us to be tempted but only up to a certain point. *"God is faithful and will not allow you to suffer any temptation beyond your powers of endurance."* (1 Cor. 10:13). God uses our temptations to test us and see whether our faith is genuine and true. Facing these tests and overcoming them builds and strengthens Christian character. *"Count it *all joy when you face manifold temptations knowing that the proving of your faith produces steadfastness."* (James 1:2-4).

Whilst we live in this world, we shall be confronted with temptations. For this reason, Jesus said to His disciples, *"Keep watching and praying so that you do not fall into temptation. The spirit is willing but human nature is weak"* (Matt. 26:41).

> *"From dark temptation's power,*
> *From Satan's guiles defend,*
> *Deliver in the evil hour,*
> *And guide me to the end."*
>
> James Montgomery (1771-1854)

NEVER LOOK BACK
Luke 9:62

"No-one who puts his hand to the plough and looks back is fit for service in the kingdom of God"

As Jesus and His disciples were walking going along the road, someone said to Him, *"I will follow you wherever You go."* Jesus said to him, *"The foxes have holes, and the birds of the air have nests, but the Son of Man has nowhere to lay His head."* Jesus said to another man, *"Follow Me."* But he said, *"Permit me first to go and bury my father."* Jesus said to him, *"Allow the dead to bury their own dead, but as for you, go and proclaim everywhere the kingdom of God."* And another also said, *"I will follow you Lord, Lord; but first permit me to say good-bye tom those at home."* But Jesus said to him, *"No one, after putting his hand to the plough and looking back, is fit for the kingdom of God."* (Luke 9:57-62. NASB).

Jesus discerned these excuses as a half-hearted attempt to follow Him. They were unwilling to give a full commitment of themselves to Him. The message of Jesus to each of us is, "Follow Me". No excuses. When we put our hand to the plough it implies a lifetime of service with Him to the very end.

A man never looks back as he ploughs the field. He keeps looking ahead. There can be no distractions otherwise his furrows are not as straight as an arrow. Our eyes must be fixed ahead on Jesus. No looking back with regrets otherwise we render ourselves unfit *"for service in the kingdom of God"*.

> *"My cross I'll carry till I see Jesus,*
> *My cross I'll carry till I see Jesus,*
> *My cross I'll carry till I see Jesus,*
> *No looking back, No looking back"*

Folk Song from India.

THE POINT OF NO RETURN
Matthews 16:24

Jesus said, "If anyone would come after me, he must deny himself and take up his cross and follow me"

The first known use of the "Point of no Return" was in 1941. It was used by pilots during the Second World War when their remaining fuel over Nazi Germany would be insufficient for their return to their home base. Turning back was not an option. They had reached the point of no return. They had to keep going. Jesus said, *"If anyone would come after me, he must deny himself and take up his cross and follow me."*

Nobody who follows Jesus can hold on to even the smallest of their own agenda, their own dreams, their own way of living in the world. They must sacrifice every ounce of self if they would choose to walk after Him. To deny ourselves is not just giving up *things* but the giving up of *ourselves unreservedly* to Jesus Christ. It is to fully identify with Him in His rejection, suffering and death and ready to lay down our own lives for Him.

"Foxes Book of Martyrs" is an account of the sufferings of protestants during the reign of Queen Mary, known in history as Bloody Mary. (1553-1558). The Martyrs Cross in London marks the place where three Protestant bishops, Nicholas Ridley, Hugh Latimer, and Thomas

Cranmer, were burned at the stake for refusing to renounce their protestant faith. As they stood back-to-back tied at the stake the last words uttered by Bishop Latimer have been recorded: *'Be of good comfort, Master Ridley, and play the man, we shall this day light such a candle, by God's grace, in England, as I trust shall never be put out.'*

Such was the love and devotion in following Christ that these three Bishops, along with countless other martyrs, faced death rather than deny Him. They had passed the point of no return in their devotion and commitment to Jesus. They were prepared to die rather than deny their Saviour. The point of no return is when our love for Christ is so great that we can never turn away from following Him regardless of personal cost.

> *"Take up the cross", the Saviour said,*
> *"if you would my disciple be;*
> *Take up the cross, with willing heart,*
> *and humbly follow after me"*
>
> Charles W. Everest (1814-1877)

"NEVER TAKE REVENGE"

Romans 12:19

"Do not take revenge, my friends, but leave room for God's wrath, for it is written: "it is mine to avenge; I will repay," says the Lord".

Each of us have been wronged in some way or another. We may have been criticised, humiliated, insulted, abused, or some other incident that unleashed within us anger, bitterness and resentment. According to the world the way we should react is to strike back. We should hurt them as they have hurt us. An eye for an eye, a tooth for a tooth" (Ex. 21:23-25; Lev. 24:17; Deut. 19: 21).

God has always declared He alone will punish those that harm us. From the very beginning it was His prerogative to take revenge on those who wronged others (Duet 32:35). Paul quotes this verse to remind his readers to leave it to God to handle justice for those who have harmed them. David could have taken revenge against Saul who tried to kill him, but David let Saul live. He left the revenge to God (1 Sam. 24). Don't seek revenge yourself.

We need to keep an eternal perspective by remembering that on Judgment Day it will be God who will vindicate every wrong committed against us. We may think that if someone gets away with a crime on earth, they get away with it forever. They do not. No one will escape the justice of the Lord. On Judgment Day they will face His anger. *"Vengeance is mine, I will repay"*, said the Lord.

Revenge doesn't give us peace. We find peace by refusing to strike back. It is God's prerogative alone to punish the evil doers. Leave it to Him. "Do not take revenge, my friends, but leave room for God's wrath, for it is written: *"It is mine to avenge; I will repay,"* says the Lord".

> *"Have faith in God, my heart,*
> *Trust and be unafraid;*
> *God will fulfil in every part,*
> *each promise He has made"*

Bryn Austin Rees (1911-1983)

DEAD TO SIN BUT ALIVE IN CHRIST

Romans 6:2

"We who died to sin; how can we live in it any longer?

For years I struggled with the words, *"We died to sin.* I did not feel dead to sin. On the contrary as a young Christian, I was very much alive to sin! If I had *"died to sin" then* why did I still sin? Sin was still very much alive in my members. As I grew in spiritual maturity, I slowly came to understand that my sinful nature was still very much alive within me. It was far from dead.

So, what does it mean that we died to sin? I learned that to die to sin was not to be dead to my sin nature but dead to its corrupting power over my life. I began to understand there were powers working within me that came from both my sinful nature and from my new nature in Christ. The greater of these powers was the power of the indwelling Christ. It was Christ's power that enables me to have the victory over the power of my sinful nature. Jesus had freed me not just from sins penalty, which is death, but also from sin's power that gives me victory in life. In that sense I am dead to sin's power over me.

This is not sinless perfection. We do fall into sin, but we do not live in sin. There is a difference. Sin is no longer habitual in our lives. If we do fall into sin, God has made provision for us. If we confess our sin, He will forgive us our sin. (1 John 1:9). Our victory over sin is through maintaining our union with Christ (John 15:9). Through the power of His resurrected life, we can have victory over sin's corrupting power.

Paul wrote, *"How can we who died to sin live in it any longer?"* He is writing to believers who have new life in Christ. Jesus has broken its power over us. We are dead to it.

> *"But thanks to God. He gives us victory through our Lord Jesus Christ".* (1 Cor. 15:57)

> *"Dead unto sin through Him who died,*
> *who rose and has gone up on high,*
> *Through Him I live to righteousness,*
> *Through Him to God I am brought nigh."*

Horatius Boner (1808-1889)

WHAT ARE WE LIVING FOR?
Philippians 1:21

"For to me, to live is Christ, and to die is gain."

Can we honestly say, "For me, to live is Christ?" It is a soul-searching question that should get a positive response from every professing Christian. If a Christian does not live their life for Christ, then their reward at the end will be less than what God had intended it to be.

Paul was torn between two desires. What should he choose? I'm torn between the two: *"For me to live is Christ, and to die is gain"*. His heartfelt desire was to depart and to be with Christ. He was getting old. For years he had travelled to different parts of Asia preaching the gospel of Christ to the Gentiles. He was tired and wanting to depart from life to be with Christ. However, he wrote to the Philippian Christians, that to go on living; is beneficial to you. Paul's reason for wanting to stay was to serve them.

"For me, to live is Christ" We either are living for Him or living for ourselves. There is only one throne in the heart of every believer and Jesus demands the right to rule from that throne. He will abide no rivals. He reigns as Lord and King in our lives, or He does not reign at all.

And to die? Well, to die is gain. No Christian should ever fear death. To die in the Lord is not just better, but very much better than life. (John.11:25-26; Rom.14:8; 1 Cor.15:49,55-57; Rev.14:13.). Some early Christians used to refer to death as "Brother Death" because death released them from all earthly sorrows and ushered them into all the blessings of heaven.

> *"Living for Jesus, a life that is true,*
> *striving to please Him in all that I do;*
> *Yielding allegiance, glad-hearted and free,*
> *this is the pathway of blessing for me."*
>
> Thomas O. Chisholm (1866-1960)

A GREAT CLOUD OF WITNESSES

Hebrews 12:1

"Therefore, since we are surrounded by such a great cloud of witnesses, let us throw off everything that hinders and the sin that so easily entangles, and let us run with perseverance the race marked out for us"

Everyone in this great cloud of witnesses has finished their race. Abel, Enoch, Noah, Abraham, Isaac, Jacob, Joseph, Moses and myriads of others have crossed the finishing line. (Hebrews: Chap.11). Is this cloud of witnesses looking down and cheering us on like they do at a football match? I don't think so. I think they are giving us an example to emulate them. They stand out as testimonies to the faithfulness of God in how He supported and encouraged them in their own race.

Despite their trials and tribulations, these witnesses obtained a good testimony through their faith in God. They have crossed the finishing line despite the many difficulties they had to endure. This vast cloud of witnesses is growing in numbers and when we cross the finishing line, we shall take our place among them.

"Let us throw off everything that hinders and the sin that so easily entangles and let us run with perseverance the race marked out for us" These sins act as obstacles that will hinder our progress as we go forward in

the race set before us. The testimonies of these witnesses are meant to encourage us to persevere to the very end. When we finally cross the finishing line and hear the words of Jesus say, '*Well done good and faithful servant, enter into the joy of your Lord*'. that will be reward enough for us.

Don't look back to the things behind,
keep your eyes on Christ till you pass the line.
Never slow down keep strong your pace,
your reward will come when you finish your race.

Peter C. Horrell (1936-

RETURN THE QUESTION
Luke 18:41

"What do you want me to do for you?"

Mark identifies the blind man as Bartimaeus. (Mark 10:41). Calling out he cried, *"Jesus, Son of David, have mercy upon me."* Jesus asked him, *"What do you want me to do for you?* Jesus asked a similar question to two other blind men who pleaded with Him to have mercy on them. *"Do you believe I am able to do this?* (Matt. 9:28). To the crippled man lying by the pool Bethesda, He asked. *"Do you want to be healed?* (John 5:6). It was obvious what he needed, so why did Jesus ask the questions in the first place?

He wanted to test Bartimaeus' faith to see if he really believed Jesus could restore his sight. He encouraged Bartimaeus to vocalize his faith. Jesus never healed anyone until they specifically asked for it. He never coerced anyone to come to Him for healing. When anyone did seek Him out to be healed, they were healed.

"What do you want me to do for you?" Jesus is still asking us that same question today. Do you need forgiveness? If you say, I do, He will say, *'Your sins are forgiven'*. (Matt.9:2). Do you need peace? He will say, *'My peace I give to you'*. (John.14:27). Do you need wisdom? *'Ask and you shall receive'*. (James 1:5). Do you need comfort? *'I will never leave you*

nor forsake you'. (Heb. 1:3-5). Do you need assurance? *'No one can snatch you out of my Father's hand'* (John 10:28).

We can never repay the debt we owe Christ. He still asks us today, "*What do you want me to do for you?*" But let us now return the question to Jesus:

LORD, WHAT DO YOU WANT *ME* TO DO FOR YOU?

PRAYER

> *"Take my life and let it be*
> *consecrated, Lord to Thee.*
> *Take my heart; it is Your own,*
> *it shall be Your royal throne.*
> *Take myself, and I will be*
> *ever, only, all for Thee".*

Frances Ridley Havergal (1836-1879)

SCORCHED BUT ESCAPING THE FLAMES

1 Corinthians 3:15

"If it is burned up, he will suffer loss; he himself will be saved, but only as one escaping through the flames"

This verse can only be understood in its context. The key verse is 13. *"His work will be for what it is, because the Day will bring it to light. It will be revealed with fire, and the fire will test the quality of each man's work"*. This judgment refers to what is known as the "Bema Seat Judgment" reserved only for believers.

The "Bema Seat Judgment" has to do with the assessment of our life when on earth. How we lived our lives on earth. The use of our gifts. What did we achieve for Christ. Did I make a difference. We were all assigned a task *"For we are God's handiwork, created in Christ Jesus to do good works, which God prepared in advance for us to do"*. (Eph. 2:10). The question will be, what good works did I do?

Christian teachers will be judged more strictly according to whether their teaching was based on the foundation of Christ. (James 3:1). Their work will be scrutinized by Christ as worthwhile of worthless. Each of us will be assessed by Christ. If our work was worthwhile there will be rewards. If our work was worthless, we shall suffer loss. Let us avoid being one who suffers loss of reward and yet still saved but only *"as one escaping through the flames."*

> *"A charge to keep I have ...*
> *As in Your sight to live;*
> *And O Your servant, Lord prepare,*
> *a strict account to give".*

Charles Wesley (1707-1788)

"CHRIST IS ALL I NEED"

1 Corinthians 1:30

"It is because of Him that you are in Christ Jesus, who has become for us wisdom from God----that is, our righteousness, Holiness and redemption"

Wisdom, righteousness, holiness and redemption are ours in Christ Jesus. We did not earn these and neither did we deserve them. They were imparted to us as a gift from God through our faith in His Son Jesus Christ.

Jesus is our *wisdom*. Wisdom is to discern truth from error and thus enable us to make correct decisions and offer wise counselling to others. It is having discernment in evaluating the needs of those seeking help. God's wisdom is available to every believer. (James 1:5; 3:14-18). It is different from knowledge. You can have knowledge without wisdom; however, both should be eagerly desired by believers.

Jesus is our *righteousness*. Our fallen sin nature has no righteousness of its own. It is completely unacceptable in God's sight (Isaiah 64:6). Paul learned this lesson (Phil. 3:9). The only righteousness acceptable to God is the righteousness imputed to us through our faith in Christ. There is no other way we can be saved but through Him. It is by His righteousness alone in us that makes us acceptable to God.

Jesus is our **holiness**. Christians have their part to play in making this a reality in their lives. We have been set apart by God to be sanctified, made holy, by the indwelling power of the Holy Spirit. God's plan and purpose for our lives is to transform us into the likeness of Jesus. This involves allowing the Holy Spirit to do His transforming good work in us that brings about God's purpose for us.

Jesus is our **redemption**. He is our Redeemer who provided salvation from the penalty of sin. Jesus paid the price for our sin. In Jesus we have received everything we shall ever need. We are complete in Him (Col. 2:10). He is our wisdom, our righteousness, our holiness and our redemption.

> *"Jesus Christ is made to me,*
> *all I need, all I need. He is all I need ...*
> *wisdom, Righteousness, and Power,*
> *Holiness forevermore,*
> *My Redemption full and sure,*
> *He is all I need"*

Charles Price Jones (1865-1949)

"ABIDE IN CHRIST"

John 15:7

"If you remain in me and my words remain in you, ask whatever you wish, and it will be given you".

How should we interpret this verse? One commentor asks, 'Is it a promise only for super-saints or is it not meant to be taken literally?" Neither is true. This promise is for every believer who has put their faith in Jesus Christ. The promise, *"whatever you wish, it will be given you"*, depends upon fulfilling the condition, *"if you remain in me and my words remain in you."*

To remain In Christ is like a branch that remains connected to a vine. As the branch depends upon the vine to produce its fruit so the believer who remains connected or in union with Christ produces the fruit of the Spirit. This is evidence that we are abiding in Him. *"By their fruit you shall know them"*. (Matt.7:16-20).

"Ask whatever you wish, and it will be given you". Has Jesus given us a blank cheque? Can we ask for whatever we want? For example, a new car? a bigger home? money? etc. No, Jesus has not given us a blank cheque. Proof of our abiding in Christ is asking in accordance with the will of God. If we are abiding in Christ, we find that we only want what God wants for us. We desire only that which will bring glory to God.

There are no selfish requests on our part. The best request we can ask of God is that His grand purpose finds it fulfilment our lives.

> "Abide in Christ –this highest blessing gain;
> Each day sweet fellowship with Him maintain.
> Abiding, He and we are joined as one;
> In constant fellowship, all barrier gone.
>
> Abide in Him, anointing then will flow;
> In fellowship, the Spirit's lead we'll know.
> Obeying, we His riches apprehend;
> Led by the Spirit, we will be His friend.
>
> Abide in Him, the light of grace will shine;
> In fellowship, all shadows will decline.
> Obey the light, His life in us will grow;
> from darkness freed, our hearts will comfort know.
>
> Abiding, we are strengthened with each breath;
> In fellowship, His life will swallow death.
> Abiding, all our sighing turns to song;
> In fellowship, our heart is gladdened, strong".

Author: Unknown

"THE EYE OF FAITH"

2 Corinthians 4:18

"So, we fix our eyes not on what is seen, but on what is unseen. For what is seen is temporary, but what is unseen is eternal"

Everything we see is temporary and destined for destruction. The things the world values such as wealth, pleasures, profits, honours, will one day be gone. Even the world itself is predestined for the fire. *"But the day of the Lord will come like a thief. The heavens will disappear with a roar; the elements will be destroyed by fire, and the earth and everything in it will be burned up".* (2 Peter 3:10).

Paul is reminding the followers of Christ not to fix their eyes on what they see. They are all temporary. In less than the blink of an eye all will disappear in an enormous flash that will light up the entire Universe. Don't set you affections upon what you see, or they will blind you to your true and eternal riches. Fix your "eye of faith" on your eternal and unseen riches that await you in heaven.

"We do not want you to be uninformed, brothers, about the hardships we suffered in the province of Asia. We were under great pressure, far beyond our ability to endure, so that we despaired even of life". (2 Cor.1:8). It was in this context of suffering that he encouraged his readers to look with the "eye of faith" to what is unseen.

Life's trials can become unbearable and lead to discouragement in the lives of Christians. But they are temporary and will come to an end. For this reason, Paul urges us to focus upon what we cannot see. With the "eye of faith" we are guaranteed the joys and glories of heaven that are eternal and will never pass away.

> *"Forever with the Lord!" Amen, so let it be:*
> *Life from the dead is in that word, 'Tis immortality.*
> *Here in the body pent, Absent from Him I roam,*
> *Yet nightly pitch my moving tent, A days march nearer home."*

James Montgomery (1771-1854)

SET APART FOR HIMSELF
Psalm 4:3

"Know that the Lord has set apart the godly for himself; the Lord will hear when I call to him"

"The Lord has set apart the godly for himself." To be set apart for the Lord is the most privileged relationship anyone can ever have. It indicates an intimate relationship between the Lord and those whom He has set apart for Himself. Setting us apart for Himself speaks of His love, care and protection over us. It also indicates that those whom He has set apart are His treasure. They are the apple of His eye (Psalm 17:8). He has a special regard for them and will hear their prayers.

In setting us apart indicates He has a plan and a purpose for us. He has already given to us a gift of the Holy Spirit in preparation for the work He has already prepared for us to do here on earth. (1 Cor. 7:7,12:7,11; Eph.2:10, 4:7;1 Peter 4:10; Matt. 28:16-20). He set us apart so we could serve Him. God set us apart for Himself and at the same time separated us from the world. Although living in the world we are cautioned not to love the world and the things of the world. (1 John 2:15-17). With the eye of faith, we see beyond this world to what Jesus has prepared for us. *"I go to prepare a place for you"* he told His disciples. (John 14:3). As the old song goes: *"This world is not our home, We're just a passing through"*.

In being set apart as His treasure we ought to seek an ever-closer walk with Him. We are indeed favoured above all people that the Lord has set us apart for Himself.

> "Set apart a chosen vessel,
> To the King of kings,
> Set apart for ever severed,
> From all earthly things.
>
> Set apart an earthen vessel,
> Empty, weak and small,
> Yet the treasure that it bears,
> Christ the Lord of all"

Author unknown

THE DAY OF VINDICATION

1 Corinthians 4:5

"Therefore, judge nothing before the appointed time; wait until the Lord comes. He will bring to light what is hidden in the darkness and will expose the motives of men's hearts. At that time each will receive his praise from God"

Paul knew there were those in the Corinthian Church who had a very low opinion of him. They were very quick to pass judgment on him. But Paul couldn't care less. He was not interested in what others thought or said about him. Nor was he concerned how others judged him or what false accusations they levelled against him. The criticisms directed at him were like water flowing off a duck's back. His attitude towards his critics was, 'Think and say what you like', *'I don't have to prove that I'm right. The Lord is my Judge'* (1 Cor. 4:3-4).

Human judgment is superficial. Only the Lord has the right to pass judgment. Only He knows the hearts of men. Only His judgment is true and impartial. *"He will bring to light what is hidden in darkness"*. We ought never to allow ourselves to be guilty of passing harsh judgment upon others. There are many things we cannot know about others. We do not know what load they may be carrying in their hearts. Many hide their regrets and pain. We can never know the motives of another person's heart.

"Wait until the Lord comes" when He will bring to light what is hidden in the darkness and expose it to the light. The secrets of every heart will be revealed. Everyone will receive justice on that Day. Christians who have been falsely accused of wrongdoing will be vindicated by the Supreme Judge of all mankind. He alone sees and knows what is in the heart of all men and will judge accordingly.

> *"And must I be to judgment brought,*
> *and answer in that Day;*
> *For every vain and idle thought,*
> *and every word I say?*
> *Yes, every secret of my heart,*
> *shall shortly be made known;*
> *And I receive my just desert,*
> *for all that I have done"*

Charles Wesley (1707-1788)

HEAVENLY MINDED

Colossians 3:1-2

"Since then, you have been raised with Christ, set your hearts on things above where Christ is seated at the right hand of God. Set your minds on things above, not on earthly things"

Every true believer has been raised to new life in Christ. (Col. 2:12). Their citizenship has already been established in heaven where they will reside with Jesus, His angels and all the residents in Paradise. (Phil. 3:20). Jesus has already prepared the place they will occupy for eternity. (John 14:3). Therefore, writes Paul, *"Set your hearts on things above where Christ is seated at the right hand of God"*. Be heavenly minded.

Let us set our hearts on Him who sacrificed His own life so that we could be with Him in heaven. To see His face. What will He look like? Will He be like any one of the thousands of faces depicted by artists over the centuries? What does an angel look like? How many are there? What do they do? What will we do in heaven? Who is the Archangel Gabriel? How big is Heaven? There is so much we don't know about heaven, but the day is coming when we shall be there in our glorified bodies. Paul encourages us to *"set our hearts on things above where Christ is seated at the right hand of God, not on earthly things."*

Earthly things are not all evil, but they can become harmful to our spiritual wellbeing if we set our minds upon them. To be earthly-minded is to be short-minded. The things of earth are temporary. Our own lives on earth are temporary. Everything, including the world itself is temporary. It has been marked for destruction. (Matt. 24:35; 2 Peter 3:10-12).

The things above are eternal. Heaven is eternal. All who dwell in Heaven are eternal. We shall be eternal. And throughout eternity we shall forever be with our Lord and Saviour, Jesus Christ.

> For ever with the Lord.
> *Amen, so let it be,*
> Life from the dead is in that word,
> 'Tis immortality,
> Here in the body spent,
> Absent from home I roam,
> Yet nightly pitch my moving tent,
> A days march nearer home"
>
> James Montgomery (1771-1854)

HUMILITY

Philippians 2:3

"Do nothing out of selfish ambition or vain conceit, but in humility consider others better than yourselves"

The more we get to know the depths of sin in our own hearts the less difficulty we shall have in considering others better than ourselves. True humility is seeing ourselves as we really are, sinners and helpless without God. In the times of Paul, humility was considered a weakness but in the eyes of God humility is of great value.

Humility is respecting the dignity and worth of others rather than catering to our own ego or protecting any sense of our own self-importance. The humble person will do nothing out of selfish ambition or vain conceit nor letting his actions be motivated by selfish pride. They value others above themselves and look out for their interests. They do not elevate themselves above others but willingly sacrifice to love them.

God *"leads the humble in what is right and teaches the humble His way"*. (Ps. 25:9) Jesus said, *"Whosoever humbles himself like this child is the greatest in the kingdom of heaven"* (Matt. 18:4). There is simple no place for pride in God's kingdom.

> *"I am persuaded that love and humility are the highest attainments in the school of Christ and the brightest evidence that He is indeed our Master"*
>
> John Newton (1725-1807)

> *"Let your grace, Lord, make me holy,*
> *Humble all my swelling pride;*
> *Fallen, guilty, and unholy,*
> *Greatness from my eyes I'll hide;*
> *I'll forbid my vain aspiring,*
> *Nor at early honours aim,*
> *No ambitious heights desiring*
> *far above my humble claim"*
>
> William Goode (1762-1816)

HOLINESS TO THE LORD

1 Thessalonians 5:23-24

"May God himself, the God of peace, sanctify you through and through. May your whole spirit, soul, and body be kept blameless at the coming of our Lord Jesus Christ. The one who calls you is faithful, and he will do it"

God is holy and those who are His family must be holy too. God is the very essence of holiness. Nothing impure or immoral can ever enter His presence. At the moment of our conversion, we were separated unto God. Then began the work of the Holy Spirit in our lives in transforming us into the image of Jesus to make us fit for heaven. This the work of the Holy Spirit within, is called sanctification that will continue up to the end of our lives.

The prayer of Paul for the Thessalonian congregation is that God Himself may sanctify them *'through and through,* that is, to make them holy in every part. The process of sanctification in our lives is the work of God and He will finish what He has started. (Phil.1:6). However, He needs our cooperation. Our obedience to Him is the key to His fulfilling His purpose in our lives.

God does not want part of us. He wants all of us. Our spirit, soul and body. We are to be sanctified until there is nothing left in us that has not been sanctified. There is some disagreement among theologians over whether there is a difference between the spirit and the soul. The spirit is unique to humans and capable of religion and worship. The soul is sometimes referred to as the personality or the heart. Let the theologians continue to debate their differences over this issue but it doesn't alter the fact that God wants us to be holy in every part of our being.

PRAYER

Complete your work of sanctification in my life, O Lord, so I may be presented faultless and complete before Your throne of glory
(Jude 23-24)

"O worship the Lord in the beauty of holiness!
Bow down before him. his glory proclaim;
With gold of obedience, and incense of lowliness,
kneel and adore him: the Lord is his Name!

John S. Monsell (1811-1875)

"I AM"

John 6:35

"I am the bread of life"

What thoughts must have passed through the minds of those who listened to these words of Jesus; *"I am the bread of life. He who comes to me will never go hungry, and he who believes in me will never be thirsty"*. They would have thought, who is this man that makes such an outrageous claim about himself? *"Never go hungry ... never be thirsty again!*

There was only one Man who could. Jesus Christ. He said to the Jews, "I most solemnly say to you *before Abraham was born*, I AM". The "I AM" was the personal name of God, revealed directly to Moses (Exodus 3:14). In declaring Himself, "I AM" Jesus claimed equality with God. (John 8:58).

In saying they will *"never go hungry ... never be thirsty again!* Jesus is obviously not referring to the needs of the physical body. He is referring to the spiritual need within the souls of all men. This need cannot be satisfied with ordinary food. Jesus said, *"I am the bread of life"*, pointing to Himself as the source of satisfying the deepest yearnings of the soul.

Just as we need our daily bread for our physical wellbeing so likewise, we receive spiritual bread by maintaining our union with Christ who is our life. We nurture and grow in our relationship with Jesus through prayer our close relationship with Him. "I am the Bread of Life

> All who eat this Bread will never die
> I am God's love revealed
> I am broken that you might be healed.
>
> All who eat of this heavenly Bread
> All who drink this cup of the covenant
> You will live forever for I will raise you up
>
> I am the bread of Life
> All who eat this Bread will never die
> I am God's love revealed
> I am broken that you might be healed.
>
> No one who comes to Me shall ever hunger again
> No one who believes shall ever thirst
> All that the Father draws shall come to Me
> And I will give them rest.
>
> I am the Bread of Life
> All who eat this bread will never die
> I am God's love revealed
> I am broken that you might be healed.
>
> John Michael Talbot (1954-

"I AM"

John 8:12

'I am the light of the world. Whoever follows me will never walk-in darkness but will have the light of life'.

The world is a dark place. Watching the news can be very depressing. There is little we can be optimistic about. Confusion, corruption and immorality. The world is a dark place full of sin and evil. Jesus said, *"the people love darkness rather than Light because their deeds were evil."* (John 3:19)

But there are seekers after truth. They don't want to remain in the darkness of ignorance. They want to find answers to their questions. Why am I here? What is the meaning of life? Is there life after death? Jesus is the answer to those questions and many more. He said, '*I am the light of the world, whoever follows me will never walk-in darkness, but will have the light of life*'. This is the second powerful declaration, "I AM" from the Son of God.

As darkness and death go together so light and life go to together. Those that live in spiritual darkness are dead in trespasses and sin. They prefer their sin remain hidden and not be exposed. They reject the light and love the darkness because the light of Christ exposes, brings to light their sin.

" *Whoever follows me will never walk in darkness but will have the light of life*" The followers of Christ do not walk in darkness. They have the light of Christ that has illuminated their minds to God's truths. They have found the answer to that age-old question. What lies after death? Jesus, the Light of the world, has revealed it to them.

> "The whole world was lost in the darkness of sin;
> The Light of the world is Jesus!
> Like sunshine at noonday, His glory shone in;
> The Light of the world is Jesus!
>
> No darkness have we who in Jesus abide,
> The Light of the world is Jesus!
> We walk in the light when we follow our Guide!
> The Light of the world is Jesus!
>
> Come to the Light, 'tis shining for thee;
> Sweetly the Light has dawned upon me;
> Once I was blind, but now I can see:
> The Light of the world is Jesus!
>
> Philip P. Bliss (1838-1876)

"I AM"

John 10:7

"I am the door for the sheep"

This is the third of the seven "I AM" statements Jesus makes about Himself. God used the "I AM" to identify Himself to His people. (Ex 3:14). By saying "I AM" Jesus was claiming equality with God. This was blasphemy for which the Jews tried to kill him. (John 8:58-59). One of the most striking doors in the world, is the door at St. Peter's Basilica in Rome. It is opened in a holy year, once every 25 years. The door is sealed from inside with a brick wall to prevent entry. Unlike the Door in Rome shut to all outsiders, Jesus is an open door to find forgiveness. He is the open door to eternal life. He is the open door to find peace with God.

Jesus said, *"I am the door for the sheep."* He has the authority to open the door and to shut the door of heaven. He opens the door to those who hear and knows His voice and He shuts the door against those who have turned their backs on Him. Jesus is <u>the</u> door not <u>a</u> door. The common thinking today is that there are many doors into heaven. The idea is all religions are like different climbers, all climbing up the same mountain towards its peak and all eventually arriving at the same place. That is one of Satan's lies.

In his allegorical painting "The Light of the World", English artist William H. Hunt (1827-1910) depicted Jesus knocking on a door. The door has no outside handle. It can only be opened from the inside. The artist is illustrating Revelation 3:20. *"Behold, I stand at the door and knock; if anyone hears my voice and opens the door, I will go in and eat with him, and he with me".* The unopened door illustrates the heart of man through which Jesus wants to gain entrance. But it can only be opened from the inside.

"Jesus is the door;
He is the gateway
everyone has access
He is the only way.

Jesus is the door
He is the bridgeway
to finding peace with God.
He is the only doorway.

Jesus is the door,
He is the invitation,
He offers to everyone.
the only way to salvation",

Deborah Ann Belka
Birth Place. **Fremont, CA USA.**

"I AM"

John 10:11

"I am the good shepherd. The good shepherd lays down his life for the sheep"

Seven hundred years before the birth of Jesus, the prophet Isaiah described what the people were like in the Southern Kingdom of Judea. *"All we like sheep have gone astray, everyone has turned aside to his own way: and the Lord has laid on him the iniquity of us all".* (Is. 53:6). Like sheep they had followed one another into idolatry. Isaiah foretold the mission and the suffering of their coming Messiah. *"He was despised and rejected by men ... he carried our sorrows ... he was smitten and afflicted ... he was pierced for our transgressions ... like a lamb he was led to the slaughter ... he did not open his mouth ... he bore the sin of many ...* (Isaiah chap. 53).

Jesus was born not to live a long life, but to die an early death. He was on a mission that would end His life on a cross in his early 30's. As a good Shepherd he lay down his life willingly for his sheep. It was His love and compassion for us for which He died.

Jesus is the good Shepherd who knows His sheep. He knows all about us. He knows us by name. He knows our weaknesses and strengths; the difficulties we face and the sufferings we must endure. As our good

Shepherd, He protects us from the unseen forces of evil. He provides our every need. He guides us and keeps us from going astray.

There are many false shepherds posing as shepherds of God's people. They have their own interests at heart rather than the spiritual welfare of those whom they have deluded into following them. Jesus said, *'Watch out for false prophets who come to you in sheep's clothing but inwardly are ravening wolves.* (Matt. 7:15).

Jesus is the good Shepherd who will lead and guide us throughout our lives. And when we take our final breath, we shall fear no evil for He shall be with us, and together we shall walk through the valley of the shadow of death into the all the glories of Heaven. (Psalm 23).

> *Oh! Christian friend, do not fear, you'll will never walk alone,*
> *Jesus, your Guide and Shepherd, will lead you safely home.*
> *He'll guide you through the Valley, the Valley of your death,*
> *And lead you to the place of your eternal happiness.*

Peter C. Horrell (1936-

"I AM"

John 11:25

"I am the resurrection and the life. He who believes in me will live, even though he dies, he shall live"

Only God could make a statement such as this. C. S. Lewis (1898-1963) wrote, *"A man who was merely a man and said the sort of things Jesus said would be either a lunatic on the level with a man who says he is a poached egg or else he would be the Devil of Hell. Either this man was, and is, the Son of God, or else a madman or something else. You must make your choice"*.

Some believe He was a good man or a great prophet. Other claim he was an angel, or a god created among other gods. Still others say he was a legend, liar or a lunatic. The Bible, however, tells us that He is God. His miracles, His resurrection, His unique attributes point to what He Himself claimed to be, "I am the Alpha and the Omega, the First and the Last, the Beginning and the End. (Rev. 22:12-13).

Lazarus was dead. He had already been in his tomb for four days when Jesus arrived in Bethany the home of Lazarus and his two sisters, Martha and Mary. Martha said to Jesus, *"Had you been here my brother would not have died"*. *"Your brother will rise again"* replied Jesus. And Martha said, *"I know he will rise again in the resurrection on the last day."* Jesus said, *"I am the resurrection and the life. He who believes in me will live, even though he dies, he shall live"*.

No mere mortal could ever make such a statement such as this. He raised Lazarus from the dead as evidence to an unbelieving world that He was all that He claimed to be. Just as He had the power of God to raise Lazarus from the dead so also, He Has the power to raise from the dead all those who have put their faith in Him.

> "In Christ alone my hope is found;
> He is my light, my strength, my song;
> This cornerstone, this solid ground,
> Firm through the fiercest drought and storm.
>
> What heights of love, what depths of peace,
> When fears are stilled, when strivings cease!
> My comforter, my all in all –
> Here in the love of Christ I stand".
>
> Stuart Townend & Keith Getty

"I AM"

John 14:6

"I am, the way the truth and the life. No-one comes to the Father except but through me"

"I am the way".

Jesus did not say He would show us the way, but that He Is the way. He isn't claiming to be <u>a</u> way. He is claiming to be <u>the</u> way. He is the only way we find forgiveness of sins. He is the only way in which we can be reconciled and find our peace with God. (Rom. 5:1-2). Jesus is the only way.

"I am the truth".

Jesus is the personification of truth. Without Jesus we do not know what the truth is. There is no half-truth or partial truth in Jesus Christ. He is the fountain of all truth. His promises are true. Those who trust Him as their Saviour will find Him true to His word. His warnings to those who refuse His free offer of salvation will find His words were true on Judgment Day.

"I am the life".

Jesus is the Author and Giver of eternal life. (1 John 5:11). Those that do not have this life are dead in their trespasses and sin. Only Jesus can raise them from this state of death and impart His life-giving Spirit of eternal life. People seek the 'good life' by appeasing their own desires. The 'good life ', however is only in Jesus who is the Giver of eternal life.

"No-one comes to the Father except through me"

This is the most controversial statements that nonreligious people and world religions have against Christianity. The claim to have an exclusive way, an exclusive truth, and the only way to the true God. They call it bigotry. If there were many roads to God, then Jesus is not one of them because He absolutely claimed there was only one way to God, and He Himself was that way. F.F. Bruce (1910-1990) said, *"If this seems offensively exclusive, let it be borne in mind that the one who makes this claim is the incarnate Word, the revealer of the Father".* (Acts 4:12).

> *"I Am the Way, the Truth and the Life,*
> *That's what Jesus said.*
>
> *I Am the Way, the Truth and the Life,*
> *That's what Jesus said.*
>
> *Without the Way there is no going.*
> *Without the Truth there is no knowing.*
> *Without the Life there is no living.*
>
> *I Am the Way, the Truth and the Life,*
> *That's what Jesus said."*

"I AM"

John 15:1

"I am the true vine and my Father is the gardener"

The Temple in Jerusalem was a magnificent structure comprising an area of about 35 acres. One of its gates was called the "Beautiful Gate" that was plated with silver and gold and much larger than the other gates. It was near this "Beautiful Gate" that Peter healed the crippled beggar. (Acts 3:1-10). Curled along the top of the Gate was a vine made of gold, hung with bunches of grapes as tall as a man.

Jesus may have alluded to this feature when He said, *"I am the vine, and my Father is the gardener. He cuts off every branch in me that bears no fruit, while every branch that does bear fruit, he trims clean so that it will be even more fruitful"*. The Gardiner represents the Father, the true vine represents Jesus, and the branches represent the followers of Jesus.

The pruning in the life of a follower of Jesus can often be a painful experience. God will use "all things" to accomplish His eternal plan for our lives. He uses all things to work together for good to those who love Him. (Rom. 8:28). His purpose is to conform us into the image of His Son. This is His ultimate plan for every follower of Jesus.

Spiritual fruit can only come from the true vine. He alone is the source of a fruitful life, and this is what God wants to see in each of us.

> "He is the vine and we're the branches,
> We should e'er abide in Him;
> And let Him abide in us,
> As the flow of life within.
>
> Oh, how precious this abiding,
> Oh, how intimate and sweet;
> As the fruit of life is added,
> And our joy is made complete."

Adapted

GOD

John 3:16

"For <u>God</u> so loved the world that he gave his one and only Son, that whoever believes in him shall not perish but have eternal life"

G<u>OD</u>. There was never a time when God did not exist. The Bible makes no attempt to offer proof that he does exist, but it does tell us how we can know that he does exist. *"In the beginning God created the heavens and the earth"* (Gen. 1:1). He created the world, he made the sun, the moon and the stars. He made the land and the sea; he made the animals, and he made people. (Ps. 33:6-9). Everything has a beginning except God and everything depends upon God.

How do we know God exists? *"The heavens declare the glory of God; and the firmament shows His handiwork. Day unto day utters speech, and night unto night reveals knowledge. There is no speech nor language where their voice is not heard. Their line has gone out through all the earth, and their words to the end of the world.* (Psalm 19:1-4).

God had no beginning. *"Before the mountains were born or you brought forth the earth and the world, from everlasting to everlasting you are God"* (Ps. 90:2). He was before the mountains were formed. God is *"from everlasting to everlasting."* Though the Bible makes no attempt to prove God exists, the apostle Paul explains, *"For since the creation of the world His invisible attributes are clearly seen, being understood by the things that are made, even His eternal power and Godhead, so that they are without excuse."* (Rom. 1:20).

The Hebrew word translated God is plural. *"Then God said, let us make man in our own image ...* (Rev. 1:26). This is the first hint in the Bible that God is Trinity. The Father, the Son and the Holy Spirit. The doctrine of the Trinity is not fully revealed until the New Testament.

God is Omnipotent. He has unlimited power. God is Omniscient. He has unlimited knowledge. God is Omnipresent. He is capable of being everywhere at the same time. Everything has a beginning and everything that has a beginning also has an end. But God has no end because He had no beginning. *"Before the mountains were born or you brought forth the earth and the world, from everlasting to everlasting you are God"* (Ps. 90:2).

> "O Lord my God! When I in awesome wonder,
> Consider all the worlds Your hands have made,
> I see the stars, I hear the rolling thunder,
> Your power throughout the universe displayed.
>
> > Then sings my soul,
> > My Saviour, God to You
> > How great You are,
> > How great You are!

Carl Boberg (1859-1940)

LOVED

John 3:16

"For God so <u>loved</u> the world that he gave his one and only Son, that whoever believes in him shall not perish but have eternal life"

L**OVED.** Love is often linked to romantic feelings of romance or affection that one has for another person or family member. But human love is often fickle and a far cry from God's love. *"God is love"* (1 John 4:8). Love is one of God's attributes. It is an essential aspect of His character. God loves because it is his nature to love.

His love is more than mere kindness. God's love moves Him to compassionate action. *"God shows his love for us even when we were still sinners, Christ died for us."* (Rom. 5:8). God *"causes the sun to rise on the evil and good and sends His rain on the righteous and unrighteous."* God gives good sunshine and good rain to an evil farmer, is an example of God loving His enemies. God's love reaches out to every single person on earth, whether they are good or bad. (Matt. 5:45). His love knows no barriers. It is endless and unconditional.

When we fall into sin, He still loves us and as a loving Father, He disciplines us because he wants us to become like his Son, Jesus. *"For the Lord disciplines the one He loves and chastises every son He receives so that they may grow to become more like Jesus."* (Heb. 12:5-6). If He did not love us, we would quickly slide into sin and loss.

It is through God's love to us that we can truly love others. Jesus said, *"A new commandment I give unto you, that you love one another; as I have loved you, so you must love one another. All men will know that you are my disciples if you love one another."* (John 13:34-35). It is relatively easy to love a fellow Christian, but Jesus also told us to *"love your enemies, bless them that curse you, do good to them that hate you, and pray for them which despitefully use and persecute you."* (Matt. 5:43-44). God's love reaches out to those that persecute us, revile us and hate us and it is His love we need to be able to do as Jesus asked us to do: Love them and pray for them. God's love is boundless.

The greatest expression of God's love is sending his only Son into the world so that we might live through him. *"This is God's love, not that we have loved God but that He loved us and sent his Son as the atoning sacrifice for our sins"* (1 John 4:7-10). Because God loves us, we have no need to fear. He is sovereign overall.

> *"Though the mountains fall way*
> *and the hills be shaken,*
> *My love shall never fall away from you,*
> *nor my covenant of peace be shaken,*
> *says the Lord, who has mercy on you."*
>
> Isaiah 54:10

WORLD

John 3:16

"For God so loved the <u>world</u> that he gave his one and only Son, that whoever believes in him shall not perish but have eternal life"

WORLD. *"In the beginning God created the heavens and the earth"* (Gen. 1:1). He used no pre-existing material to create the world. God created the world out of nothing. It was His world, and it was a paradise. He created it for the habitation of His people that they might know Him, love Him and serve Him.

The creation account is divided into seven days. God creates light (day 1) the sky (day 2); dry land, seas, plants (day 3); Sun, moon & stars (day 4); Birds & sea creatures (day 5); Land animals & humans (day 6); The Sabbath of rest (day 7). God saw all that He had made, and it was very good. And there was evening, and there was morning – the sixth day" (Gen. 1:31).

Biblical creation is not compatible with the belief that the world just haphazardly came together over 4.6 billion years ago out of a mixture of dust and gas around a young sun. Neither do biblical creationists view the Bible or the book of Genesis as a mythological or allegorical document. We uphold the Bible as God's eyewitness account of actual creation events as recorded in Genesis 1.

No longer can God look upon the world and say it is "very good". What was once a created paradise is today a nightmare. Since the Fall of Adam, we live in a world of evil and suffering. Earthquakes, tsunamis, hunger, pollution, terrorism, genocide, threats of nuclear war, greed, hatred, corruption, misuse of drugs and alcohol and poverty and inequality are world-wide. But even though the world has fallen into such a state of wickedness God's love for the world has never diminished.

His world was stolen from Him by the craftiness of Satan who rules it as the prince of this world. (John 14:30) He is responsible for all the misery and suffering in the world. He holds the souls of hundreds of millions as slaves under his power. God's love for the world was so great that "He sent His only Son, the Prince of Peace to save the world and set the prisoners free.

> "I was once a slave to Satan,
> And he worked his will in me,
> But I'm bound by sin no longer,
> For the Son has set me free.
>
> All my fear, all condemnation,
> All that stood 'twixt God and me,
> Praise His name! are left behind me,
> For the Son has set."
>
> William A. Stewart. (1864-1942)

SON
John 3:16

"For God so loved the world that he gave his one and only <u>Son</u>, that whoever believes in him shall not perish but have eternal life"

S<u>on</u>. We were given a hint of the Trinity in the Old Testament when God said, *'let <u>us</u> make man in <u>our</u> own image."* (Gen. 1:26). In the New Testament more is revealed about the role of each member of the Trinity. The Trinity does not mean that three persons are united in one person but rather that there are three eternal distinctions in the substance of God. There is but one God; and the Father, Son and Holy Spirit are this one God. Neither is God without the others; each with the others is God. 1. The Father is recognized as God. (John 6:27; 1 Peter 1:2). 2. Jesus Christ is recognized as God. (John 1:1; John 1:18). 3. The Holy Spirit is recognized as God. (Acts 5:3, 4; 1 Cor 3:16).

> And in this Trinity, none is before, or after another;
> none is greater, or less than another;
> but the whole three Persons
> are co-eternal together: and co-equal.
>
> The Athanasian Creed (AD 325)

God so loved the world that He gave His one and only Son Jesus Christ to save mankind. To do so He chose to assume a human nature and became a man in the form of Jesus Christ. He humbled Himself by laying aside His glory and privileges (Phil 2:6-8). He became human because it was part of His plan to die in our place as a man and to be resurrected from the dead. (Heb.9:22). Whilst on earth Christ was both fully human and fully divine.

He was truly human and able to identify with the sufferings of humanity; Jesus experienced sorrow and wept tears. He was tempted. He experienced hunger and thirst. He knew what it was to be rejection, criticised and betrayed. (John 11:55; Matt 4:1-11; Heb 4:14-16; Mark 3:1-6).

And He was truly divine: His miraculous birth, His eternal existence His miracles His authority to forgive sin His acceptance of worship His ability to predict the future and His resurrection from the dead What God was, He was. Jesus was divine. All creation took place through Him. Not a single thing was created without Him. (Luke 1:26-31; John 1:1-3; Matt.9:24-25; Matt. 9:6; Matt. 14:33; Matt.24:1-2; Luke 24:36-39).

> "Oh, the deep, deep love of Jesus,
> Vast, unmeasured, boundless, free,
> Rolling as a mighty ocean
> In its fullness over me
>
> Samuel T. Francis (1834-1925)

WHOEVER

John 3:16

"For God so loved the world that he gave his one and only Son, that <u>whoever</u> believes in him shall not perish but have eternal life"

WHOEVER. One of the most gifted and colourful poets of the 18th century was Scottish Robert Burns. (1759-1796). Burns enjoyed using his pen to ridicule the theological beliefs of Scotland's Reformed Presbyterian Church with its Calvinistic interpretation of predestination. In one of his poems, "Holy Willie", he ridicules their frigid stand on predestination.

> "O Thou, who in the heavens does dwell,
> who as it pleases best Thyself.
> Sends one to heaven and ten to hell,
> all for Thy glory."

Calvinists believe that God chooses certain individuals for salvation because it's His prerogative as Sovereign to choose whom He wants to save. His choice is based solely upon His grace and mercy. Suppose we have a large hall filled with one thousand people, and these one thousand represent the whole of humanity waiting to be born. Before they are born, however, God has already chosen one hundred for salvation. The remaining nine hundred are left to suffer eternal damnation. Reformed Presbyterians believe that those nine hundred were predestined to damnation even before they are born. Many Christian denominations find that interpretation of predestination abhorrent.

God doesn't love some and reject others before they are born. His love is not partial. He loves every single individual on earth equally. And He want all to be saved. (1 Tim 2:4). Jesus died for the <u>"whosoever"</u>. Hence the great commandment to go out to every nation and make disciples (Matt 28: 16-20). This is based upon giving everyone equal opportunity to be saved. But only those who respond to Christ are saved.

> To go beyond the furthest star,
> Far past all worlds above;
> Though lost within the depths of space,
> I'm still within God's love.
>
> No mortal souls beyond His reach,
> It knows no depth, nor height;
> No borders to its width nor length,
> God's love is infinite.
>
> His love revealed on Calvary's Cross,
> I cannot comprehend;
> When Jesus died to save my soul,
> T' was love that knows no end.

Peter C. Horrell (1936-

ETERNAL LIFE

John 3:16

"For God so loved the world that he gave his one and only Son, that whoever believes in him shall not perish but have <u>eternal life</u>"

ETERNAL LIFE. John 3:16 has long been famous as a powerful declaration of the gospel. It is the most popular single verse used in evangelism. It has been called "the golden text of the Bible", "the gospel in a nutshell", and" everyman's text" and the best-known Bible verse in the world. It reveals God's purpose for sending Jesus.

John 3:16 tells us about the unconditional love that God has for His creation. It teaches us about the sacrifice God made for us, and it helps us understand the eternal blessings of being a follower of Jesus. This verse is a promise and affirms the hope we have as Christians that there is an eternal life waiting for those who believe in Jesus. God wants to save the world so desperately that He became part of the world in the form of a man – Jesus Christ.

God looks at fallen humanity. He does not want it to *perish*, and so in love He extends His gift of salvation in Jesus Christ. It is God's love that actually saves man from eternal destruction. *"Whoever believes in the Son has eternal life, but whoever rejects the Son will not see life, for God's wrath remains on him".* (John 3:36). God's wrath can be defined as righteous anger. It is in response to man's sin. He is responding to godlessness and wickedness. And He responds angrily to those with unrepentant hearts who have rejected His Son Jesus who died to give them eternal life in heaven.

God stands as the judge of all mankind. Each of us will have to give an account for what we have done and how we have lived. To those who believe in Him shall not perish but have eternal life. And O what a glorious life that shall be.

> "Now is eternal life,
> if risen with Christ we stand,
> in him to life reborn,
> And holden in his hand;
> No more we fear death's ancient dread,
> In Christ arisen from the dead.
>
> Unfathomed love divine,
> Reign thou within my heart;
> From thee nor depth nor height,
> nor life nor death can part;
> My life is hid in God with thee,
> and through all eternity."
>
> George W. Briggs (1875-1959)

THE SEVEN DEADLY SINS
Proverbs 6:16-19

<u>PRIDE</u>

Leading the list of these seven deadly sins is pride. God hates six things, but the seventh the worse. It is the worst of the seven deadly sins and is considered the father of all sins because it was the sin of pride that led to Lucifer's rebellion and subsequent expulsion from heaven. In his epic poem, "Paradise Lost", John Milton writes about the pride of Satan who declared, *"I will exalt my throne above the stars of GOD: I will be like the HIGHEST"*. (Is. 14:13-15). Milton goes on to quote Satan as saying, *"Better to reign in hell than to serve in heaven"*. Satan would rather *'reign'* than *'serve,"* and his pride cost him his place in heaven and brought sin, death and untold suffering into the world.

Pride is the sin from which all other sins originate because it can lead into other sins such as envy, greed and anger. It is the sin of thinking oneself more important and superior to anyone else. It is the attitude of a person who is arrogant and egotistical causing them to look down their nose at others. But God will not be mocked. He hates the proud and loves the humble. C S. Lewis wrote, *"As long as you are proud you can never know God. A proud man is always looking down on things and people: and of course, if you are looking down, you cannot see something that is above you."* "In the pride of his face the wicked does not seek him; all his thoughts are, there is no room for God." (Psalm 10:4).

Whoever says they have no pride is full of it. No matter how committed we are to Christ, none of us are free from pride in our hearts. Martin Luther said, "*I have within me that great pope, SELF*". Pride is essentially self-worship. Thoughts of self-grandeur have their roots in pride. There is a difference however, between sinful pride and good pride. Parents can be proud of the academic achievements of their children. You can be proud in the accomplishment of a job well done. One can have pride in their country. Sinful pride is deeply rooted in the heart and self-serving.

To acknowledge before God that pride within us is sin and something we hate is a step towards humbling ourselves before God. "*Humble yourselves under the mighty hand of God, that he may exalt you in due time.*" (1Peter 5:6). Far better for us to humble ourselves than to leave it to another to humble us. We shall struggle with pride till our dying day. But it need not control us. The only pride we should ever cherish in our hearts is what God has done for us in Christ. (2 Cor. 10:17-18).

> "*Show me, as my soul can bear,*
> *The depth of inbred sin.*
> *All the unbelief declares,*
> *The pride that lurks within:*
> *Take me, whom Thyself has bought,*
> *And bring into captivity*
> *Every high aspiring thought*
> *That would not stoop to Thee*"
>
> Charles Wesley (1707-1788)

THE SEVEN DEADLY SINS
Proverbs 6:16-19

LIES

God hates lying. The Ninth Commandment states do not bear false witness. (Deut. 5:20). Lies are a most detestable evil to God because He is the source of all truth. The tongue can do enormous damage. James likens it as to fire that can set aflame a whole forest. He likens it to deadly poison. Like poison that slowly spreads through the body the tongue can spread lies and slanderous words that poisons minds against others. *"Life and death are in the power of the tongue."* (Proverbs 18:21).

Lies are an abomination to the Trinity. They are contrary to God's nature as He is the God of truth. They are contrary to Jesus, who is truth itself. They are contrary to the Spirit of truth who leads us into all truth. Liars are dishonest, deceptive and destructive. Their lies by gossip and slander are a devastating force of evil. They wreck marriages, ruin careers, destroy reputations, create suspicion and cause untold grief and pain. We can see that there are genuine reasons God hates a lying tongue. *'Life and death are in the power of the tongue'* (Pro.18:21).

Revelation 21:8 says that all liars shall have their part in the second death (in the lake that burns with fire and brimstone). A lying tongue is a reminder that all words count. All words have consequences and that all our words will be judged by God. Isaac Watts writes,

"Oh, it's a lovely thing for youth,
To early walk-in wisdom's way;

To fear a lie, to speak the truth,
That we may trust to all they say!
But liars we can never trust,

Even when they say what is true;
And he who does one fault at first,
And lies to hide it, makes it two.
Have we not known, nor heard, nor read,
How God does hate deceit and wrong?
How Ananias was struck dead,
Caught with a lie upon his tongue?
So did his wife Sapphira die,
When she came in, and grew so bold;
As to confirm that wicked lie,
Which just before her husband told.
The Lord delights in them that speak,
The words of truth; but every liar
Must have his portion in the lake,
That burns with brimstone and with fire."

THE SEVEN DEADLY SINS
Proverbs 6:16-19

MURDER

The sixth commandment says, "*You shall not murder.*" (Gen 5:17). "*Hands that shed innocent blood*" refers to the cold-blooded killing of the innocent. The law of God makes provision for the execution of the murderer. (Gen.13:4; Ex. 21:12; Rom.13:4). Having been found guilty of murder, the shedding of their blood is not the shedding of innocent blood. They have been found guilty of murder and must pay the price for their crime.

Murder goes against God's commandment and His value for human life. (Gen. 9:6). Life is sacred to God because He created it and defends it. The devil was a murderer from the beginning, and so are his children who are under the condemnation of God. (John 8:44; Rev 21:8; 22:15). The greatest example of innocent life lost is Jesus. When He was killed, even Pilate who sentenced Him to death knew there was nothing Jesus had done wrong to deserve to die. (Matt 27:23-24).

Another form of shedding innocent blood is the sin of abortion, the silent holocaust, as it has been called. It is the killing of an unborn child. This is sinful and morally wrong, because it violates the sanctity of human life. The Bible makes it clear that God places a lot of value on un-born life. In Psalm 139:13 we read '*you made all the delicate, inner parts of my* body, and knit them together in my mother's womb...' The prophet Isaiah cried out 'listen to my words all you nations ... the Lord called me before my birth ... from within the womb he called me by my name". (Isaiah 49:1-5). Other biblical references show that God is involved from the very beginning in the birth of a child. The bringing to life and development of a baby is God's own workmanship. (Jeremiah 1:5; Job. 33:4).

The reason why there is no mention of abortion, infantile, genocide or suicide in the Bible is simple that God's people, the Hebrews, did not practice these things. Abortion is not mentioned because the Hebrews did not practice abortion. They treated un-born life as precious and the birth of the child as a gift from God. Abortion is destroying the potential of a life that could have had a huge effect for good in the world. God will hold accountable those that endorse this practice. To deny the killing of babies, the slaughter of a whole race of people, is contrary to moral decency and order.

"There is an evil game;
A game that no one can win,
Abortion is its name,
Oh! What a terrible sin?

All they want is a chance to live;
but pain and hatred are all you give;
They are to live in your womb;
But you have made it their tomb".

Author unknown

THE SEVEN DEADLY SINS

Proverbs 6:16-19

WICKEDNESS

The fourth thing God detests is a heart that devises wicked plans. David feared for his life and prayed, *"Rescue me, O Lord, from evil men, protect me from men of violence, who devise evil plans in their hearts and stir up war every day."* (Ps 140:1-2). Men who have a lust for power that is not of this world devise evil plans in their hearts to achieve that power at any cost. Tyrants such as Stalin, Hitler, Mugabe, Qaddafi, Mussolini, to mention just a few, were consumed with greed and a lust for power. Their hands are stained with the blood of their innocent victims. They were men of violence who set their hearts to get what they wanted. God hates a heart that devises evil and along with present day tyrants they are under the condemnation of God.

A thief devises evil in his heart as he plans to steal from a neighbour. A businessman devises evil in his heart when he plans to swindle his customers. There are evil thoughts in all men's hearts; but the devising of them is the mark of utter depravity and wickedness and is detestable to God. The devises of the heart, though in secret, are clear to God. Nothing is hidden from Him. There are no secrets that lurk within the heart that He cannot see. It is the heart that forms sinful thoughts and lustful affections and emotions. To mull over unclean thoughts of evil, to ponder over them in the imagination of your mind is hateful to God.

God described Noah's generation with these words: *"Every imagination of the thoughts of man's heart was only evil continually"* (Gen.6:5). We must guard and rule our hearts, or our hearts will rule us. (Prov. 4:23).

> **"Create in me a clean heart, O God, and renew a right spirit within me. Lord God, you know better than anyone that my heart needs cleansing every single day. I am so grateful that you have taken my sins away from me and chosen Not to remember them anymore."**

THE SEVEN DEADLY SINS
Proverbs 6:16-19

EVIL

"*Feet that are quick to rush into evil*". Who are quick to do harm. If evil thoughts and imaginations are nurtured and fed, they eventually lead to outward acts of sin. Our feet follow where our hearts and minds and thoughts have already gone. To rush into evil is to demonstrate a great delight and enjoyment of evil and an eagerness to participate in it without any restraint or delay. They have a greedy desire for it, for they not only lack conscience and self-control but crave for it. "*Having lost all sensitivity, they have given themselves over to sensuality so as to indulge in every kind of impurity, and they are full of greed.*" (Eph. 4:19). "*As a man thinketh in his heart, so is he.*" (Prov. 23:7).

This verse refers to impulsive sinners who rush from sin to sin. They are bent on evil. "*Apart from Christ all people have a desire to do evil, some unregenerate people give into these desires via sinful actions more often and more readily than others. Many sinners keep their sinful impulses in check even if they never come to Christ. This does not mean they are innocent, but only that much of the evil they consider remains in their heart and never comes to fruition in their deeds. We are thinking here of the virtuous pagan who is a good neighbour and a relatively upstanding member of society. Others, however, do not control their sinful impulses. Both groups are guilty of sin, but those who act on the evil thoughts earn a *greater judgment because their evil has a bigger effect on others."* (Ligonier Ministries)

Solomon warns against enticement by sinners to follow them. He spoke about their feet. *"My son, do not go along with them, do not set your foot on their paths; for their feet rush into sin, they are swift to shed blood"* (Prov. 1:15-16). We can be swift to run into all kinds of failings that later we regret. The psalmist prayed, *"For you have delivered my soul from death and my feet from stumbling, that I may walk before God in the light of life."* (Psalm 56:13). The psalmist again tells us, *"I have refrained my feet from every evil way, that O might keep Your word."* (Psalm 119:101). Our choice is involved in deciding which way our feet will work.

> "Oh! For a closer walk with God,
> A calm and heavenly frame;
> A light to shine upon the road,
> That leads me to the Lamb!
>
> So shall my walk be close with God,
> Calm and serene my frame;
> So purer light shall mark the road,
> That leads me to the Lamb."
>
> William Cowper (1731-1800)

THE SEVEN DEADLY SINS
Proverbs 6:16-19

FALSEHOOD

To bear false testimony is a direct violation of the ninth commandment. God hates lying, particularly when it comes to a matter of justice. In legal proceedings a witness who lies puts an innocent person in danger that could result in imprisonment or even death. In the Old Testament we read how Jezebel plotted the death of Naboth who refused to sell his ancestral vineyard to the king. Jezebel, his wife, falsely accused Naboth of cursing God and the King, and hired two thugs to act as witnesses against him. Pronounced guilty, Naboth was taken out and stoned to death so that her husband Ahab could possess his vineyard. (1 Kings 21:8-14).

God hates lies, but not all lies are done with a wilfully evil intent. This type of lying always has an evil intent in perverting justice. They have been the cause of the condemnation on many innocent people They have also been the reason many people go unpunished. *"A corrupt witness mocks at justice, and the mouth of the wicked gulps down evil."* (Prov 19:28).

The Bible gives many warnings about false witnesses. Bearing false witness is the most grievous sin. To speak falsely against someone to damage them civilly or criminally; framing them, requires a special kind of evil: a lack of decency and empathy so profound that they must be possessed by evil. Jesus Himself faced false accusations from the Pharisees and their followers. Many bore false witness against Him, but their testimony did not agree." (Mark 14:56). Even Pilate, the Roman governor, who oversaw Jesus' sentence. Know that Jesus had done nothing wrong, but he pandered to the Jews and allowed the false accusations to stand. (Matt 27:22-26).

As followers of Christ, we can expect that people will sometimes make false accusations against us but hear the encouragement of Jesus. Blessed are you when people falsely say all kinds of evil against you because of me. Rejoice and be glad, because great is your reward in heaven. (Matt. 5:11-12). No matter what others say about us falsely, we can rely upon God's Word. Christians who have been falsely accused of wrongdoing will be judged and vindicated by the Supreme Judge of all mankind. He alone sees and knows what is in the heart and will judge accordingly. Christians who have been falsely accused of wrongdoing will be judged and vindicated by the Supreme Judge of all mankind. He alone sees and knows what is in the heart and will judge accordingly.

> "Deceit and falsehood I abhor,
> but love Thy law, Thy truth revealed;
> my steadfast hope is in Thy word;
> Thou art my refuge and my shield;
> the paths of sin I have not trod,
> but kept the precepts of my God"
>
> Martin Luther (1483-1546)

THE SEVEN DEADLY SINS
Proverbs 6:16-19

TROUBLEMAKER

A man that *stirs up dissension among brothers*," obviously refers to someone who is causing division between family members or within the church. It is one of the highest among the seven things that God hates and regards as an abomination. He despises dissension and division among His people. Christians are meant to live in unity together without conflict. Throughout church history there have always been conflicts, strife and divisions within churches. One reason is because of some doctrinal differences, and another, and more prevalent in our day, is immorality in leadership that devastates the church's testimony and desecrates the name of Christ.

Discord can be caused from a casual conversation. Without thinking of the harm it can do, gossip about others can sow discord. Airing other people's dirty laundry to unrelated parties is subjecting them to humiliation and scorn. Gossip regularly shows poor restraint and a lack of consideration for other feelings. It is poisonous in its influence and is an abomination to God.

We all have our own opinions that at times can clash with the opinions of others. Some are intractable in their opinions that can lead to heated debate. Although there is no intent to sow discord in the church it inevitably has occurred and needs to be quickly resolved. *"If it be possible, as far as it depends on you, live at peace with everyone."* (Rom 12:18). This command recognizes that conflict is sometimes unavoidable. Some people are just not interested in making peace with us. They are hot-tempered and stir up dissension. But we ourselves should never be the reason for an un-peaceful relationship with another person that leaves a rift between us. As best we can let us as act as peacemakers to stem any discord or strife in our church.

<u>Matthew 5:9</u>

Blessed are
the peacemakers:
for they shall be called
the children of God.

"Now peacemaking is a divine work. For peace means reconciliation, and God is the author of peace and of reconciliation. It is hardly surprising, therefore, that the blessing which attaches to peacemakers is that "they shall be called sons of God." For they are seeking to do what their Father has done, loving people with his love."

John R.W. Stott (1921-2010)

THE MOUNT OF TEMPTATION
Matthew 4:1-11

Shortly after Jesus was baptized by John the Baptist, the Spirit of God descended upon Him like a dove, and the voice of God from heaven declared, *"This is my dearly loved Son, with whom I am well pleased."* Jesus was then led by the Spirit into the desert to be tempted by the devil. The temptation He was to endure was part of God's plan so Jesus could identify with us in our temptations and to demonstrate to all His holy and sinless character. (Heb 2:18; 4:15).

After fasting for forty days and forty nights, Jesus was hungry. The devil came and said, *"If you are the Son of God, tell these stones to become bread."* Jesus replied, it is written: *"Man does not live on bread alone but on every word that comes from the mouth of God."* (Deut. 8:3). Jesus shows that every word that proceeds from the mouth of God was more precious to Him than food itself. It means that people need more than material things to truly live.

The devil then took Jesus to the pinnacle of the temple that ascended some 200 feet from the floor of the Kidron Valley. *"If you are the Son of God, "throw yourself down, for it is written": He will command his angels to lift you up, so you won't strike your foot against a stone.* To leap from there and survive would be an astonishing accomplishment. But the devil misquoted the verse and left out the words: "To keep you in all your ways", so making the promise say what in truth it never suggested. (Psalm 91:11-12). Jesus said, it is also written, do not put the Lord your God to the test."

Again, the devil took him to a high mountain from the top of which could be seen *"all the kingdoms of the world and their glory." "All this I will give you, if you will bow down and worship me."* This is what the devil wanted from the very beginning. Worship and recognition from God Himself. The devil is the prince of the world and controls its kingdoms. So, they were his to give. Adam and his descendants gave the devil this authority because of their sin. Away from me, Jesus said, for it is written: *"Worship the Lord your God, and serve him only."*

The devil leaves and the angels came and ministered to Jesus. Jesus had triumphed over the devil by using the word of God as a sword against Satan. "It is written", "It is written", Jesus said on numerous occasions to show that the Old Testament Scriptures have authority. He wanted to make it clear that the words He said were not His own but were God's words.

The Bible is God's Word. It is likened to a sword. A two-edged sword. Therefore, it is essential for the believer to become familiar with this 'sword of the Spirit' by reading and meditating upon it as the Word of God. Only then can the follower of Christ be effective in their witness for Christ and in their warfare against the enemy of their soul. (Eph. 6:17).

> "Go, study the Bible, God's Word is a light,
> That brightly will shine in your way;
> Twill warn you of dangers, 'twill lead you aright,
> From time to eternity's day."

Eliza E. Hewitt (1851-1920)

THE MOUNT OF TEACHING

Matthew 5:1-12

In His sermon on the Mount, we have eight beatitudes of Jesus that act like a map to guide us into the kingdom of God.

1. *Blessed are the poor in spirit, for theirs is the kingdom of God"* The poor in spirit are those who are conscious of their sins and their failures. They know in their hearts that they are unworthy of the grace and love of a holy God. To be poor in spirit is to acknowledge a need in asking for God's mercy.

2. **Blessed are they that mourn, for they shall be comforted.** Jesus is referring to 'godly sorrow'. When someone takes sin seriously in their lives and are sorry and ask for forgiveness they are forgiven. In this way they are comforted.

3. **Blessed are the meek, for they shall inherit the earth.** Meekness is not weakness. Moses was called the meekest of all men and he certainly was not weak. The meek and gentle are not given to vengeance. It will be the meek who will inherit the earth when they reign with Christ at His coming kingdom.

4. **Blessed are those who hunger and thirst for righteousness, for they shall be satisfied.** Some of the rich and famous are

bitterly unhappy having discovered that their wealth and their fame do not satisfy. They hunger after the wrong things. To hunger after righteousness is to be in accordance with what is: honourable, upright, virtuous, noble, morally right, and ethical.

5. **Blessed are the merciful, for they shall obtain mercy.** One who is truly merciful gives a hungry man food and a lonely person companionship. Being merciful is meeting a need – not just feeling it. And In return they will receive mercy.

6. **Blessed are the pure in heart, for they shall see God.** Only the pure in heart can see God. Jesus came, not only to save us, but to make us pure and acceptable in God's sight.

7. **Blessed are the peacemakers, for they shall be called the sons of God.** God's peacemakers are those who already have made their peace with God through faith in Christ. They are the peacemakers who are able accomplish peace by bringing others to submit to God's truth.

8. **Blessed are they that suffer persecution for justice's sake, for theirs is the Kingdom of God.** To be a Christian in some countries carries the death penalty. There is evidence that proves that more Christians around the world have been martyred for their faith in the 20th century alone, than in the combined previous 2000 years of the church's history. The promise to those who suffer for Christ is: *"theirs is the kingdom of God."*

'The Beatitudes are an encouragement to those who experience various KINDS of oppression. The promise of blessings is to each of these oppressed groups. Each of these eight Beatitudes highlight the qualities and attitudes valued in the Kingdom of God.'

THE MOUNT OF PRAYER
Matthew 14:23

Jesus spent much of His time with His disciples and with people. But there were times He sought solitude and would dismiss the crowds, and even His own disciples, that He might spend time in alone with His Father. He chose a place where He could have His mind free from having to think about the needs of the crowds that always followed Him. Unlike us, He did not have the same reasons for prayer as we do. He did not have to confess sin for He was without sin. (John 8:45-47)

Jesus was subject to all the temptations of man. Having taken on the form of a human being He endured temptation like all men, yet without sin (Heb. 4:15). He would have prayed for strength in facing and overcoming the many temptations He had to face. And He would have prayed for the courage He would need to finish His Father's mission that would end on a cross. The fact that Jesus was aware of His need to seek solitude and prayer should also motivate us to do likewise. The lesson for us is clear. If Jesus prayed how much more, we should make prayer a part of our lives. What is prayer?

> Prayer is the soul's sincere desire,
> Unuttered or expressed;
> The motion of a hidden fire,
> That trembles in the breast.

> Prayer is the burden of a sigh,
> The falling of a tear;
> The upward glancing of an eye,
> When none but God is near.
>
> Prayer is the Christian's vital breath,
> The Christian's native air;
> His watchword at the gates of death -
> He enters heaven with prayer.
>
> James Mongomery (1771-1854)

There are times when we need to disengage ourselves from the outside world. As we shut the door on all its distractions we are inwardly refreshed as we wait before God, meditating on who He is and what He has done for us. Prayer is as vital to our spiritual lives as oxygen is to our bodies. A prayerless believer can never know a close walk with God.

> Restraining prayer, we cease to fight,
> Prayer makes the Christian's armour bright;
> And Satan trembles when he sees,
> The weakest saint upon his knees."
>
> William Cowper (1731-1800)

THE MOUNT OF TRANSFIGURATION

Matthew 17:1-5

Six days after foretelling His death, Jesus takes Peter, James and John and leads them up a high mountain. Early tradition identifies Mount Tabor as being the Mount of His transfiguration. It rises to a height of about (1,900 feet, 2835 meters). Today, it is the location of the "Church of the Transfiguration", built on the ruins of a fourth-century church.

The word 'transfigured' in Greek means a change that comes from within. In His transfiguration, the glory of Jesus radiated from within and shone through His physical body revealing His divine nature. His face shone like the sun and his clothes became as white as light. He shone with heavenly brightness so much so that there was no adequate earthly description for it. Peter, James and John had a glimpse of the glory that Jesus had in heaven before he was sent by God into the world to die for the sins of the world. (John 3:16). Later, Peter was to write, *"they were eyewitnesses of His majesty."*

The patriarch Moses and the prophet Elijah appeared with Him on the mount. Moses had lived about 1400 years before Jesus, Elijah some 900 years yet they were alive and in a resurrected, glorified state. They talked with Jesus about what He would accomplish in Jerusalem. They did not converse with the three disciples but with Jesus, their Lord and Master.

Perhaps Peter was so overwhelmed by the scene he was witnessing that he didn't know what he was saying: *"Lord it is good for us to be here. If you wish, I will; put up three shelters, one for you, one for Moses and one for Eijah."* The effect of his words put Jesus on an equal footing with Moses and Elijah in building shrines for each of them. God would have none of it. *"This is my beloved Son, whom I love, with him I am well pleased. Listen to him."*

Everything points us to Jesus. He is the centre of God's plan for the coming of a new age. No one is before Him, no one is equal to Him, and no one will come after Him. He is the Alpha and the Omega, the beginning and the end, and to Him, and Him alone every knee will bow and call Him Lord.

> "At the Name of Jesus every knee shall bow,
> every tongue confess Him King of glory now;
> 'tis the Father's pleasure we should call Him Lord,
> Who from the beginning was the mighty Word.
>
> In your hearts enthrone Him; there let Him subdue,
> all that is not holy, all that is not true.
> Look to Him, your Saviour, in temptations' hour;
> let His will enfold you in its light and power.
>
> Caroline Maria Noel (1817-1877)

THE MOUNT OF PROPHECY
Matt 24:1-44

When Jesus left the Temple, his disciples called his attention to its size and splendour. It wasn't just big; it was also beautiful. Herod the Great (who ruled when Jesus was born) greatly expanded and improved on Zerubbabel's temple. (516 BC. After Herod's work, the temple was enormous: 450 metres long and 450 metres wide. The sight was the centre of Jewish life for almost a thousand years. Do you see all these things? Jesus asked, *"I tell you the truth, not one stone here will be left on another, every stone will be thrown down."*

Jesus then climbed the Mount of Olives with his disciples where they had a panoramic view of the Temple 80 meters below from where they were sitting. *"Tell us,"* they asked, *"when will this happen, and what will be the sign of your coming and the end of the age?"* Jesus replied, *"Watch out that no-one deceives you."* He then began to tell them of future events that would occur in the world prior to His second coming and the end of the age.

There will be false prophets who will claim to be Christ and will appear to perform great signs and miracles that will deceive whole nations. Nations will be at war against other nations world-wide. Famines, pestilences and earthquakes will become more frequent and more intense before the end of the age. There will be a time of great tribulation such as the world has never known. It will be a time unparalleled in cruelty and catastrophe. Lawlessness will abound, and the love of many will grow cold.

There will be standing in the holy place an abomination that causes desolation spoken of through the prophet Daniel. Immediately after the tribulation the sun shall be darkened, the moon shall not give her light, and the stars shall fall from heaven, and the powers of the heavens shall be shaken. Then will appear in the heaven the sign of the Son of man and all the peoples of the world will cry out in fear. All the nations of the world will see the Son of Man coming in great power and glory. And the angels will gather the people of God from one end of the heavens to the other.

Jesus then said to his disciples now learn a lesson from the fig tree. When you see the leaves, you know summer is near. Likewise, when you see all these signs the end of the age is near. In AD 70, about 40 years after Jesus spoke these words, there was a widespread Jewish revolution against the Romans in Palestine. The Romans brutally crushed the rebel; Jerusalen was levelled and the temple destroyed. Not one stone was left on another just as Jesus said would happen. So, it shall be in the future events.

> "Live close to Him and trust His love,
> Assured that while on earth we roam,
> whatever may come, He bends above
> To guide His children safely home.
> Live close to Him and trust His love"
>
> James Rowe (1865-1933)

THE MOUNT OF TRIUMPH

Matt 27:32-56, John 19:30

Condemned to death by a man who knew He was innocent; Jesus was made to carry his cross to Mount Calvary situated outside the wall of Jerusalem to be crucified. Death by crucifixion was the cruellest and most humiliating form of punishment in the ancient world widely used across the Roman Empire. It was designed to make the victim die publicly, slowly, with great pain and humiliation. This was the method of death God intended for Jesus to die for our sins. His last sayings from the Cross:

1. *Father, forgive them; for they know not what they do."* (Luke 23:34). **Forgiveness**. On His mind there was no hatred, revenge or self-pity, but eternal forgiveness. Jesus demonstrated a depth of forgiveness that passes our understanding.

2. *"Truly I say to you, today you will be with me in paradise."* (Luke 23:43) **Salvation**. A crucified sinner prays to a crucified Saviour. For the one who turned to him in repentant faith, received the promise of life.

3. *"Woman, behold your son. To the disciple. Behold your mother."* (John 19:26-27) **Relationship**. As he dies, he settles his earthly obligations as best he can. With His thoughts on Mary's future

security and protection, Jesus entrusted her into the care of John, His beloved disciple.

4. *"My God, my God, why have you forsaken me?* (Matthew 27:46. Mark 15:34) **Abandonment**. He was made a curse for us and felt the full flood of God's righteous wrath upon Him. It is difficult to understand in what sense Jesus was abandoned by God.

5. *"I thirst."* (John 19:28) **Distress**. It reminds us again of the incredible physical suffering that Jesus suffered on our behalf. He accepted a tasted of diluted wine; to wet His parched lips and dry throat so He could make one final announcement to the world with a clear, loud voice.

6. *"It is finished."* (John 19:30) **Victory**. The words 'It is finished" were not spoken in a whisper. It was a shout of triumph, a cry of victory. The task of earning the salvation of the world was completed in his work on the cross. The types, promises, and prophecies, sacrifices and ceremonies were finished. The power of Satan, sin and death was finished. The work His Father had entrusted to Him was finished.

7. *"Father, into thy hands I commend my spirit."* (John 19:30) **Reunion**. No one took Jesus' life from Him. Jesus said, *"I lay down my life that I may take it again. No one takes it from Me, but I lay it down of Myself. I have power to lay it down, and I have power to take it again"* (John 10:17-18). Jesus gave up His spirit and breathed His last. He was buried and three days later He rose from the dead and returned to His Father in Heaven.

THE MOUNT OF COMMISSION
Matthew 28:18-20

In His resurrected body Jesus walked and talked and ate with those to whom He appeared to show them He was physically alive. He was able to appear and disappear, even behind closed doors. The 40 days between Jesus' resurrection and ascension He appeared to many people. He made Himself known to Mary Magdalene and to the women near the tomb. He walked and talked with two of His disciples on the Road to Emmaus. He appeared to Peter and the Apostles behind locked doors. And to doubting Thomas. He provided a miraculous catch of fish for His disciples. And He appeared to more than 500 people at the same time. (Matthew 28, Mark 16, Luke 24, John 20 +21).

The eleven disciples were told by Jesus to go to Galilee, and to a mountain where they would see Him. The text doesn't indicate which mountain it was where Jesus gathered His disciples. He spoke to them, saying, *"All authority has been given to Me in heaven and on earth. Go therefore and make disciples of all nations, baptizing them in the name of the Father and the Son and of the Holy Spirit, teaching them to observe all things that I have commanded you: and lo, I am with you always, even to the end of the age".*

"Who is to go out of that first band of disciples? It is Peter, the rash and the headstrong. It is John, who sometimes wishes to call fire from heaven to destroy men. It is Philip, with whom the Saviour has been so long, and *yet he has not known him. It is Thomas, who must put his finger into the print of the nails, or he will not believe him. Yet the Master says to them, 'Go; therefore, all power is given unto me, therefore go.' You are as good for my purpose as anybody else would be. There is no power in you, but then all power is in me, therefore go."* (C H. Spurgeon).

It is His authority and power that enables us to step out boldly to proclaim the gospel to the world. There is no place on earth where the gospel of Jesus should not be preached and where disciples are not made. His promise is ever sure: *I am with you always, even to the end of the age"*. In His command to *"baptize them in the name of the Father and of the Son and of the Holy Spirit," He* uses the singular noun *name* (not 'names') highlighting the unity of the Trinity. Baptism is a symbol of Christ's burial and resurrection. It is a symbol of our new life as a Christian.

> "Lord, You give the Great Commission:
> Heal the sick and preach Your word.
> Lest Your Church neglect its mission,
> And Your gospel goes unheard.
> Help us witness to Your purpose,
> With renewed integrity:
> With the Spirit's gifts empower us,
> For the work of ministry."
>
> Jeffery W. Rowthorn (1934 -)

LET US FEAR

Hebrews 4:1

"Therefore, since the promise of entering his rest still stands, let us fear that none of you be found to have fallen short of it"

The writer of Hebrews has a word of warning for the Christians to whom he sends his letter. The letter is addressed to a Christian community whose faith was faltering because of strong Jewish influences. This verse continues the line of thought from chapter 3. This is made clear by use of the word *"therefore"* meaning what follows is an application of what has come before. What came before is the example of Israel's failure. The Hebrew people failed to fully trust in God, and as a result they were denied entry into the Promised Land. Because of their disbelief and their disobedience, they were left wandering in the desert for 40 years.

God saved His people from their slavery in Egypt so they could enter all the blessings He had prepared for them in the Promised Land. For forty long years they wandered in the dry and barren wilderness far from delights God had planned for them so long before under the leadership of Moses He rescued them from Egyptian slavery. God bought then *out* of Egypt so they would enter Canaan. But because of their unbelief and disobedience they were drifting around in a desert place.

Sadly, that is the experience of many believers. They have been saved but they are wandering around in a spiritual desert. Their spiritual lives are dry. Through their unbelief or disobedience, they are missing out on all the blessings that God wants to give them. God has an eternal plan for those who trust in Jesus as their Saviour. But His plan can only come to completion through our total commitment to Him. He needs our co-operation in aligning ourselves with His will for our lives. His ultimate intention for all His people is that they be transformed into the image of His Son, Jesus Christ. Nothing is more important in our Christian lives than that.

"Let us fear" lest we fall short of God not being able to fulfil His purpose in our lives because of our unbelief or disobedience. The rest that He promises is found in Christ alone but only to those who have made Him Lord of their lives and live only for please Him.

> "Jesus! I am resting, resting,
> In the joy of who You are,
> I am finding out the greatness,
> of Your loving heart.
> You have bid me gaze upon You,
> And Your beauty fills my soul,
> For by Your transforming power,
> You have made me whole."
>
> Jean S. Pigott (1844-1882) Adapted

LET US BE FAITHFUL
Hebrews 4:14

"Therefore, since we have a great high priest who has gone into heaven, Jesus the Son of God, let us hold firmly to the faith we profess."

We face many difficulties in our pilgrimage to the celestial City. Our lives on earth are fraught with troubles and temptations no matter how close we walk with God. We are not wrapped in cottonwool! We live surrounded by evil and its effects inevitable interferes with our own lives. We need the help of our great High Priest who sits at the right hand of the Father to face life's difficulties. (Heb. 1:3). Jesus became the High Priest for every believer. He stands above the priests of the Old and New Testaments. He is "great" in the sense that it puts all other priesthoods in a minor status. He symbolizes power, authority and acceptance. Jesus ascended into heaven and now ministers there for our sake.

"We do not have a High Priest who is unable to sympathize with our weaknesses, but we have one who has been tempted in every way, just as we are, yet was without sin." (Heb 4:15). Jesus knows and feels what we go through. He suffers along with us. He feels our pain. This should encourage us to hold fast our confession of faith. This means holding firmly to what we believe about Jesus. We believe that His sacrificial death on the cross was for the sins of the whole world. We believe it is by faith alone in Jesus that we are saved from the penalty of sin which is spiritual death.

We believe that He alone is the only way to God. No one can come to God but through Him. We profess that in Him alone is salvation, eternal life and happiness, and that He will return in glory to judge the world. And we are encouraged to *"hold firmly to the faith we profess."*

As our High Priest He never ceases to intercede for us. It is the intercession of our Great High Priest that keeps us in the faith. It is the intercession of Jesus that recalls and renews us when we have sinned, it is the intercession of Jesus that gives us access into the very presence of God. It is the intercession of Jesus that makes our prayers acceptable to God (1 Peter 2:4-5).

> *"Before the throne of God above,*
> *I have a strong, a perfect plea;*
> *A Great High Priest, whose name is love,*
> *Whoever lives and pleads for me.*
> *My name is graven on His hands,*
> *My name is written on His heart;*
> *I know that while with God He stands,*
> *No tongue can bid me thence depart."*
>
> Charitie L. Bancroft (1841-1923)

LET US BE BOLD

Hebrews 4:16

"Therefore, let us boldly approach the throne of grace with confidence, so that we may receive mercy and find grace to help us in our time of need."

The Holy of Holies was the innermost and most sacred area of the ancient tabernacle of Moses and the temple of Jerusalem. Only on one day of the year, Yom Kippur, the Day of Atonement, was the high priest permitted to enter the Holy of Holies. He had first to be consecrated and ordained via a ritual that emphasized the need for cleansing him symbolically before putting on his robes and taking up his work. He had to bring the blood of a sacrificed bull and sprinkle it on the Ark of the Covenant to atone for his sin, and the national sins of the people of Israel. (Leviticus 16). There was a Jewish tradition that the high priest would enter the Holy of Holies with a rope tied to his foot. The purpose of the rope was to retrieve the high priest's body in case he died in the course of his duties within the Holy of Holies.

Behind the curtain inside the Holy of Holies was the Ark of the Covenant which had always been a symbol of God's presence throughout Jewish history. The curtain was a constant reminder that sinful humanity could not enter the presence of a holy God.

When from the cross Jesus cried, *"It is finished,"* it was not with a whisper, but with a mighty shout of triumph, a cry of victory. All the types, the promises, the prophecies, sacrifices and ceremonies in the Old Testament were finished. There was no longer any need for the sacrifice of sheep, goats, bulls, doves or pigeons. Jesus had paid the ultimate sacrifice for the sins of the world.

When Jesus cried out *"Father, into your hands I commit my spirit", and yielded up His spirit the curtain of the temple was torn in two from top to bottom.* The temple curtain symbolized the separation of God from sinful man. The tearing of the curtain symbolized the start of a new relationship with God. He tore the curtain that separated us from Him. Jesus has opened a new way, the only way, for us to find peace with God. He said, *"I am the way, no man can come to the Father but by me."* (John 14:6). We are encouraged, t*herefore, to come boldly to the throne of grace with confidence, so that we may receive mercy and find grace to help us in our time of need."*

> *"Come, you who from your hearts believe,*
> *That Jesus answers prayer,*
> *Come boldly to a throne of grace,*
> *And claim His promise there.*
> *That if His love in us abides,*
> *And we in Him are one,*
> *Whatever in His name we ask,*
> *It surely will be done".*
>
> Fanny Crosby (1820-1915)

LET US BE MATURE
Hebrews 6:1-2

"Therefore, let us leave the elementary teachings about Christ and let us press on to maturity, not laying again the foundation of repentance from acts that lead to death, and of faith in God, instruction about baptisms, the laying on of hands, the resurrection of the dead and eternal judgment".

Some scholars believe this letter was written for Jewish Christians who lived in Jerusalem about 64 AD. It appears that some had difficulties in leaving behind the ceremonies and sacrifices of the Old Testament. There were some similarities between Judaism and Christianity that made it possible for converted Jews to think they could hold to both simultaneously. Repentance from dead works, faith toward God, instructions about washings, laying on of hands, the resurrection from the dead, and eternal judgment represent basic Christian doctrines that would correspond to some Jewish teaching. These things are what the writer calls the elementary teachings about Christ. In short, they are basic doctrines.

"Therefore, let us leave the elementary teachings about Christ and let us press on to maturity." This directive to press on to maturity is not just for those early Jews but for every Christian. We should never forget the elementary teachings that we have already learned about Christ, but

the writer urges us to go beyond the basics and press on to a fuller and greater understanding about God and His will for us. Many Christians have never risen above the elementary teachings of the gospel. Spiritually speaking, even after 20, or 30 years they are still spiritually immature, and living like spiritual paupers unaware of all the riches in Christ they are missing.

"Mark time" was an order given out by the Regt. Sargent Major to a marching group of soldiers under his command. Left-right, left-right on the spot. There can be no "marking time" in our spiritual lives. We are urged to press forward on to spiritual maturity. There is no such thing in the Christian life as standing still. A fervent prayer life, quiet meditation upon His Word and a thirst to know more of Christ are evidence that we are pressing on to spiritual maturity. As we do so we shall grow in our knowledge of God, have a deeper intimacy with God and a greater enjoyment of God.

> "I asked the Lord that I might grow,
> In faith, and love, and every grace;
> Might more of His salvation know,
> And seek, more earnestly, His face."
>
> John Newton (1725-1807

LET US BE SINCERE
Hebrews 10:22

"Let us draw near to God with a sincere heart in full assurance of faith, having our hearts sprinkled to cleanse us from a guilty conscience and having our bodies washed with pure water."

"*Let us draw near to God with a sincere heart in full assurance of faith.*" Our confidence in drawing close to Him rests on what Christ has done for us - what He has accomplished on our behalf when He laid aside his glory and came to earth as a Man. We have absolutely nothing that makes us acceptable to God but only our repentance and faith in His Son, Jesus, as our Saviour and Lord. A sincere heart means being true and loyal to the Lord. In full assurance of faith means being fully persuaded that God will accept us based upon what His Son, Jesus has done for us.

"*Having our hearts sprinkled to cleanse us from a guilty conscience and having our bodies washed with pure water.*" This symbolic cleansing is referred to by David. "*Purge me with hyssop, and I shall be clean; was me, and I shall be whiter than snow*" Psalm 51:7). The inward cleansing of the heart took place when a repentant sinner was redeemed by faith in Christ. Both *"sprinkled"* and *"washed"* refer to the spiritual, not material.

It is not the simple practice of water baptism to which this verse is referring when it speaks of *"having our bodies washed with pure water."* *"Baptism is the outward sign of an inward cleansing, and it is the latter that was more important."* Leon Morris. (1914-2006). That inward cleansing took place when we were born anew by the Spirit of God. The washing of the body through water baptism is simple a sign of one's testimony to the world that they are now a follower of Christ. We now have a High Priest to represent us before God. (Heb. 4:16). As we draw near to Him with a sincere heart, in full assurance of faith, He will draw near to us. (James 4:8).

> "O for a heart to praise my God,
> a heart from sin set free;
> a heart that's sprinkled with the blood,
> so freely shed for me.
>
> A heart resigned, submissive, meek,
> my great Redeemer's throne;
> where only Christ is heard to speak,
> where Jesus reigns alone.
>
> A humble, lowly, contrite heart,
> believing, true, and clean,
>
> which neither life nor death can part,
> from Him that dwells within."
>
> Charles Wesley (1707-1788)

MY LORD - MY STRENGTH - MY REDEEMER

Psalm 19:14

"May the words of my mouth and the meditation of my heart be pleasing in your sight, O Lord, my Strength and my Redeemer"

David pours out praise to the glory of God displayed throughout His creation. He looks above and sees the entire heavenly vista - the sun, the stars, the planets - that tell of God's presence, God's wisdom, and God's power to all earths inhabitants. There are no places on earth that His handiwork is not seen. (vv.1-6). David also praised God for the wisdom offered through His Law. About 300 years earlier, God gave His Law to Moses beginning with the Ten Commandments. (Exodus 31:18). God's law was more desirable to David than gold. (v.10). *"The Law of the Lord is perfect, restoring the soul; the testimony of the Lord is sure' making wise the simple; the commandment of the Lord is pure, enlightening the eyes. (vv 7-8).*

David longed to have a closer walk with God. He knew that real godliness was not only a matter of what a man did, but also of what he said and thought in his heart. He prayed, *"May the words of my mouth and the meditation of my heart be pleasing in your sight, O Lord, my Rock and my Redeemer."* There are so many ways we can sin with our words, James writes, *"The tongue is a fire, the very world of iniquity; it is set among our members as that which defiles the entire body, and sets on fire the course of our life, and is set on fire by hell."* Who can tame the tongue? *"No one can tame the tongue. It is a restless evil, and full of deadly poison"* (James 3:1-12). It is a reminder to us all to carefully weigh up our words before we speak for Jesus said, *"I tell you, on the day of Judgment people will give an account for every careless word you speak, for by your words you will be justified, and by your words you will be condemned."* (Matthew 12:36-37).

"Let the meditation of my heart be pleasing in your sight, O Lord, my Strength and my Redeemer." David desired purity of mind and heart. He wanted only to speak words that were pleasing and acceptable to God from a pure mind. His petition was that the meditation of his heart would be pleasing in God's sight. There is so much that the followers of Christ can meditatre upon. We can meditate upon what He has done for us. His love and His mercy and sacrifice for us. And we can meditate upon His Word. As we do so we can say with full assurance, Jesus is *my* LORD. Jesus is *my* STRENGTH and Jesus is *my* REDEEMER.'

"He is my Refuge, my Rock, and my Tower,

> He is my Fortress, my Strength and my Power;
> Life everlasting, my Saviour is He,
> Blessed Redeemer – Jesus for me."

>> William J. Kirkpatrick. (1838-1921) Adapted

POETRY

Beyond The Furthest Star

To go beyond the furthest star,
Far past all worlds above;
Though lost within the depths of space,
I'm still within God's love.

No mortal souls beyond His reach,
It knows no depth, nor height;
No borders to its width nor length,
God's love is infinite.

His love revealed on Calvary's Cross,
I cannot comprehend;
When Jesus died to save my soul,
T' was love that knows no end.

Exalted high above all angels,
Raised to heaven above;
Jesus shall rule the universe,
In righteousness and love.

Resplendent In Your Holiness

Resplendent in Your holiness,
The saints gaze on Your splendour;
Saved solely by Your grace,
Their praise endures forever.

Blessed are they who dwell with You,
Your face they now can see;
Made perfect in Your likeness, Lord,
In love and purity.

Like the saints in heaven above,
Who were saved by grace;
Make me pure in heart, O Lord;
That I might see Your face.

Create in me a clean heart, Lord,
Free from sin and guile;
That when I see Your face, O Lord,
I'll also see Your smile.

Lord Of All Creation

Lord of all creation,
You sit on heaven's throne;
Heaven and earth and all above,
Belongs to You alone.

All power is in Your hands,
With all authority;
All peoples shall confess you, Lord,
And all on bended knee.

What love could make You leave,
Heaven's eternal Throne?
It was your love for lost sinners;
To claim them for Your own.

You died on Calvary's Cross,
You appeared in human form;
You exchanged Your
crown of glory,
For a crown of thorns.

When my time on earth is done,
I'll join the host in heaven;
With them I'll raise my voice,
In praise and adoration.

No eye has seen no ear has heard,
What Heaven's treasure be;
To dwell in Your eternal presence,
Shall be enough for me.

The brightness of Your glory,
Fills heaven with Your light;
The saints of heaven
dwell with You,
Robed in dazzling white.

They worship and adore You,
On earth I join their praise;
Lord of Lord, King of kings,
My songs to You I raise.

Sovereign Lord, King Of Kings

Sovereign Lord, King of kings,
You rule the Universe;
Seated on Your royal Throne,
You reign in righteousness.

Lord, I lift my heart to You,
Your name be blessed forever;
You are the Saviour of mankind,
Almighty to deliver.

The Sun and Moon and stars above,
Created by Your Hand;
Kept by Your mighty power;
They move at your Command.

In time they all shall pass away,
And all the world shall see;
When you return to earth,
In power and majesty.

No mortal mind can comprehend,
The depth of Your great love;
Its deeper than the deepest sea,
And higher than heaven above.

No forces in the Universe,
No superpowers on earth;
Can ever part me from your love,
In this life nor in death.

Your handiwork seen in the stars,
For all the world to see;
Proclaims Your wisdom and your power,
To all humanity.

Let all the dwellers on the earth,
Proclaim their love for You;
In songs of everlasting praise,
In anthems old and new.

My Tower Of Strength

You are my Tower of Strength,
Throughout the storms of life;
My Refuge and my Guide,
In times of calm and strife.

My Rock and my Defender,
In You I find my peace;
I rest in You, my Saviour,
My thanks will never cease.

My future is in Your hands, O Lord,
No safer place to be;
Content am I to leave it there,
You know what's best for me.

The path for me You've chosen
Will work out for my gain;
Though it be a path of thorns,
May it glorify Your Name.

From North and South, East and West,
May songs of praise be sung;
To Jesus, Saviour of the world,
Our God's beloved Son.

You are the Lord of lords,
You are the King of kings;
You shall rule the Universe,
All praise to you I bring.

Jesus The Light Of The World

Jesus, Light of the world,
You shine in this world of sin;
Your peace and full salvation,
Dispels all fears within.

Send out your truth and light,
To guide us on our way;
That as we walk in Your light,
We'll never go astray.

Jesus, O King of kings,
You came from heaven above;
The Light of life, the bread of life,
The Fount of Life and Love.

O teach us how to live our lives,
Your truth and love proclaim;
Your light and love shine through us,
Brings glory to Your Name.

Jesus, Guide of our lives,
Your will in us be done;
That we might be like You,
God's Beloved Son.

You died to save us from our sin,
To save the human race;
May our lives reflect, O Lord,
Your life, Your love, and grace.

Thank You, Lord

Thank you, Lord, for choosing me,
a wretch of little worth;
You breathed new life into my soul,
and gave me second birth.

The life You now have given to me,
I want to live for You;
Lord let it be a life well lived,
to do what You would do.

Help me Lord, to walk Your way,
in love and purity;
Fulfil your will throughout my life,
the life you planned for me.

Create in me a heart made pure,
a copy of Your own;
Where You alone will reign supreme,
my heart your royal throne.

Teach me Lord to love your Word,
a light that guides my way;
Your Word my chart and compass,
that will not let me stray.

Open O Lord, my darkened eyes,
to see Your truths within;
Write them upon my heart and mind,
to keep me from all sin.

When O Lord, my death draws near,
my peace I'll find in Thee;
As I exchange my mortal life,
for immortality,

Lead me through the realms of Light,
what joy when at Your feet,
To kneel before You, O my Lord,
both faultless and complete.

Spirit Of God

Sent into this world, O Spirit of God,
You were sent from the Father above;
You came to impart the second birth,
God's life - God's peace - God's love.

You came to exalt Jesus on high,
As our Saviour and our Lord;
To show He is the only way,
The only way to God.

You came to dwell in our hearts,
To transform us from within;
To keep us from all evil,
That we might be like Him.

You are our Teacher, O Spirit of God,
To teach us how to live;
That we should live like Jesus,
Our thanks to Him must give.

Prince Of Life

Great is Your love, O Prince of life,
For us You came to save;
To impart to us eternal life,
And hope beyond our grave.

Great is Your peace, O Prince of peace,
The peace that You convey;
A peace that only You can give,
Nor the world can take away.

Great is Your power, O Lord of lords,
Before You all shall kneel;
You alone will reign supreme,
When Your power You reveal.

Great is Your majesty, O King of kings,
Matchless is Your fame;
All monarchs of this world will bow,
And pay homage to Your name.

From Every Nation

From every nation, tribe and tongue,
The saints in heaven meet;
They join with heaven's angels,
To worship at Your feet.

Ten thousand times, ten thousand,
All saints in heaven proclaim;
We've saved by grace alone,
And sing praises to His Name.

They wear the robes of righteousness,
Arrayed in robes of white;
And stand before Your Mercy Seat,
Accepted in Your sight.

You came to earth to save us,
All thanks to You be given;
From sin and death you raised us up,
To be with You in heaven.

Glory, wisdom, honour and power,
To You alone belong;
Thank You Lord for saving us,
Endless is our song.

Alpha & Omega

Jesus, the Alpha and Omega,
The Beginning and the End;
The eternal God incarnate,
My eternal Friend.

You left behind Your glory,
To obey Your Father's will;
To die for our salvation,
On the Cross on Calvary's Hill.

When You return in glory,
And time will cease to be;
Your reign will never end,
Throughout eternity.

You're the Alpha and Omega,
The Beginning and the End;
At Your name, Lord Jesus,
Every knee will bend.

Endless Is The Universe

O Lord, God Almighty,
Worthy of all praise;
Your awesome power and wisdom,
The Universe displays.

Great is Your creation,
Sustained by Your own Hand;
It's majesty and splendour,
Revealed to every land.

Endless is the Universe,
As countless stars I see;
In Your wisdom; Almighty God,
You know its destiny.

You are its great Creator,
The Author of its birth;
Its stars surpass in number,
The grains of sand on earth.

We give You thanks, O God,
We praise Your holy Name;
Great Your mercy, great Your love,
For us Your Son was slain.

Jesus will rule the Universe,
As Saviour, Lord and King;
All power is in His hands,
Endless praise to Him we bring.

How Great You Are Lord

How great you are, O Lord,
On heaven's throne above;
Awesome in Your holiness,
Endless in Your love.

Your sacrifice upon the Cross,
Gave us peace and rest;
Removed our sin; so far from us,
Far as east is from the west.

In place of death; You gave us life,
In place of guilt; Your peace;
In place of darkness; You gave us light,
And our fears You made to cease.

Jesus, Saviour of the world,
You saved us by Your grace;
To be with You in heaven,
Where we shall see Your face.

Let all the angels worship You,
All creatures here on earth;
With all the heavenly hosts in heaven,
Throughout the Universe.

Offer up their praises, Lord;
To You, who set us free;
And we on earth shall join their praise,
Throughout eternity.

Your Love

Your love, O Lord, reached out to us,
You called us by our name;
You gave us peace and joy,
In place of guilt and shame.

We thank you, Lord, we thank You,
We long to see your face;
Your mercy that has saved us,
'Twas only by Your grace.

Our hearts in love o'er flow to You,
Our Shepherd, Guide and Stay;
You are the Bread that feeds our souls,
The Light that guides our way.

O Jesus, Saviour, Lord and Friend,
Our Source of Peace and Rest;
Our Helper throughout all our days,
In You we're truly blessed.

Forever In Your Debt O Lord

Forever in Your debt, O Lord,
I shall ever be;
In place of condemnation,
You have pardoned me.

I was not even good enough,
that you should die for me;
A sinner and a rebel,
yet you set me free.

Not all the riches of this world,
could my ransom pay;
Your sacrifice on Calvary's Cross,
was the only way.

You shed your precious blood for me,
this, my ransom paid;
To free my soul from sin and death,
on You, my sin was laid.

Forever in your debt, O Lord,
I shall ever be;
Both in my life upon this earth,
and through eternity.

O my Saviour and my God,
my life you have reclaimed;
Let it be a life well lived,
to glorify your name.

From Eternity Into Time

You stepped from eternity into time,
Leaving Your glory behind;
You took the form of a human,
To die on a Cross for mankind.

You did not come to be our Judge,
To judge us for our failures;
Love and mercy brought you,
To come and be our Saviour.

The price you paid for our sin,
That salvation we would gain;
Was Your precious blood,
Shed on the Cross of shame.

You knew there was no other way,
To save from condemnation;
T 'was only by Your sacrifice,
Could give us full salvation.

O Son of Man, O Son of God,
Lord of Life and Prince of Peace;
Creator of the Universe,
Your reign shall never cease.

I Am His New Creation

I am His new creation,
all praise and thanks to Him;
The old has gone, the new has come,
He changed me from within.

He saved me from a life of sin,
and from its condemnation;
Shed His blood on Calvary's Cross,
and purchased my salvation.

His promise to the burdened
"I will give you rest';
Free from guilt and fear,
and a heart of heaviness.

This is Christ's own promise,
To those who make this plea;
"Forgive me Lord, accept my life,
And let me follow Thee".

His load is light and easy,
His promises are true;
He is my Helper all through life,
He'll lead me safely through.

It's not my hold on Him I trust,
but His firm hold on me;
He'll not forsake me now in time,
nor through eternity.

And when on Judgment Day,
as I kneel before His throne;
He'll not turn His back on me,
He'll claim me for His own.

With all the saints in heaven,
this my song I'll sing;
How great is Your mercy,
my Saviour and my King.

The Lord Of Hosts

The Lord of hosts is with us,
Jehovah is His Name;
The God of light and power,
Whose victory we proclaim.

He sent His Son, Lord Jesus,
To conquer sin and death;
He broke the power of Satan,
By rising from the dead.

The power of hell couldn't hold Him,
The Prince of darkness failed;
The Hand of God His Father,
Upon His Son prevailed.

Jesus now is Conqueror,
Angelic hosts now sing;
That at his Name shall every tongue,
Confess Him Lord and King.

All praise to God our Father,
Who sent His Son to give;
Salvation full and free,
That man with Christ might live.

All praise to Christ our Saviour,
Whose victory we proclaim;
Worthy of all praises,
We magnify His Name.

You Gave Me Life

You gave me life, eternal life,
that I might live with You;
You raised me from the state of death,
and gave me life anew.

You set my feet upon life's path;
with joy I now can sing;
O grave where is Your victory?
O death where is your sting?

You gave me peace, eternal peace,
the world could never give;
A peace that stills my anxious heart,
and drives away all fear.

I know not what my future holds,
my times are in Your hands;
Your peace assures me I am safe,
held fast in Your right Hand.

You gave me hope, eternal hope,
the anchor of my soul;
Holds me steadfast through life's
trials, and bids me onward go.

This world is not my final home,
I'm just a passing through;
My destiny is heaven above,
For ever-more with You.

You gave me joy, eternal joy,
with joy I now can sing;
A song of praise to You my Lord,
my Saviour, Friend and King.

You are a friend to all who grieve,
you are the Prince of peace;
O King of kings and Lord of lords,
your reign will never cease.

Your Love Reached Out To Me

Your love, O Lord, reached out to me,
it touched my heart and set me free;
Free from sin, from guilt, and shame,
now free to praise Your holy Name.

Restored, forgiven, my life made new,
with songs of praise I worship You;
Forever in Your debt I live,
my life, my all, to You I give.

Your glory and Your love divine,
in my life, O let them shine;
That searching souls in me shall see,
the likeness of Your life in me.

And when my life on earth is run,
to hear Your welcome words: 'Well Done',
Will fill my soul with boundless joy,
to dwell with You for evermore.

Precious Is Your Love

Precious is your love,
endless beyond all measure;
It far exceeds in value,
all of earthly treasure.

You came to save our souls,
from heaven you came to earth;
You came to free us from our sin,
and give us second birth.

Your love knows no limits,
it reaches all mankind;
The vilest of all sinners,
You always had in mind.

You long to change our lives,
you long to liberate;
From sin's awful power,
transforming sinners into saints.

Your promise of eternal life.
to those who do Your will;
Can never, ever fail.
that promise You'll fulfil.

Heaven and earth will pass away,
but not a word You've spoken;
Your word is everlasting,
and never shall be broken.

The peace you give to those,
who trust you and obey;
a peace the world can never give,
and neither take away.

And when our lives draw to a close,
and with our final breath;
Your lasting peace will comfort us,
through the valley of our death.

God's Purpose

O God, my life was known to you,
from the cradle to the grave;
You chose me for Your purpose,
before the world was made.

To make me in the likeness,
the likeness of Your Son;
Holy and blameless in Your sight,
like Your beloved One.

Passing through life's bitter storms,
my peace I found in Thee;
Your still small voice within my heart,
speaks of your love for me.

Your love for me shown on the cross,
to me you did impart;
No power can ever break that bond,
that binds me to Your heart.

You are the Keeper of my soul,
for whom You came to save;
You rescued me from Satan's power,
when once I was his slave.

The unseen forces of this world,
before Your presence flee;
All power in heaven is given to You,
with all Authority.

When I take my final breath,
In that moment I shall see;
Your purpose for my life, O Lord,
now fulfilled in me.

In Your presence I shall kneel,
a trophy of your grace;
Both faultless and complete,
as I see Your smiling face.

Eternal Spirit

Eternal Spirit of the living God,
sent from heaven above;
You are the Spirit of holiness,
of wisdom, truth and love.

In the Name of Christ my Saviour,
you came to impart;
The truths revealed by Jesus,
and write them on my heart.

You teach me from God's Word,
lest I should go astray;
You reveal His truths to me,
that keep me in His way.

The purpose of Your work in me,
Is to free me from my sin;
To create Christ's image in my life,
that I shall be like Him.

You are God's seal of ownership,
you sealed me as God's own;
Your still small voice within my heart,
ensures I'm not alone.

The cosmic powers of this dark age,
against my soul can stand;
No power in all creation,
can snatch me from God's Hand.

O Spirit of the living God,
sent from heaven above;
Help me grow in holiness,
in wisdom, truth and love.

You came from heaven to teach me,
to glorify God's Son;
To complete God's work within my
life, His will, not mine, be done.

Saviour And Lord

My Saviour, and my Lord,
My source of peace and rest;
When I am weak, and downcast,
and weighed with heaviness.

I find in You the strength I need,
that You impart each day;
You change my heart of heaviness,
for the garment of Your praise.

I know You'll ne'er forsake me;
you are my faithful Friend;
Your presence always with me,
and will be to the end.

I know not what my future holds,
I'm yours at your commands;
I know that you will guide me,
my times are in Your hands.

When I come to You in prayer,
my petitions You always hear;
as I draw near to You, my Lord,
To me You've always near.

I cherish times of fellowship,
when in quiet we converse;
Your silent whisper in my heart,
fills me with gratefulness.

When my eyes close in death,
in that moment I shall see;
What You my Lord and Saviour,
have prepared for me.

T 'was by Your grace alone,
I unworthy of Your love;
Have led me through my pilgrimage,
to my heavenly home above.

Christ's Return

When You return in glory with archangels at your side,
an awesome sight that all the world shall see;
Joy will fill the hearts, of those who trusted You,
when as Conqueror, You claim Your victory.

The rulers of this earth, the kings and mighty lords,
the rich and poor to You will bend the knee;
None surpasses You, in wisdom, love, and power,
and none surpasses Your authority.

Every eye shall see You, and every knee shall bow,
and every tongue confess that You are Lord;
You will rule the world, in righteousness and truth,
and all the nations praise with one accord.

Ten thousand times ten thousand, Angelic voices sing,
to You be all the glory, Our Saviour and our King;
You died to save the world; returned to claim Your own,
Your rule is everlasting from your Royal Throne.

Christ - The Image Of God

Christ, the image of the living God,
took the creatures place;
The God of all creation,
now has a human face.

God so loved His world,
and all humanity;
He sent His Son as Saviour,
to die on Calvary's tree.

He died a ransom on the Cross,
to save the human race;
He is the Saviour of mankind,
He took the sinner's place.

No power on earth could take His life,
until His hour had come;
Then freely sacrificed His life,
His Father's will was done.

Christ is our resurrection,
with Him we all shall reign;
We shall die, yet shall we live,
when raised to life again.

When we exchange our mortal life,
for immortality;
we'll share His life in glory,
throughout eternity.

How Excellent Your Name

How excellent is your Name,
Almighty God and King;
Creator of the Universe,
Over which you reign supreme.

Your power, your love and beauty,
Are in your works displayed;
By your spoken word, O Lord,
Heaven and earth were made.

The heavens declare your glory,
For all the world to see;
Reveals to earth Your presence,
To all humanity.

Your breath of life upon the earth,
Brought life abundantly;
To flourish and to grow,
Over land, and in the sea.

How great Your love, O Lord,
That in Your eternal plan;
You created this world a paradise,
For the dwelling place of man.

When Adam sinned against You,
And all seemed at a loss;
You died as Saviour of the world,
To regain what he had lost.

Holy Communion

Calm my heart and mind, O Lord,
your voice I long to hear;
As I draw close to You, dear Lord,
to me You will draw near.

Search me, O Lord, and know my heart,
reveal my faults within;
Let me not take this bread and wine,
if conscious of a sin.

A broken and a contrite heart,
Lord, you'll not despise;
Repentance of my sin,
is precious in Your eyes,

Your promise is forever sure,
for those who come to You;
In sincerity and in faith,
they'll find You ever true.

These symbols of Your flesh and blood,
take, You said, and eat;
In remembrance of My sacrifice,
at this Table; where we meet.

The new covenant You have made,
sealed with Your own blood;
You are the Way, the Truth, the Life,
the only way to God.

I thank You; O I thank you, Lord,
for coming to my aid;
Without Your love and sacrifice,
I'd never have been saved.

I offer You myself,
as a living sacrifice;
Grant me strength and courage,
till we meet in Paradise.

How Wonderous Your Love

How great, how wondrous is Your love,
it searched me out, and found me;
A sinner shackled as a slave,
my sins, like chains, had bound me.

How great, how wondrous is Your love,
T' was by Your grace alone;
Your love and mercy set me free,
and claimed me for Your own.

How great, how wondrous is Your love,
it spans all time and space;
It reaches out to all mankind,
endless is Your Grace.

How great, how wondrous is Your love,
Your face I long to see;
That I can praise you as I ought,
throughout eternity.

Thanksgiving & Petition

You are my shield and hiding place,
midst sorrow, pain and strife;
Thank you for Your presence,
as You walk with me through life.

My faith grows strong, my body weak,
as I grow old in years;
Before me lies Your glory,
behind me, toil and tears.

I long to be free from my weakness,
my spirit released like a bird;
To soar into Your presence,
where only Your praises are heard.

Grant me a peaceful ending,
as I close my eyes in death;
A happy passage from this world,
Into my eternal rest.

Poem For A Christian Funeral

Do not grieve too much for me, I'm where I want to be;
I have exchanged my mortal life, for immortality;
I'm in my Saviour's presence, a trophy of His grace,
I kneel before my Lord and God; I see His smiling face.

My love for you, my family, ends *not* within my grave,
Tis stronger than the strongest steel that earth has ever made;
No power can ever break that bond, that binds you all to me,
From heaven, it reaches out to you and from eternity.

My life has ended, my race complete, the crown of life I've won,
was time for me to go and hear, my Saviour's words: 'Well Done."
I wait for you, my family; my friends, to join me here,
there is no grief, no pain, no tears, and here there is no fear.

My final message to you my friends, comes from heaven above,
Live your lives for Jesus; for you He showed His love;
So, when your hour of death draws near, this your song you'll sing,
O grave where is your victory? O death where is your sting?

And so, my family and my friends, grieve not too much for me,
Rejoice; I'm with my Saviour: I'm where I want to be.

A Christian's Lamentation In Old Age

Why am I still here, my Lord? Why am I still here?
I've passed my three score years and ten, of death I have no fear
My fear is that I'll live too long: What lies ahead for me?
My mortal frame is weak, and frail my memory.

I've lost my dear life's partner, who now is in Your care,
I lie awake at night and think of the life we use to share;
Grief overwhelms my spirit, and tears begin to flow,
My heart is filled with sorrow that only you can know.

My life is now behind me, I've passed my three score years,
You've been with me in times of joy, and in times of tears;
I know you have a plan for me that one day will be clear,
Then you'll show the reason why I was still here.

Until that day arrives, O Lord, sustain me from above,
When I feel my loneliness reveal to me your love;
What joy will fill my heart, when you call me home,
I long, O lord to be with You, and kneel before your throne.

Perfect Peace

Perfect peace, in my hospital bed,
Swinging between life and death;
Grant me strength to praise Your Name,
With my final breath.

A lasting treasure awaits me,
That nothing on earth can afford;
My end is ever closer,
It's time to meet my Lord.

We're walked life's path together,
My Lord, my Life, my King;
I long to enter Your presence,
Endless praises there to sing.

(From Peter's hospital bed when he was seriously ill with little chance of recovery)

ABOUT THE AUTHOR

Peter C. Horrell was born in England in 1936. He served in the British Army in Kenya in the mid-50s during the Mau Mau conflict. As a traveller, and adventurer, he hiked around Europe, immigrated to Australia and later moved to New Zealand in the early 60s. In New Zealand he had, what he called, a "Damascus Road" encounter with Christ. He felt a call to foreign missionary service and spent time at the Missionary Training College in Tasmania where he met his future wife, Caroline. Together they served in South America and Spain. Upon their return to Australia, Peter completed his theological studies at the Baptist Theological College of Queensland. He has been a Baptist pastor of churches in Australia and New Zealand. He has written several Christian articles including his autobiography. His interests are poetry, archaeology, early European history and succulents plants. He and his wife Caroline have 'retired' and live in Maleny, Queensland, Australia. They have been married over 50 years and have 3 children.

www.ingramcontent.com/pod-product-compliance
Lightning Source LLC
Chambersburg PA
CBHW031306150426
43191CB00005B/100